THE
Light
TOUCH

How to Use Humor
for Business Success

MALCOLM L. KUSHNER

Simon and Schuster
New York   London   Toronto   Tokyo   Sydney   Singapore

Simon and Schuster

Simon & Schuster Building
Rockefeller Center
1230 Avenue of the Americas
New York, New York 10020

Designed by Karolina Harris
Manufactured in the United States of America

1 3 5 7 9 10 8 6 4 2

Library of Congress Cataloging in Publication Data
Kushner, Malcolm L.
The Light Touch : how to use humor for business success /
Malcolm L. Kushner.
p.   cm.
1. Success in business.   2. American wit and humor.   I. Title.
HF5386.K95   1990
650.1—dc20   *90-31639*
                                                           CIP

ISBN 0-671-68625-9

For Chris,
whose sense of humor was confirmed
when she married me.

Contents

Preface

This is not just another book about humor in public speaking. Success as a manager requires much more than public-speaking ability. That's why this book gives you *all* the knowledge you need to be successful.

This is the first book that explains how to use humor in a full range of management functions. It includes the following:

- How to use humor to manage conflict
- How to use humor to motivate people
- How to use humor to handle awkward and embarrassing situations
- How to use humor to improve productivity
- How to use humor to influence corporate culture
- How to use humor to improve letters, memos, and reports

The emphasis is on simple, practical techniques that anyone can use. You don't have to be a comedian. You don't have to be "naturally funny." You don't have to know how to tell a joke. In fact many of the techniques can be employed without uttering a single word.

There's only one requirement: You must want to develop new skills that will give you an edge over your competition.

The book also includes everything you need to know for using humor successfully in a speech. But again the emphasis is on simple techniques. An entire chapter is devoted to methods for incorporating humor into your remarks even if you can't tell a joke. These powerful methods can also improve your performance in one-on-one or small-group meetings. And this is very important because it's in these settings that you probably do most of your communicating. After all, how many formal speeches do you actually give?

This book will introduce you to a wide cross-section of businesspeople who have mastered the power of humor. You will learn how they succeeded. And how you can too.

Anyone can learn to use humor successfully. You don't need to possess anything more than an average sense of humor. If you have ever laughed or smiled—at anything—then you qualify.

How can I make such a claim? Simple. I have spent the past eight years researching and developing techniques for using humor to improve business performance. During that time I have trained managers, executives, and professionals in organizations ranging from start-up firms to Fortune 500 companies. My clients have included everyone from missile engineers, bank presidents, and attorneys to sheriff's deputies and IRS executives. These are not "yuck-a-minute" people. They are very serious about their work. And even more serious about their careers. Today all of them are utilizing my humor techniques to gain a competitive edge.

How did I discover these techniques? As an attorney with one of San Francisco's largest corporate law firms, I noticed that certain people consistently used humor to their advantage. And they tended to be the most successful and admired members of their organizations. Whether it was a fellow attorney negotiating a settlement or a client structuring a business deal, these people had a light touch that produced solid results. They used their sense of humor as a magnet to draw people into their orbit. People wanted to be around them. The value of this effect cannot be overestimated in a business environment. Managing, selling, negotiating, planning, decision making—all of the fundamental tasks associated with business life become a little bit simpler when people are prejudiced in your favor.

Fascinated by this phenomenon, I devoted myself to learning more about it. I combed the stacks of university libraries and read all the scientific literature available on humor. I interviewed numerous professors, business leaders, judges, politicians, government executives, engineers, accountants, salespeople, and a wide variety of managers. I sought out people with a reputation for using humor effectively and cross-examined them about their methods.

An analysis of my data produced a startling result. Although some people were naturally funny, many more were not. Many of the people who used humor effectively employed remarkably simple devices. They also avoided making common mistakes that could sabotage their efforts. I realized that humor was a skill that could be learned and developed.

That realization led me to a new career. As a humor consultant, I have dedicated my efforts to identifying the basic principles of successful humor use. My focus has been on practical applications. How can a person who is not "naturally funny" use humor effectively? What are the rules? What are the tricks? How do basic principles translate into easy-to-apply techniques? Over the years I have turned the answers to these questions into a system for harnessing the power of humor.

And that's why I've written this book—to share my system with you. In the following chapters you will learn the basic humor principles and how to make them work for you. You will learn how humor can improve your communications, mitigate conflicts, increase productivity, and enrich corporate culture. You will also learn numerous proven techniques for incorporating humor into your management style.

If you've always thought that humor was a talent you could never possess, then this is the book for you. Even if you are naturally funny, the book will be useful. It will help you understand and expand what you've been doing instinctively.

Now I'm not saying that reading this book will transform you into a comic genius. Don't expect people to suddenly be charmed by your every word. That would be magic. And there's nothing magic about the techniques and principles discussed in this book. They have been used successfully by thousands of managers and professionals no different than yourself. What this book does offer is a *method* for turning your sense of humor into a powerful business asset. Its simple rules and easy-to-apply formulas will enable you to use humor to command respect and attention, build morale, and create a productive work environment.

One final caveat: Although this book contains all the information you need to use humor effectively, it can only serve as a guide. Simply reading the book is not enough. You must put its lessons into action. By applying my techniques and principles, you can turn your sense of humor into a tool for success.

Just remember, after employing my system, thousands of managers, executives, and professionals have had only two words to say: "It works."

It will work for you too.

ONE

Humor Is a
Winning Strategy

If you would rule the world quietly, you must keep it amused.
—Ralph Waldo Emerson

Joe DiNucci had just been named U.S. workstation sales manager for Digital Equipment Corporation. A vice president arranged a dinner so that DiNucci could meet Digital's senior research managers. During the dinner an engineering manager known for his blunt opinions said that Digital would produce the world's best workstations in three years. DiNucci was not impressed. He said, "If we don't do it in two years, it will be too late." The tough-talking manager replied, "You know, you're really full of [expletive deleted]."

A dead silence reigned. No one knew what to say. So DiNucci broke the ice. "You know that's an amazing insight," he said. "Most people take months to reach that conclusion. You came to it in forty-five minutes." The engineering manager laughed and the dialogue opened up again. By the end of the evening the manager was completely won over. He even invited DiNucci to give a motivational speech to the engineering research group.

That dinner took place in 1987. At the time Digital was enjoying little success with its workstation products. Despite the company's status as the second largest U.S. computer maker, the trade and business press ignored Digital's presence in the workstation market. The company wasn't considered a "serious" player. As a result many potential customers weren't even aware that Digital made workstations.

By 1989, just two years later, Digital's status had changed dramatically. A plethora of new workstation products had captured the attention of the entire computer industry. And the press took note. In a single month highly favorable stories appeared in *Business Week, PC Week,* and *The Wall Street Journal.* Suddenly Digital was viewed as a major player in the hottest market segment of computing.

Was Joe DiNucci's use of humor responsible for the company's success? If he hadn't poked fun at himself, would his relations with the engineering manager have remained strained? Would his advice have been ignored? Would Digital have waited too long to introduce the new workstations? You be the judge.

Humor is a powerful management tool. It can gain attention, create rapport, and make a message more memorable. It can also relieve tension, enhance relationships, and motivate people, if it's used appropriately. In today's competitive business environment, success requires developing your full potential. Every skill counts. And humor can provide the winning edge.

Have you ever dealt with someone who really knows how to use humor effectively? I mean really knows. A person who can walk into a room full of angry people and release the tension with a perfect quip. A person who can be tough, firm, and demanding without ever seeming abrasive. A person who can display a graceful, self-effacing wit during the most stressful situations. This person might be your boss, a customer, or someone you manage. It might be a colleague or a competitor. No matter who it is, the person always says the right funny thing at the right time. And he or she is always a winner.

Such people are modern business warriors who wear their sense of humor like a suit of golden armor. Their humor draws attention. It distinguishes them from the crowd. And it shields them from attack. You can easily spot these people in any organization. Their counsel is eagerly sought. Their opinions are highly valued. And if they're not already at the top, they're moving rapidly through the ranks.

Why You Don't Have to Be Naturally Funny

Did you ever wonder how these people came to use humor so successfully? It's usually assumed that they were born with a special talent, that they're "naturally" funny. They either have it or they don't, right? Absolutely wrong! This is a big myth that has survived far too long. Sure, some people are born with a special talent for making others laugh. They become famous as clowns and comedians. But for many other people, particularly businesspeople, humor is an *acquired* trait. It's a skill that is learned, developed, and honed.

Unfortunately too many people believe the myth that you must be born with a talent for humor. Maybe you're one of them. Maybe you believe that humor is beyond your capabilities. Why do you feel this way? Because you can't tell a joke? You're not naturally funny? You don't have a quick wit? You don't have the right personality? You can't think of amusing observations? You feel ill at ease with humor? You're too old to develop a new skill?

Stop worrying. You don't have to be a comedian to use humor successfully. All you need is a sense of humor—and an understanding of how to communicate it.

Being Funny Versus Having a Sense of Humor

Have you ever worked with anyone who seemed to lack a sense of humor? These people never smile, never respond to amusing remarks, and certainly never offer any. They are always *very serious*. And you usually try to minimize your contact with them. Then one day, out of the blue, they smile or laugh at a joke. The effect is incredible. Suddenly our view of them is totally transformed. They have a sense of humor after all!

We completely reevaluate our opinion of them. Perhaps they're not as bad as we thought.

Numerous social science studies have demonstrated that a little humor can increase a speaker's likability. Veteran Silicon Valley computer executive Ronald Braniff confirms this from practical experience. "Managers who use humor in their presentations with employees come across as more approachable, and people are more likely to open up with them," he states. "If you manage a lot of people, it's easier to maintain morale and enthusiasm by showing you have a good sense of humor."

And it's common sense. Just ask yourself these questions: Do you know someone who lacks a sense of humor? How do you feel about this person? Do you try to minimize your interactions with him or her? Do you try to avoid doing business with this person? Your answers should suggest why humor can play such an important role in establishing business relationships.

Now let's make an important distinction. Distinguish between being funny and communicating a sense of humor. Most of us have known people who couldn't tell a joke. Yet we knew that they had a sense of humor. They couldn't tell a joke, but they could "get" a joke. They could appreciate the humor of others. They could see the absurdity in a situation. There are many ways of displaying a sense of humor without being "funny."

Your goal as a manager, executive, or professional is *not* to be a comedian or a clown. Your goal is to communicate the fact that you have a sense of humor. That's what will increase your likability and make people more willing to listen to you. Let's look at how powerful communicating a sense of humor can be.

A start-up company begun by a charismatic entrepreneur grew dramatically. The founder brought in a seasoned executive to guide the company past the $100-million level. Although the new president had an excellent track record, he was cut in the traditional mold—cautious and conservative. Employees perceived him to be the exact opposite of the company's dynamic founder and they worried about the company's future.

A pep talk on the eve of a major trade show did little to dispel employee fears. The new president thanked the gathered troops for their team effort and hard work and piled cliché upon cliché. The "rousing" climax was a plea to keep up the good work so that "we can make our numbers this quarter." The response was predictably dismal, when suddenly he added, "Because I want to keep my job." The employees burst into laughter and applause.

"Because I want to keep my job." These seven words did not constitute a joke. They were uttered without any comic delivery. And they transformed the pep talk from a total failure into a major triumph. The words were simple yet powerful. Anyone can use humor in this manner.

You don't have to be a professional comedian to use humor successfully. In fact as a businessperson you have a tremendous advantage: No one expects you to be funny. If you can't tell a joke, you can still slip a light remark into a speech or conversation. Even if it's not that funny, it will communicate the fact that you have a sense of humor. Remember, your goal isn't to be hilarious, it's to communicate your sense of humor.

How Humor Can Advance Your Career

If you're looking for scientific evidence to support the commonsense conclusions about humor, recent surveys abound. Performed by various executive recruitment firms, the surveys confirm the importance of humor in building a successful career. For example, Robert Half International surveyed vice presidents and personnel directors at one hundred of America's largest corporations. The results: 84 percent thought employees with a sense of humor do a better job than people with little or no sense of humor. Robert Half interpreted the survey as follows: "People with a sense of humor tend to be more creative, less rigid and more willing to consider and embrace new ideas and methods."[1] In other words a sense of humor may give you an edge in your career.

A Hodge-Cronin & Associates Inc. survey of 737 chief executives of large corporations produced similar results. The survey found that 98 percent of the respondees would hire a person with a good sense of humor over a person who lacks humor.[2]

In a 1988 letter to *The Wall Street Journal*, executive recruiter Russell S. Reynolds, Jr., explained how he looks for a sense of humor in job candidates he interviews: "You'd be amazed at how some people respond if an interviewer, for example, says, 'Come in, have a seat. How did you get here?' One individual might say, 'I walked,' and another might respond... 'It all started with my mother.'" Reynolds concluded that in addition to playing an important role in executive recruitment, humor stimulates creativity and helps people manage change.[3]

One company that takes humor seriously is Integral, which counts having fun among its corporate goals. The software company, based in Walnut Creek, California, describes its objectives as "the pursuit of excellence, profitability and enjoyment," according to marketing director George Proudfoot. Unlike many other companies, Integral actually looks for job candidates who want to have a good time at work. "When we interview, we give people a statement of our corporate philosophy and gauge their reaction as they read it," says Proudfoot. "If someone remains very straight-faced, they probably won't be that happy here."

Nancy Hauge, director of human resources for operations at Sun Microsystems, uses a similar strategy. "Generally in interviews I mentally note how long it takes someone to laugh," she states. "How long does it take the interviewee to find something funny, tell me something funny, or share his or her sense of humor? Because humor is very important to our corporate culture." She believes that people who can find the humor in a difficult situation can probably handle tough problems without being overwhelmed.

Common Fears

If humor is so powerful, then why isn't it used more extensively by managers and executives? There are two answers to this question. First, humor *is* used extensively by a certain segment of managers—successful ones. Second, its use is inhibited by the fear that humor may backfire.

Concern that humor may produce unintended and undesired results is not unfounded. Humor used inappropriately can distract, offend, increase tension, lower credibility, or be misinterpreted. In working with managers and executives for the past eight years I've heard all these objections and numerous others. However, they can all be boiled down to one major fear: "I'm not funny, I'll 'bomb.'" That's the primary reason that most businesspeople are reluctant to use humor.

Allow me to address this fear by pointing out something that you may not have considered before: You don't have to tell a joke to bomb. Every time you open your mouth, you're at risk. You can be silly, boring, obnoxious, or irrelevant without ever attempting to use humor.

A Sense of Humor Means More Than Telling Jokes

The use of humor as a management tool is not limited to dispensing quips and anecdotes during presentations or conversations. A sense of humor encompasses a much wider range of activities in business, including problem solving, stress reduction, and improving communication. You can use your sense of humor to do all this and more without ever telling a joke.

Creative problem solving provides a good example. It is sense of humor, not comic delivery, that offers the fresh perspective that is critical to solving problems. A sense of humor means looking at things from an offbeat angle. It means perceiving relationships that other people overlook. It means exercising flexibility in your thinking. It's no coincidence that all of these aspects of humor double as creative-problem-solving techniques.

A case in point involved a bank plagued by low morale. Tellers constantly complained about a few horrendous customers. So the bank created a "Worst Customer of the Week Award." Each Friday afternoon the employee with the best horror story won the award and a bottle of champagne. Both morale and customer satisfaction improved. Tellers seeking to win the award actively solicited the worst customers. The customers responded to the increased attention by becoming more bearable.[4]

Comic vision often leads to serious solutions. That's why successful brainstorming sessions are marked by laughter. After the brainstormers stop laughing, they often realize that an outrageously funny idea is actually a long-sought solution.

An extreme example of a sense of humor as a problem-solving device involved a potential lawsuit. A friend of mine who is an attorney applied for a position as a staff counsel with a legal organization. Her job interview was conducted by two attorneys—one male and one female. During the interview the male interviewer—a "macho good old boy"—asked if she had any children. The female interviewer instantly became pale and nervous. And with good reason. Asking that question during a job interview is a violation of federal laws against employment discrimination. My friend solved the problem with her sense of humor. She replied, "None that I know of."

Her answer pleased both interviewers. The female interviewer calmed down because the humorous answer indicated that a lawsuit would not be forthcoming. And the male interviewer liked the "macho" spirit of the reply. My friend got the job.

Humor Relieves Stress

Humor's ability to change perspective also makes it a valuable asset in the battle against stress. Termed the disease of the 1980s, stress has become an ever-growing monkey on the back of American business. A recent article in *Newsweek* reported that stress-induced job-health-care costs in California corporations have doubled in the last five years.[5] And the trend is expected to escalate as corporate mergers and restructurings continue to produce layoffs, cutbacks, and anxiety.

The role of humor as a stress reducer cannot be overestimated given today's climate of corporate calamity. By directing your comic vision inward, you can change your perceptions of stressful situations and secure a degree of momentary calm. The endeavor is worthwhile, not only from a health perspective but from a purely management standpoint. Stress interferes with objectivity and clouds business judgment. Humor, used judiciously, can help you maintain the perspective necessary for successful decision making.

The classic example involves industrialist Joseph P. Kennedy, patriarch of the famous American clan. When asked how he kept his cool while negotiating with the top business leaders of his day, Kennedy reportedly revealed a simple technique. He said that he imagined his adversaries wearing red flannel underwear. Viewed in that way, they were much less threatening.

The major advantage of directing humor inward is that you need only amuse yourself. You don't have to worry about the reactions of other people. You don't have to explain why you're smiling. You don't have to wonder if anyone else will "get" it. It's *your* stress, and you can reduce it by thinking about things that *you* find humorous.

Of course you also have the option of going public with your humorous approach to stress. That was the course chosen by Fred Joseph, chief executive of Drexel Burnham Lambert Inc., when his company faced a federal indictment for securities violations in 1988. At the time Drexel—a major investment banking and securities firm—was at the center of the insider trading scandal that had rocked Wall Street for more than a year. Joseph faced a particularly thorny dilemma. He could avoid racketeering charges by pleading the company guilty to other felonies. However, several top revenue producers at Drexel opposed such a settlement. They hinted that they would leave the company if Joseph settled. But if Joseph didn't settle, the company might be indicted for racketeering and go bankrupt.

Joseph eased some of the tension by sporting a lapel button that read, "STRESS." The button also carried a definition: "That's what happens when the mind overrides the body's need to kick the [expletive deleted] out of someone who justly deserves it."[6]

Joseph eventually decided to settle. I don't know what happened to the button.

How Humor Affects Channels of Communication

Humor can also play a significant role in assessing the channels of communication in a business organization. Many books have been written about formal and informal methods of communication within a corporate structure. Forests have been decimated to provide paper for this pursuit. But no matter which book you read or which theory you choose, the basic idea remains . . . well, basic. Some people want to send messages, some want to receive messages, and some want to block messages. And no matter what channel of communication you select—the memo, the meeting, or the grapevine—you need to confirm that your message got through.

A fascinating example of testing a communication channel with humor involves two top government executives. Former secretary of state George Shultz used to include a joke in every cable he sent to Ronald Reagan. When Shultz returned to Washington, he knew that his message had gotten through if the president said, "That was a great joke, George."[7]

The mere presence or absence of laughter can communicate important information. A good example involves a friend who took the landscape-architect license test. One multiple-choice question asked, "Why should you avoid planting pyrocanther along a highway?" One possible answer was, "Because birds will eat the berries, get drunk, and fly into cars." When my friend saw that answer, she laughed out loud and immediately eliminated it. Later during the test, while reviewing her answers, she realized that no one else had laughed. So she changed her answer. Her reasoning was impeccable. No one else had laughed at the answer about drunk birds because it was the *correct* choice!

Perhaps the most dramatic example of sense of humor greasing the channels of communication comes from the 1987 Soviet-American summit that resulted in the historic intermediate-range nuclear forces treaty. An excellent summary is provided by columnist Hugh Sidey in the December 28, 1987, issue of *Time*:

> When historians write of this summitry between once glowering superpowers, they may decide that the sense of humor shared by the two leaders played as much a part as any other human quality. "He has a good sense of humor," Reagan declared. "I told him the speeding joke. The Soviet police were told to give tickets to speeders, no matter who they were. One day Gorbachev is late leaving home for the Kremlin, and he hurries to his car and tells the driver that he will drive to save time. So the driver sits in the backseat and Gorbachev takes off lickety-split down the road and passes two cops on the side. One of the officers gives chase but in a short time returns to his partner, who asks if he gave him a ticket. 'No,' the cop answers. 'Well, who in the world was it?' asks the other cop. 'I don't know,' replies the first cop, 'but his driver was Gorbachev.' Gorbachev loved it. He just howled."[8]

If humor has the power to ease the Cold War, then it has the power to improve your business relationships. Because, in the final analysis, business comes down to people. Making deals, giving speeches, conducting meetings, solving problems, getting ideas, communicating visions—the world of commerce is a shifting maze of human interaction. And humor provides a powerful tool for navigating the maze—a tool that you can learn to use successfully.

So let's get to it. For as an old philosopher once said, "You should never finish anything you haven't started."

Make Your Point with Humor

The shortest distance between two lines is a point.
—C. A. Griger

"Have you heard the one about the priest, the minister, and the rabbi who went fishing in the same boat? The fish weren't biting. So the priest got out of the boat and walked across the water to another spot. Then the minister got out of the boat and walked across the water. The rabbi got out of the boat and he started to sink. He tried again and almost drowned. Finally the priest said to the minister, 'Don't you think we should tell him where the rocks are?' ... Now I'd like to talk about the effect of export restrictions on the balance of trade in the emerging global economy...."

How many times have you heard a speaker begin a presentation with a joke that has nothing to do with the speech that follows? The joke is totally irrelevant. What's your reaction?

If the joke is funny, it's a distraction at best. It does nothing to further the speaker's message. If the joke isn't so funny, then that's called bombing. It's obvious that the speaker wanted to be funny. No one laughed. And the speaker is left twisting in the wind as an uncomfortable silence emanates from the audience.

That's why the cardinal rule for using humor effectively is *make it relevant.*

Avoiding the Biggest Mistake

Although this rule is commonsense, it is routinely violated by many businesspeople. In fact the single biggest mistake made in public speaking today is the use of irrelevant humor. It's become a national epidemic. Fortunately a few simple precautions can help us keep it from spreading.

Carriers of irrelevant humor come from all walks of business life. They are managers, executives, salespeople, and engineers. They speak at annual meetings, industry conferences, training sessions, and employee banquets. And they are well-intentioned. They are good people who want to communicate successfully. But they have a problem. After taking weeks or months to prepare an important presentation, they take only ten seconds to throw in their favorite joke. Inevitably they use it as the opening and inevitably it bombs.

This unfortunate event produces two reactions. One group of business speakers swears off humor forever. They decide that they "can't tell a joke" or that they "aren't funny." So they take a vow of seriousness and revert to the stuffed-shirt school of business communication. The other group has an even worse reaction. They remain undaunted. They continue to inflict irrelevant humor on the world at large.

Neither reaction is desirable or necessary. A few preventive measures enable anyone to use humor in a safe and effective manner.

Your first step in harnessing the power of humor is to use it for a purpose. Irrelevant humor is a distraction. Whether you're speaking to one person or one hundred, humor is more effective if it makes a point.

Here's why: Relevance reduces resistance. A basic principle of audience psychology is that people resist humor if they think someone is *trying* to be funny. They put a comedy "chip" on their shoulders. This is a problem faced by professional comedians every time they stride up to a microphone. The typical audience attitude is: "You think you're funny—prove it!" The professional comedian works very hard to overcome this automatic resistance.

In contrast, when humor is used to make a point, our reaction is likely to be more generous. We're more open to accepting the humor. We realize that the person is using humor to make a point and only secondarily to be funny. Our resistance decreases. Consequently there is a much greater chance that we will be amused by the speaker's humor.

Most important, even if we don't think the speaker is funny, the humor still makes a point and moves the presentation forward. The speaker isn't left in the embarrassed limbo called bombing. He or she simply moves on to the next part of the presentation. As long as the humor makes a point, it will always have a place in the speech, even if it doesn't get a laugh.

Let's consider an example. A Phillips Petroleum Company executive addressed a group of chemical-industry producers about the problems of government regulation. Specifically he discussed how environmental restraints had slowed construction of a Phillips chemical plant. He summed up his main point by saying, "I got to feeling a little like Moses crossing the Red Sea with the Egyptians in hot pursuit. When Moses asked God for help, God looked down and said, 'I've got some good news and some bad news. The good news is that I'll part the sea, let your people pass through, and then destroy the Egyptians.' 'That's great,' said Moses. 'What's the bad news?' God said, 'First you have to file an environmental impact statement.'"[1]

If his audience thinks the joke is funny and tries to remember it, then they're remembering his main point. If they don't think it's funny, he has still reinforced his point. The story won't bomb, because the audience will recognize its relevance. It supports and illustrates a major theme of the presentation.

How to Make Humor Relevant

How can you ensure that your humor is relevant? Just follow my simple three-step method: Authorize, Analyze, and Analogize.

Authorize means that you as author should write your serious message first. Don't start with the humor. Add it after you develop what you're going to say. Humor should complement and augment your basic points. It shouldn't determine them.

Analyze means that you carefully review the points presented in your serious message. You can't make your humor relevant if you haven't carefully analyzed the points you're making.

Analogize means that you relate a quip or anecdote to one of your points. Your humor should help introduce, summarize, or highlight one of these points. This process ensures that you won't force irrelevant jokes into your presentation.

The three-step method requires a small investment of time in order to be used effectively. You need time for thinking about the humor in your presentation. Slapdash efforts won't work. Throwing in your favorite joke without much thought is a prescription for disaster. Think of the process as an insurance policy. It reduces the risk of bombing. The "premium" you pay is preparation.

Let's examine the process in action with a real example. An executive had to give a speech to the shareholders at her software company's annual meeting. During the fiscal year the company had lost several million dollars by acquiring a small subsidiary and running it into the ground. The speech had to acknowledge and explain this mistake. When the executive asked me for advice, I suggested using the three-step process.

Step 1: She wrote a detailed explanation of how the subsidiary had been acquired, including what went wrong.

Step 2: An analysis of her explanation quickly revealed the main point that she wanted to make in her speech: She wanted to admit that her company had made a mistake by purchasing the subsidiary.

Step 3: I suggested that she explain the events leading up
to the subsidiary's failure and then analogize it to
the following story:

>It's like the fellow who went to a florist and ordered a floral
arrangement for a friend who had opened up a new office.
Then he went to the new office, and there was a wreath that
said "Rest in Peace." Well, this fellow was mad. He went back
to the florist. And he screamed and raved and ranted. Finally,
the florist said, "All right, I made a mistake. But calm down. It's
not that bad. Just think. Somewhere today, someone in the city
was buried under a floral arrangement that said, 'Good Luck in
Your New Location.'"

The story had the desired effect at the annual meeting. It admitted the mistake while provoking laughter from the shareholders. The story eased their tension and helped them accept
the executive's explanation.

The power of the analogy method is limited only by your
imagination. After all, any quip or anecdote can be analogized
to an infinite number of points. It's up to you to make the
connections.

A good example comes from the sales force of a company
that sells storage space for backup tapes of computer data.
They break the ice with prospects by using this anecdote:

One of the most important things to consider with any information system is your backup plan. A consultant asked a group
of people how many of them had one. One brave soul raised
his hand and said, "I've got a disaster plan—complete and ready
to go into action. It's real simple—just one page." And the
consultant said, "A one-page disaster plan? What would you do
if your computer center blew up, or flooded, or caught on fire?
How could you recover with just a one-page disaster plan?" He
said, "Well, it's really very simple. It's a two-step plan. First, I
maintain my resume up-to-date at all times. And second, I store
a backup copy off-site."

The story is effective because it illustrates the storage company's key selling point: Be prepared. But note that the story could illustrate other ideas. It would be equally effective for making points about resourcefulness, looking out for number one, career change, and the superiority of simplicity. In fact the story can be used to illustrate any point to which you can analogize it. Its effectiveness is limited only by your inventiveness.

A side benefit of using the analogy method is that it forces you to examine your serious message carefully. It keeps you focused on your key points. And it helps you discover the parts of your message that don't clearly make a point. In other words, it's a wonderful editing tool that compels you to stay on track.

How to Use Old Jokes

But is staying on track really enough? Does making a joke relevant guarantee success? What if it's an old joke? What if everyone has already heard it? People often ask me if old jokes should be avoided. They worry that the joke won't be funny if it's too familiar. Nothing could be further from the truth.

First, recognize that part of what your audience will find funny is the way that you've analogized a joke to one of your points. Using an old joke in a new way is a creative act. It can produce surprise and amusement. Second, old, funny jokes are like old hit songs—most people enjoy hearing them once in a while. Third, what's old to you may be new to someone else. The bottom line is that an old joke will work if it makes a point.

A good example comes from the 1984 presidential campaign. Senator John Glenn of Ohio talked about an old man sitting on a porch in a fenced-in yard watching a dog run around. A visitor came up and said, "Does your dog bite?" The old man said, "Nope." So the visitor walked in. As soon as he did, the dog ran up and bit a chunk out of his leg. The visitor said, "I thought you said your dog didn't bite." The old man said, "It's not my dog."

Glenn then analogized the story to Ronald Reagan and the federal budget deficit: "He says it's not his dog that's biting us." Detailed accusations followed.[2]

The story about the dog in the yard is an old joke. But after Glenn started using it, he received a lot of favorable media coverage about his "newfound" sense of humor. In addition his campaign message reached new voters every time the media quoted the story. The old joke worked for Glenn because it made a point.

Why Personal Anecdotes Work Better Than Jokes

What if you can't tell a joke to save your life? If you were trapped in an alley and a mugger said, "Tell a joke or die," you'd start planning your funeral. Are you forever condemned to a prison of serious utterances? Will you never experience the joy of hearing laughter at one of your remarks? Is there no reprieve?

Stop worrying. Even if you can't tell a joke, you can tell a humorous personal anecdote relevant to your presentation. Anyone can.

My claim is based on the assumption that you have at least one mildly amusing story that you've been telling for years for no particular purpose. You tell it when you meet people. It's an icebreaker. You tell it at parties and social functions. The story may involve something that was embarrassing years ago but seems funny now. It may relate to home, school, or work. It may even be a story about something that happened to someone else.

Whatever the form of your personal anecdote, it will possess two important traits. First, it will be real. That's what makes it so valuable. And second, you will be comfortable telling it. After all, you've already been telling it for years, so no special comic delivery will be required.

The key to success with personal anecdotes is developing points that your story can illustrate. An exercise I conducted for managers at an educational software company demon-

strates the process. After explaining the value of personal anecdotes I asked for a volunteer to share a story with the group.
In exchange the group promised to come up with a point that
the story could make.

The volunteer turned out to be the company's chief programmer—the person who oversees development of the software. He was a soft-spoken, shy individual and his colleagues
seemed surprised that he had volunteered. His delivery was
not dramatic or embellished. He possessed no special comedic
skills. And he told his story in a matter-of-fact way as follows:

> I had an uncle who had a big brass bed in his house with big
> brass knobs. And when people came over to visit, he would
> challenge them to try and get their mouths around one of the
> knobs. And nobody ever could. Then one day some cousins
> came over. And they all got drunk. And my uncle challenged
> them to get their mouths around a knob. And one of them did.
> And he got stuck. So they sawed it off and they were taking him
> to a hospital when a cop stopped them. The cop said, "I'm
> arresting all of you for disturbing the peace, especially that guy
> with the trumpet in his mouth."

During the programmer's recitation his coworkers listened
intently to every word. Their full attention was focused on this
tale about a crazy uncle. And they began laughing long before
the ending. Why? Because the story is real. And it comes across
as real. You just can't make up stuff like that.

In order to keep our end of the bargain, I asked the group
what points the story could be used to illustrate. Immediately
the company's marketing manager jumped up and said, "Don't
bite off more than you can chew."

When the laughter died down, the chief programmer noted
that he could use the story to make that point. He said that
one of his major tasks as a manager was warning new pro-
grammers not to be hotshots. He can now accomplish this task
by telling them the story about his uncle. By doing so he will
achieve something even more important than making a point

about work habits: He will begin to establish rapport with his new subordinates.

The story of the weird uncle is the type of information that starts a bonding process. New employees will feel honored that the chief programmer has chosen to share something so personal. In addition the story has a humanizing effect. It's self-effacing. It admits that the chief programmer has strange relatives. So it helps bridge the gulf between boss and subordinate.

Most important, the chief programmer can *tell* his personal anecdote. He can't tell a joke, but it doesn't matter. He can tell the story about his uncle. He's been telling it for years. Now he can tell it to make a point.

The personal anecdote is one of the most powerful tools in your humor arsenal. It never fails to gain attention and it can be used by anyone. Take advantage of it. Try to recall key events in your life—your first date, your first job, your first driving lesson. All of them offer potentially amusing stories. Mine your memory for anecdotes. They are a precious resource that each of us possesses in great abundance.

So now you know the secret. Using humor successfully is not very difficult. It's no different than using any other type of communication. It will work if it makes a point. Whether you're talking to one person or one hundred, you will better serve your audience if your jokes serve a purpose. And if you can't tell a joke, use a personal anecdote. Just remember to analogize it to your message. As long as you make it relevant, you'll be on your way to using humor for business success.

Personal-Anecdote Checklist

Personal anecdotes are easy to deliver but sometimes difficult to recall. The following checklist will help jog your memory.

- Your most embarrassing experience
- Your first date

- Your first day on the job
- The funniest thing that ever happened to a friend
- The biggest mistake you ever made
- A strange dream
- The most bizarre thing you've ever seen or heard
- Your wildest vacation story
- Hobbies
- The funniest thing that ever happened at a business meeting
- Eating out: strange restaurant, waiters, food, poor service
- Relatives
- Learning to drive
- High school: prom, teachers, classes
- College: dorm, professors, exams
- Something that seems funny now but didn't when it happened
- Your first job interview
- The strangest gift you've ever received

Nine Powerful People Make Their Points

1.
Bernard Randolph, Commander, Air Force Systems
Command: at the Interservice MTAG/IMIP 1988
Conference, Atlanta, Georgia, November 29, 1988

It's great to be here and to share the platform with Norm Augustine [vice president of Martin-Marietta]. Giving a speech right before Norm does makes you feel like those two cows grazing along a highway when a tank truck of milk passed by. Big red letters on the side of the truck read, "Pasteurized, Homogenized, Vitamins A and D Added." One cow turned to the other and remarked, "Makes you feel sort of inadequate."[3]

2.
David T. Kearns, Chairman and CEO, Xerox Corporation:
at the University of Chicago, Graduate School of Business,
34th Annual Management Conference, April 8, 1986

There's a story about a Frenchman, a Japanese, and an American who face a firing squad. Each gets one last request. The Frenchman asks to hear "The Marseillaise." The Japanese asks to give a lecture on the art of management. The American says, "Shoot me first—I can't stand one more lecture on Japanese management."

You'll be glad to hear that I'm not going to talk about Japanese management today. In fact if we keep on the right road, we may wind up listening to the Japanese give lectures on American management.[4]

3.
Congressman Richard Gephardt: at the City Club of Cleveland, March 20, 1989

Recently I heard a story about George Bush being in a coma for three years and waking to find Dan Quayle standing at his bedside. Upon seeing the vice president, the president asks how long he has been asleep and then inquires about the state of the U.S. economy. To his surprise Quayle tells him that the budget and trade deficits have been reduced to zero. Then President Bush asks about inflation, which he figures must be at an all-time high. Again, to his surprise, Quayle says that inflation is not a problem. Having his doubts, the president asks for specifics. "How much," he asks, "does a first-class stamp cost?" "Very reasonable," Quayle responds. "Only thirty yen."

Unfortunately this anecdote contains a kernel of truth. When I look at America today, I see some of the real challenges confronting us.[5]

4.
Harold Sundstrom, Vice President, Public Affairs and Publications, Export-Import Bank of the United States: at the Adrian College School of Business Administration, Adrian, Michigan, December 6, 1988

But the main point I hope you'll keep in mind as you study how businesses operate in a global economy is that it creates a tremendous opportunity for U.S. companies—now and in the future. It's an opportunity that's fraught with challenge and uncertainty and stiff competition. But it's an opportunity with potentially great rewards for those who take advantage of it.

It's like the three men who had adjacent businesses in the same building. The businessman who ran the store at one end of the building put up a sign reading, "Year-End Clearance." At the far end of the building, the other businessman followed with a sign that said, "Closing-Out Sale." The businessman in the middle knew his business was going to be hurting bad, so he put up a sign that said, "Main Entrance."[6]

5.
Howard Goldfeder, Chairman and CEO, Federated Department Stores, Inc.: at the Edison Electric Institute, Cincinnati, Ohio, June 8, 1987

The competitive environment is illustrated by the two merchants who set up shop across the street from each other in New York City. One had moved to his newly expanded location from an older and smaller site. And he proudly hung the sign that read, "Murphy and Sons, Established 1875." His competitor across the way, seeing a good opportunity, responded with a sign of his own: "Johnson and Company, No Old Merchandise."

Each, in fact, appealed to a certain set of customer values and perceptions. I will, however, try to avoid giving you advice on how to do so—keeping in mind the unconsciously profound conclusion of a report given by a small grade-school student, who wrote, "Socrates was a Greek philosopher who went around giving people good advice. They poisoned him."[7]

6.
D. Wayne Calloway, Chairman of the Board and CEO, Pepsico Inc.: at the Better Business Bureau, Winston-Salem, North Carolina, January 29, 1987

We just couldn't make it in the business world if we couldn't take a few hard knocks, tolerate some frustration—and still be optimistic about the future. It reminds me of two cowboys they still talk about in Dallas, where I used to live. It seems that Tex and Waco had fallen on hard times in the Old West. And try as they might, they just couldn't find work. Then Tex heard that the U.S. Cavalry was looking for bounty hunters and was paying ten dollars for each Apache a bounty hunter brought in. So Tex and Waco signed on as bounty hunters and rode off into Apache territory. Their first night out they camped in the desert. Waco heard noises outside their tent, so he peered outside. And there, by the light of the moon, he saw a thousand Apaches surrounding the tent, all of them armed to the teeth. Waco reached back into the tent and shook his partner. He yelled, "Tex! Tex! Wake up! We're rich!"

That story certainly illustrates optimism. And it also illustrates another characteristic that we businesspeople share. And that's a focus on results.[8]

7.
Joseph N. Hankin, President, Westchester Community College, Valhalla, New York: at the American Association of University Students, 1987 South Regional Conference, Tuscaloosa, Alabama, November 24, 1987

Speaking of perspective, this is how one college student sought to help her parents gain proper understanding and perspective. She wrote them as follows: "Dear Mom and Dad, I'm sorry to be so long in writing, but all my writing paper was lost the night the dormitory burned down. I'm out of the hospital now, and the doctor says my eyesight should be back to normal sooner or later. The wonderful boy, Bill, who rescued me from the fire, kindly offered to share his little apartment with me until the dorm is rebuilt. He comes from a good family, so you won't be surprised when I tell you we are going to be married. In fact you always wanted a grandchild, so you will be glad to know you will be grandparents early next year." Then she added this postscript: "Please disregard the above practice in English composition. There was no fire. I haven't been in the hospital. I'm not pregnant. And I don't have a steady boyfriend. But I did get a D in French and an F in chemistry, and I wanted to be sure you received the news in proper perspective. Love, Mary."[9]

8.
Robert L. Clarke, Comptroller of the Currency: at the Annual Convention of the American Bankers Association, Honolulu, Hawaii, October 10, 1988

A woman from the far reaches of west Texas arrived in Austin one day to talk to the governor about getting her husband out of the penitentiary. After a long wait she was ushered into the governor's office, where she stated her request.

"What is he in for?" the governor wanted to know.

The woman replied, "Fer stealin' a ham."

"Well," said the governor, "that doesn't sound too bad. Tell me, is he a good husband?"

The woman replied, "Fact is, in the twenty-odd years we've been married, he's never had a kind nor gentle word fer me."

"Well," asked the governor, "is he a good worker?"

"No," said the woman, "I wouldn't say that. He's pretty lazy— I can't remember him keepin' a job fer mor'n a week."

"Well," asked the governor, "is he a good father—good to the children?"

"No," said the woman, "he's pretty mean to the young 'uns, if you want to know the truth. Don't notice 'em till he's drunk— when he kicks 'em out of the way."

"Ma'am," said the governor, "I have to ask you: Why do you want a man like that out of prison?"

And the woman earnestly replied, "Governor, we're about outta ham."

Necessity isn't what you want to do. Necessity isn't what you don't mind doing. Necessity is what you have to do when circumstances require you to take action.[10]

9.
G. Michael Durst, President of Training Systems, Incorporated: at the 34th Annual Convention of the

American Association for Respiratory Care, Orlando, Florida, November 5, 1988

I should say I have another type of challenge, and that is trying to present a lot of material in a very short period of time, so I don't know quite what to say to whom!

The story I love to tell to explain how I feel at this point is the story of a woman who had two children. One was five and one was three. These two little guys were constantly swearing. She tried everything to get them to stop swearing. She tried taking them to a child psychologist. After months of frustration she said to the psychologist, "Well, nothing's working. The M & M's didn't work. Ignoring their behavior hasn't worked either. They're even swearing more. So I'm going to treat these guys the way my mom treated my brothers when they were swearing. I'm going to spank them. You can call it negative reinforcement, if you like, but that's what I'm going to do!" So the next morning the first little guy got up, the five-year-old, and he went into the kitchen. Mom said, "Honey, what would you like for breakfast this morning?" He just looked up and said, "Ahh, gimme some of those damn old Wheaties." With that she swatted the kid, and across the kitchen he flew. His three-year-old brother watched this and looked up rather quizzically. "Yeah," Mom said, "so what do you want for breakfast?" He looked up and said, "Well, you bet your sweet ass it's not the Wheaties!"

So that's my challenge at this point: What to say, how to say it, and to whom.[11]

THREE

Seven Types of Humor Anyone Can Use

An onion can make people cry, but there has never been a
vegetable invented to make them laugh.

—Will Rogers

A new convict is sitting in his cell at the state prison. Suddenly someone yells out, "419." The whole cellblock starts laughing. Someone yells, "78." Everyone laughs. "642." Hysteria. And this goes on every afternoon between two and three o'clock. The new guy can't figure it out. He asks his cellmate what's so funny. "There's only one book in the prison library," the cellmate explains. "It's a jokebook. We've all read it so many times we memorized all the jokes. All we have to hear are the numbers." So the new guy goes to the library and studies the book. A few weeks later he's ready. Two o'clock arrives. Someone yells, "316." Everyone's howling. "56." Gales of laughter. The new guy yells, "237." There's dead silence. He asks his cellmate what happened. The cellmate says, "Some people just don't know how to tell a joke."

It's true. Some people can't tell a joke. Most of us have probably met such people—usually when they were demonstrating their deficiency. You may think you are one of them. Does this mean that you can't use humor to become a more powerful communicator? No!

There are seven simple types of humor that anyone can use.

They are easily delivered without any special comic ability. They are used by people such as Bank of America president A. W. Claussen, GM chairman Roger Smith, and Monsanto president Richard Mahoney. They are: quotes, cartoons, letters, lists, analogies, definitions, and observations.

Quotes

"I often quote myself," George Bernard Shaw once said. "It adds spice to my conversation." Quotes do more than that. They provide one of the simplest ways to introduce humor into a presentation. They are easy to find and use. And most important, they gain immediate audience attention. After all, that's what name-dropping is all about.

If you must give a talk that threatens to be a snoozer, throw in a funny quote. The effect on an audience can be electrifying. Eyes open. Heads move forward. Expectation fills the air. Let's face it, an audience may not be interested in what the average business speaker has to say, but they're always interested in the words of Mark Twain, Winston Churchill, or any other celebrity.

Here's how Monsanto Company president Richard Mahoney used the quote technique to liven up a speech about the economy:

> As I reviewed my notes from that talk [referring to an earlier speech], I was right on seven of the eight trends I suggested. Unhappily I missed one—the recession. You'll forgive one small oversight out of eight! I listened to the economists on that one instead of watching the Federal Reserve policies—and I now agree with what Murray Weidenbaum said in a piece in Sunday's *New York Times:* "If all the economists in the country were laid end to end, we'd be a lot better off!"[1]

What if Mahoney's audience doesn't find this quote funny? No problem. Mahoney can blame it on Weidenbaum. It's a great way of ducking responsibility and creating an immediate distance between yourself and the offensive quip. You only take the rap for picking it in the first place.

Like jokes, quotes should be analogized to points in your presentation. Again, this process is limited only by your imagination. For example, my favorite quote for opening a statistical talk comes from Yogi Berra. It concerns the time Yogi walked into a pizza parlor and ordered a pie. The waitress asked him if he wanted it cut into four slices or eight. Yogi said, "Better make it four. I don't think I can eat eight."

You will not find that quote listed under "statistics" in any quote or jokebook in the world. Yet it's perfect for beginning a statistical presentation. Statistics are inherently boring. By entertaining your audience with the Berra quote, you buy a small amount of their attention. In return for your effort, they will listen to some of your statistics. In addition, the Berra story works on a more basic level. It admits that anyone can manipulate statistics and that your manipulations will follow. By acknowledging this fact at the outset, you defuse your audience's arguments in advance and make them more receptive to your version of the statistics.

Just for practice, list all the points you might illustrate with the following quote:

> I believe it was Neil Armstrong, the first man to walk on the moon, who was asked if he had been nervous before he went into space. He said, "Of course, who wouldn't be? There I was sitting on top of 9,999 parts and bits—each of which had been made by the lowest bidder."

My list includes government spending, pessimism, courage, capitalism, economics, and realism. And that just scratches the surface.

One final point to note about quotes is the gray area of attribution. Look at the first four words of the Armstrong quote: "I believe it was." This is a very powerful qualification. The speaker doesn't actually tell us who said the funny line. We only learn that it might have been Neil Armstrong.

This qualification creates two immediate benefits. First, it absolves the speaker of potential charges of incorrect attribution. If it turns out that Neil Armstrong didn't say the line, then the speaker can say it was only a belief. Second, and more important, the attribution enables the speaker to use the power of Armstrong's name. In addition to gaining attention, it improves the chances that the audience will laugh at the quip. After all, Neil Armstrong is someone we like and respect. We are inclined to laugh at *his* jokes.

And this leads directly into the gray area. Is it proper to falsely attribute a quip to a celebrity and qualify it by saying, "I believe it was"? The answer is a matter of individual conscience. I can only offer my own experience as a guide. When I taught communication at the University of Southern California, I attributed all my jokes to Aristotle. Even if no one laughed, they thought I was smart. And to this day the football team believes it received a classical education.

Cartoons

If you still think that you need to "tell a joke" to use humor, try a little experiment. Flip through the pages of your favorite newspaper and pick a cartoon you find particularly funny. Now describe it to someone and see if he laughs. My guess is that he will.

Most people, even those who can't tell a joke, have no problem describing cartoons to friends. That's because the process is much less ego-involving than telling a joke, and it doesn't require any special comic ability. Telling a joke is a performance. You have to put yourself into it. Describing a cartoon is just the opposite. You function as a detached observer of the scene, a reporter of events.

And like the quote, a cartoon has a built-in insurance policy: You didn't originate it, you only selected it. In fact it was first selected by an editor of the publication in which it appeared. So an audience who dislikes your choice disagrees not only with you but also with a distinguished editor. If you say a situation is like a cartoon you saw in *The Wall Street Journal* or *The Washington Post*, you've got some real heavyweights on your side. You also communicate your erudite reading habits.

Of course like all forms of humor, the cartoon must be analogized to one of your presentation points. It also helps to choose a cartoon with a very graphic image. For example, a lawyer had to give a talk about the escalating cost of medical care in the United States. One of his major points was the problem of unnecessary medical tests. He said it was like the cartoon of a skeleton sitting in a doctor's office. "Well, Mr. Jones," the doctor is saying, "your X rays came back, but they didn't tell us anything we didn't already know." The audience of claims adjusters got the point.

Cartoons make ideal speech material because of their wide variety of styles and topics. You can always find one that relates to your message. Here's how Roger Smith, chairman of GM, used a cartoon in a speech about leadership:

> ... In business, on the other hand, intellectual activity has a lot to do with persuasion and consent. Businesspeople do differ— often vehemently—as to the proper course of action. But before action can be taken, there must be agreement among individuals. And these individuals often come from different disciplines, each with its own orientation, each with its own decision criteria.
>
> I recently saw a cartoon in *The Wall Street Journal*. It shows what are clearly two business executives, sitting in plush chairs, sipping drinks. And one of them says to the other, with obvious indignation, "What I find hard to accept is that there are two sides to every issue."
>
> Well, we're not all that rigid! In fact one of the hallmarks of the competent manager is the ability to tolerate ambiguity.[2]

Notice how Smith used the cartoon as a bridge from one point to another. It illustrates the point about differing orientations among executives and leads into a discussion of ambiguity.

The cartoon technique isn't limited to single-panel cartoons.

An entire comic strip can be used if it makes a point. That's how Congressman Dan Angel began an address on product liability to the Southeast Michigan Wholesale Distributors Association:

> In August of this year one of my favorite cartoon characters, Snoopy, was pictured by Charles Schulz in his *Peanuts* column playing tennis. In picture one Snoopy was shown with a brand-new tennis racket. In picture two he had committed a double fault and was obviously angry. In the next series of panels he smashed the racket to the court, banged it on the net pole, kicked it and stomped on it. Finally, in great anguish, he tore out the strings in the racket by smashing it over the tennis net pole. In the final frame of the cartoon he is seen addressing a letter: "Gentlemen, under separate cover I am returning a defective tennis racket."
>
> Although it's meant to be humorous, I am not convinced that this Snoopy cartoon does not show a great deal of understanding of the product-liability program that has arisen over the past two years, both nationally and in the state of Michigan.[3]

Again notice how a cartoon functions similarly to a quote. Traditional public-speaking advice suggests that the speaker begin with a provocative quote that establishes the theme. Congressman Angel accomplished that goal with the Snoopy comic strip. He also endeared himself to his audience by his reference to *Peanuts*, one of the most beloved comic strips in America.

The affinity between the cartoon and the quote is best demonstrated by an address given by P. L. Smith, former president and CEO of General Foods Corporation. In a speech about creativity presented to advertising executives, he analogized a cartoon to one of his points and then analogized the cartoon to a quote:

> Well, where I'm going this morning is to talk a bit about the relationship of leadership and the creative process. Awhile back I noticed a cartoon in *The New Yorker* magazine. Two secretaries

are preparing a conference room. One says to the other, "And don't forget the little pads. *In case* one of them has an idea!"

That sounds much like the words of Robert Frost, the famous American poet, who once said, "The brain is a wonderful organ; it starts working the moment you get up in the morning and does not stop until you get to the office."[4]

No matter what time of day *your* brain starts working, the cartoon provides a simple way of expressing your humorous thoughts. Even if you *can* tell a joke, it never hurts to "say" a few cartoons. After all, brevity is the soul of wit. And if a picture is worth a thousand words, a cartoon is worth two thousand.

Letters

One of the most effective yet overlooked forms of humor is the funny letter. It is a simple device that can become the highlight of any business presentation.

You can find a wealth of funny letters every day if you read the newspaper. In addition to letters to the editor, there are letters to columnists who advise on health, pets, plants, love, and any other subject that will sell a paper. A perennial favorite is the queen of funny letters—Dear Abby. If you supplement the newspaper with books of funny letters—kids' letters to God, from camp, to Santa Claus—you have quite an arsenal from which to choose.

Speakers who can't tell a joke will find a friend in the funny letter. It doesn't require any special comic ability to deliver. You just read it aloud like any other letter. It also provides the option of using a prop. You can hold up the letter and wave it around when referring to it. This is a nice dramatic touch that works well even if you're holding up a blank piece of paper. And like the quote and cartoon, the letter is "safe," because you didn't write it, you only selected it.

Funny letters are a favorite device of Rose Resnick, executive director of the Rose Resnick Center for the Blind. She employs such letters in the numerous fund-raising speeches that she delivers on behalf of the Center. One letter that would be perfect for her next engagement appeared in Juliet Lowell's book *Dear Candidate*:

Mrs. Ladybird Johnson
The White House
Washington

Dear Mrs. Johnson:

I like the idea of beautifying American cities and I want to help you in your project, so I am enclosing my check for $8.

You'll pardon me for not signing it, but I want to remain anonymous.

Millie D.[5]

By coating her appeal in humor, this particular letter would give Resnick an edge over the hundreds of other people seeking money from the same pool of contributors. The letter would reduce the tension associated with asking for money and make an audience become more inclined to give a donation.

What if you can't find funny letters to make your point? Take a cue from Bruce Rounds, former New Hampshire House majority leader. He was picked to be master of ceremonies at a salute to retiring New Hampshire Speaker Pro Tem Marshall French. But there was a problem: Rounds wanted humorous introductions for the featured speakers, and his staff kept coming up dry. The solution: a brainstorm two days before the event. Rounds would use thank-you letters to French from youngsters who had toured the statehouse. Of course the letters were "improved" somewhat.

Here is how it sounded when Rounds introduced the speakers at the banquet: "I can't think of any greater tribute to Marshall French than to read some of the letters he has received from youngsters in his constituency. I'd like to read the first one. It says, 'Dear Mr. French. Thank you for taking us through the statehouse. I liked the hall of flags. I also was interested in all those things you told us about the governor that nobody knows.' Ladies and gentlemen, may I present the governor of New Hampshire."

After the governor finished, Rounds continued: "Dear Mr. French. Thank you for the tour of the statehouse. We liked Concord. The bus trip was nice. I got sick because I ate a marshmallow sandwich. Thank you for explaining to us that *pro tem* means you're in charge of everything."

By the third letter the audience was laughing as soon as they heard the words "Dear Mr. French."

Lists

Let's talk about the geometry of humor. Two points make a line. Three or more points make a trend. This simple principle provides a powerful tool for coating dry material with humor. It allows you to build informational points right into a quip or anecdote.

The following joke illustrates the principle in its classic form:

> There are three ways to get things done: (1) do it yourself; (2) ask someone else to do it; (3) ask your kids not to do it.

The first two points are serious and mundane. They set up the expectation that more of the same will follow. The third point is funny because it violates these expectations. It catches us off guard. The technique isn't limited to three items. Three is just the starting point, the minimum number needed to create false expectations of a trend.

In a talk to the Louisiana Trial Lawyers Association, speech professor Waldo Braden demonstrated a four-item variation. Braden began by noting that all the other speakers had highly technical backgrounds related to the practice of law. Then he analogized his position to William Howard Taft's great-granddaughter:

When she was asked to write her autobiography in the third grade, the young lady responded, "My great-grandfather was president of the United States, my grandfather was a United States senator, my father was an ambassador, and I am a Brownie."

On this morning at this elegant hotel here in the French Quarter in this distinguished company, I feel like a Brownie.[6]

The technique is easy to apply anytime your presentation contains a list. If the items are boring, just add something funny at the end. Your audience will appreciate the effort. Here's how W. B. Renner of Alcoa livened up a list in a commencement address at Spring Garden College in Philadelphia:

President Delucca. Members of the board of managers. Distinguished guests. Honored graduates. Friends. And finally, parents whose tuition payments are ended.[7]

It's a small but effective touch that doesn't require any special comic ability.

Another example comes from a speech delivered by Dr. David Margulies, vice president of information systems at Boston Children's Hospital. Speaking at a conference devoted to UNIX—a computer language that has been touted as the wave of the future for the past twenty years—Margulies expressed his doubts about it:

You've heard of vaporware, then there's hopeware, then prayerware. But UNIX is beyond all that—it's nowhere.

Does your presentation include lists of budget items, courses of action, or questions for review? Tag on a funny ending. The technique is particularly effective for listing product features: "Our new minicomputer-based manufacturing management information system will decrease inventory levels, increase inventory accuracy, improve on-time delivery rates, and reduce personnel costs. But it won't do your dishes."

The technique can be used for maximum impact by constructing quips around important informational points. Let's see how this could work for the San Francisco Police Department. The officer in charge of public education receives a new assignment: to tell senior citizens how to protect themselves against crime in San Francisco. He puts together a half-hour presentation outlining several practical techniques. It is an extremely serious message. But in a dramatic ending here is how he calls his audience to action:

> There are three ways you can start preventing crime on yourself today: (1) Put a deadbolt lock on your door; (2) put a peephole in your door; and (3) move your door to Fresno.

If the audience thinks the quip is funny and tries to remember it to tell their friends, then what are they remembering? Get a peephole and get a deadbolt lock—the two most important points in the presentation!

Analogies

The fifth simple type of humor that anyone can use is the analogy. We have previously discussed analogizing humor to presentation points. I now use the word *analogy* to refer to a specific type of humor—a concise statement that highlights the similarities between two objects. Think back to those irritating questions on your college entrance exams. "Attila the Hun eating a hamburger is like the Loch Ness Monster: (a) playing a violin; (b) singing in a bathtub; (c) driving a pickup truck; or (d) swinging a golf club." Remember the test instructions? You were supposed to complete the *analogy*! Humorous analogies are particularly attractive because they are easy to deliver and they automatically make your point. When used properly, they can become the highlight of a presentation.

Let's look at an example. Several years ago Sam Armacost, then president of Bank of America, gave a speech at San Francisco's Commonwealth Club about the economy. In the speech he warned about the growing federal budget deficit. He also pointed out two especially troublesome areas of federal spending. "Defense and entitlements," he observed. "They stand out like two sumo wrestlers at an anorexia clinic."

Although the presentation lasted nearly one hour, the media focused on that single analogy, which lasted only a few seconds. For the next week Armacost's analogy continually popped up in radio, television, and newspaper reports. Why? It was short, funny, and made a point. In today's overcommunicated society, a simple analogy is a precious commodity. A simple analogy that is also funny is a rare jewel.

Judge Ira Brown of San Francisco's Superior Court recalls how a clever analogy garnered the attention of a bored jury. He tells of an older, distinguished-looking litigator who was the fifth defense attorney to make a closing argument at the end of a very long trial. There was nothing he could say that hadn't been said, and the jury knew it. However, the litigator's opening analogy ended the boredom: "I feel sort of like Zsa Zsa Gabor's fifth husband," he began. "I think I know what to do, but I don't know if I can make it interesting." The jury cracked up and listened to every word of his closing argument.

Analogies need not be limited to formal presentations. They are equally effective in adding color to the most informal conversations. Van Purdy, a regional sales manager with ASK Computer Systems, described a problem to a colleague like this: "Trying to get information out of Marie is like trying to suck a bowling ball through a fifty-foot garden hose." The line stood out. It had sparkle. It was more effective than saying Marie didn't tell us what we wanted to know.

Humorous analogies are like seeds that you plant in people's minds. The manure of the mundane ensures that they will flower in memory and keep your points paramount in the mind of your listener. Admittedly it is difficult to create concise, witty analogies. That's why it's important to jot them down when you come across them in newspapers, magazines, or conversation. File them away for future reference and then adapt them to your own points when needed.

For example, Carol Saunders, an ASK Computer Systems

manufacturing consultant, trains her company's customers how to implement computer systems. She begins by acknowledging that the task involves top executives and may be difficult. "Installing a manufacturing management information system is like mating elephants," she says. "It's done at a real high level and there's a lot of bellowing."

Saunders's analogy can be easily adapted to fit any program or decision that requires top management cooperation and generates resistance. Try adapting the analogy. Instead of "installing a manufacturing management information system," plug in your own phrase. Are you developing a new product? Are you creating a new marketing strategy? Are you asking for a raise? All of these can be like mating elephants.

The power of the humorous analogy is best exemplified by an incident that occurred during the presidential election of 1948. Incumbent president Harry Truman was not generating much voter enthusiasm. Pundits universally predicted that challenger Thomas Dewey would be the next president of the United States. But then something strange happened. A reporter pointed out that Dewey looked like the little man on a wedding cake. The analogy, which captured Dewey's stiff and pompous character, transformed the campaign. It became hard to think about Dewey without thinking about the analogy and laughing. And it became hard to vote for a person who looked like the little man on a wedding cake. Did the humorous analogy win the election for Truman? Who knows. One thing is certain, it didn't hurt.

Definitions

The sixth type of humor that anyone can use is the definition. Definitions provide a simple way of breaking up long chunks of dry material. Just take a key word or phrase from your message and define it in a funny way. Then follow it with a serious definition if necessary.

Here's how Bank of America president A. W. Claussen has

used the technique to liven up an extended discussion of the economy:

> Inflation is the process that enables you to live in a more expensive neighborhood without going to the trouble of moving.[8]

It's easy to see how this line, slipped into a weighty economics talk, can perk up an audience.

Where do you find funny definitions? Newspapers, magazines, jokebooks. Or you can create your own. Any strange-sounding word or phrase is a candidate for your consideration. For example Ronald Reagan often talked about changing the status quo. "Status quo," he said. "You know, that's Latin for 'the mess we're in.'"

An extended version of this technique was employed by Frank G. Wells, president and CEO of the Walt Disney Company, at a Travel Industry Association meeting in October 1987. In a speech to the association Wells explained the term *soft adventure* as follows:

> One market expected to grow in importance in the future is "designed experience" vacations, and a segment of this marketplace—which is expected to increase tremendously—is the so-called soft-adventure area.
>
> *Soft adventure.* . . . I must confess that my first reaction in hearing that expression is, "What a contradictory term!" It reminded me of the old word-association tests given by psychologists, so I tried it on one of the young Hollywood bachelors I work with. "I'm going to throw out a phrase," I said, "and I want you to give me the first words that come to mind: 'Soft adventure.'"
>
> "Dolly Parton," he said.
>
> Actually *soft adventure* in the tourism sense consists of "safe" versions of what may once have been considered challenging and dangerous undertakings.[9]

Notice Wells's classic use of the technique. He stated his funny definition of *soft adventure* and immediately followed it with the actual definition of that term.

The definition technique can be used to pace an entire presentation. Anytime you think you've droned on too long, just insert a funny definition. The technique is particularly applicable to "tech talk"—that strange amalgam of language that emanates from research-and-development departments around the world: "automotive-release interface"; "fourteen gigabytes of random access memory"; "on-line transaction processing"; "network systems architecture." Even "techies," who understand this stuff, don't want to listen to an endless stream of it. Instead of spouting a wall of words, break it up with an amusing definition.

Software engineer David Eisenman demonstrates the technique in his oratory about improving product quality through statistical process controls. His audiences consist of finance and manufacturing managers at technical conferences. "You don't have to be a statistician to understand quality," he tells them. "After all, what is a statistician? A person who didn't have enough charisma to be a cost accountant."

If you find it difficult to locate or create definitions for key words and phrases, try defining acronyms. Acronyms are abbreviations such as FBI (Federal Bureau of Investigation) and CIM (Computer Integrated Manufacturing). They dominate the worlds of government and technology, as well as almost every other area of human endeavor. IBM. IRS. DNA. OPEC. UN. CBS. FCC. The primordial fluid of our business universe must have been alphabet soup.

Despite the minor annoyance produced by today's overabundance of standard abbreviations, the acronym can serve as a powerful ally in your quest to communicate your sense of humor. Just pick an acronym from your presentation and change the words that it represents. A good example comes from a speech delivered by Senator Frank Lautenberg of New Jersey. In the Democratic response to Ronald Reagan's weekly radio address, Lautenberg criticized Republican handling of environmental matters. He made his point by talking about the EPA—"the Environmental Procrastination Agency."

If your presentation doesn't include an acronym, make one

up. Let's say you're talking to financial types. Tell them that you're full of CRAP—Creative Recognized Accounting Principles. Or, if you're making financial projections, you might mention that your forecasting is OWNID—Often Wrong, Never In Doubt.

Definitions can also be used in combination with some of the other techniques we've already discussed. For example, it's easy to turn a list into a definition. That's what I did for an executive who had to present an award at an Anti-Defamation League dinner:

> I'm happy to be here tonight helping your organization present this award. The Anti-Defamation League: you're an organization opposed to extremist groups—like the IRA, the KKK, and the IRS.

Definitions can also serve as the raw material for analogies. This Ronald Reagan example is a classic:

> Government is like that old definition of a baby. It's an alimentary canal with an appetite at one end and no sense of responsibility at the other.

A simple device for inserting definitions into a presentation is the dictionary formula. Just pick a word or phrase from your presentation and say that you looked it up in the dictionary. For example, "The other day somebody told me I had a warm personality. I thought it was a compliment. Then I looked up *warm* in the dictionary. It means 'not so hot.'"

You can use the dictionary formula whenever you hit a "dry patch" in your talk. It works for any topic. It works for any audience. ("*Audience,* that's the only group of people in the world who get tired *after* they sit down.")

Observations

The last, but definitely not least, simple type of humor that anyone can use is the observation. This is a catchall category that ranges from maxims, proverbs, and pithy sayings to colorful comments and observations of the absurd. The operative word is *clever*. Observations are generally short, clever lines that can be inserted almost anywhere in a presentation. The phrase "pearls of wisdom" is a good way to describe them.

For example a businessperson explaining his reluctance to speculate about the future might comment, "They say that he who lives by the crystal ball will eventually have to eat glass." That's an observation—short, clever, to the point. It doesn't require any comic delivery, yet it communicates a sense of humor. In this case the observation takes the form of a maxim or proverb.

A variation on the maxim style of observation is fortune-cookie wisdom. The observation is phrased like a fortune found in a Chinese fortune cookie and attributed to an ancient philosopher. A good example comes from a speech given by Weber State College president Stephen D. Nadauld to the Utah Bankers Association. Pertinent details appeared in a *Deseret News* account of the speech:

> Finally, said Nadauld, there is no substitute in today's competitive marketplace for "hustle." Quoting what he said was an ancient Chinese philosopher, Nadauld said, "Man stand for long time with mouth open before roast duck fly in."[10]

The line makes a point and could be successfully delivered by anyone.

The colorful comment is an entirely different breed of observation. Unlike the maxim or proverb, the colorful comment is not phrased as a universal rule or law. It pertains to an individual person or situation. For example, "He carries around a garden hose so he can always walk on water." Often the colorful comment is based on exaggeration. South Carolina senator Jesse Helms offered a good example when he described a political opponent as "so scared he is living on a diet of fingernails." Another gem was a criticism voiced by political spokesman Paul Begala: "It's not just pie in the sky, it's a whole floating bakery."

Finally we come to observations of the absurd. An observation based on absurdity, while easy to deliver, is less simple to produce. It requires a certain degree of comic imagination— an ability to see the absurdity in the world around us. Government bureaucracy provides a fertile ground for this type of observation. A speech by Senator Robert Griffin at the 1977 Annual Meeting of the Michigan Association of the Professions and the American Association of the Professions illustrates the technique:

> When I was a junior member of the House of Representatives, I once attracted national attention by offering an amendment to a very costly farm bill that would be administered by hiring many thousands of new federal employees. My proposed amendment to the funding language in the bill went like this: "Provided, however, that in no event shall the number of employees in the Agriculture Department be allowed to exceed the number of farmers in America."[11]

The line is funny because it reveals the potential absurdity of the legislation. And no comic delivery is required.

You can produce humorous observations by stepping back from your work and viewing it from a broader perspective. Forget about budget battles, due dates, phone calls, typos, paperwork, fax machines, meetings, and memos. Don't worry—none of that trivia will disappear. Just stop for a moment and lift your head above the fray. The view will be enlightening. And your ability to spot absurdities will increase dramatically.

Just Listen

A young psychiatrist and an old psychiatrist had offices across the hall from each other. Every morning they would meet in the elevator, both looking fresh and dapper. But by day's end the young man looked exhausted and disheveled while the old man looked just as fresh as he did in the morning. Finally the young psychiatrist said to the old psychiatrist, "I don't understand how you look so fresh all the time. How do you put up with listening to these patients all day?" The old man shrugged his shoulders and said, "So, who listens?"

Many businesspeople share the old psychiatrist's attitude toward listening. They consider it an effort. That's why listening is the simplest way of communicating your sense of humor— it shows that you've made an effort to appreciate another person's quip or anecdote. And your effort is essential to that person's success. To paraphrase an old philosophical question, If someone told a joke in the forest and nobody heard it, would it be funny? I don't think so. Communication is a two-way street that requires receiving as well as sending. So if you can't tell a joke, then listen to one. And laugh at it. You will quickly achieve a reputation for having a great sense of humor.

The seven types of humor discussed in this chapter, as well as listening, offer you a wide range of options for communicating your sense of humor without telling a joke. Use them often. And keep adding to your storehouse. Make a note of funny analogies you read in the newspaper. Clip cartoons from magazines. Jot down amusing quotes you hear on the radio. The world is full of possibilities. They're all around you. As Yogi Berra once said, "You can observe a lot just by watching."

A Few Analogies to Get You Started

Amusing analogies can be challenging to create, but they are easy to adapt. Here are a few analogies to start your collection. They made the points for the people who used them and they can make your points for you.

Investment banking has become to productive enterprise in this country what mud wrestling is to the performing arts.
    —Leigh B. Trevor, quoting William Proxmire quoting Mark Russell

I slept like a baby last night. I woke up every hour and cried.
—George Lefferts, on his reaction to the stock market crash

UNIX in the commercial world. It doesn't feel right. It's like seeing a Volvo with a gun rack.
—Howard Anderson, Chairman, Yankee Group

It's like solving a Rubik's cube without color coding.
—Shiraz Kaderali, Manager Public Affairs, Pacific Gas & Electric Company

If you ask me, TV executives have done for television what painting by numbers has done for art.
—David Brenner

Dealing with the Russians is like dealing with a defective vending machine—you can kick it or jar it, but talking to it does no good.
—Ken Adleman, former director of the U.S. Arms Control and Disarmament Agency

Thank you. I feel like a friend of mine, who had to ride his bicycle home after a vasectomy.
—Joe DiNucci, Vice President, MIPS Computer Systems, Inc., after a presentation to a hostile audience

FOUR

Putting Punch
in a Punch Line

Dying is easy, comedy is hard.
—Edmund Gwenn

President Woodrow Wilson was once asked how long it took to prepare his speeches. His reply: "If I am to speak ten minutes, I need a week for preparation; if fifteen minutes, three days; if half an hour, two days; if an hour, I am ready now."

His point was well made. The shorter the presentation, the longer it takes to organize it. You can't afford to be sloppy if all your points must be packed into a few minutes instead of a few hours. You must carefully plan, analyze, hone, shape, and craft your message. You must think about whom you're addressing, what you want to accomplish, and how you will construct a concise message that achieves your goal.

What does this have to do with humor? Everything. Think of quips and anecdotes as extremely short presentations. In order to carry them off successfully, you will have to organize them precisely. There's an old saying in the real estate business: The three keys to successful investment are location, location, and location. In the humor business it's preparation, preparation, and preparation.

Preparation can be divided into two main areas: audience analysis and editing. Audience analysis involves learning about the people who will receive your humor. Editing involves honing humor into its most effective form.

Analyze Your Audience

A group of Digital Equipment Corporation managers from the United States visited one of their company's facilities in Asia. The official welcome was provided by an Asian executive. "In Asia we begin a presentation with an apology," he said. "We apologize that our humble words cannot be important enough for the ears of our honored audience. But in America it is customary to begin a presentation with a joke. So I will begin today by apologizing for not having a joke."

That executive had analyzed his audience!

Your audience is your starting point. *You must know who you're talking to before you decide what to say and how to say it.* Humor that may be very effective with one audience may be totally inappropriate with another. Unless you're talking to yourself, don't rely solely on your own taste in humor. Let your audience be your guide.

So how do you choose the most effective humor for your audience? Just follow four simple rules.

RULE 1: LEARN AS MUCH ABOUT YOUR AUDIENCE AS POSSIBLE.

Do your homework. Become an expert on your audience. The more you know about them, the more you can tailor your humor directly to their interests. After all, it's hard to hit a bull's-eye if you can't describe the target.

Start by creating a general profile of your audience. Sketch in variables such as age, sex, education, race, ethnic group, occupation, religion, political view, and organizational affiliations. Then supplement that data with specific information about their beliefs, attitudes, and values. Think of yourself as a police sketch artist. You want to portray the suspect in as much detail as possible.

Is it really necessary to do so much audience research? Absolutely. In addition to helping you prepare effective humor, extensive audience analysis can improve your rapport with that audience. By using "inside information" you communicate that you've taken the time to learn about the audience. It indicates that you consider your audience important. They will be flattered that you made the effort. They will begin to like you immediately. And they will be more predisposed to appreciate your humor and listen attentively to your message.

RULE 2: AVOID OFFENSIVE HUMOR.

Don't use humor that will offend your audience. Start by eliminating racist, sexist, ethnic, and off-color humor from your repertoire. Be appropriate.

You're probably thinking this is pretty obvious stuff. Someone would have to be fairly obtuse to use racist, sexist, ethnic, or off-color humor. Of course it's going to offend any audience. Your point is well taken. So why am I making such a big deal out of rule 2? Two reasons: First, despite the "obviousness" of the rule, speakers continue to use blatantly offensive humor on an alarmingly regular basis. And second, not all offensive humor is obvious.

Let's examine this second point. I recently gave a speech about humor at a convention of high school principals in Yakima, Washington. When I concluded, one of them came over to discuss a presentation he had given at a meeting on leadership in education. His audience had been superintendents, principals, and community leaders. He claimed to have "bombed" despite following the basic rules. He said he used a story that made a relevant point. And he didn't announce that he was going to tell the joke. Yet his anecdote drew an audience reaction of dead silence and obvious discomfort.

"What point were you trying to make?" I asked.

He said his point was that education is important. "You can have the tools to do something, but they're useless if you don't know how to use them," he replied.

That seemed like an appropriate point to make at a meeting

about educational leadership. "What was the anecdote?" I asked.

He replied that his story went as follows:

Two old-maid English teachers retired and pooled their money to buy a farm upstate. They had a cow and wanted to raise livestock. Turns out that a farmer down the road had a prize-winning bull. So they asked if they could borrow the bull to mate with their cow. The farmer said okay. He brought his bull over to their barn. But the farmer couldn't stay. And he worried that the women couldn't handle the job. "Don't worry," they said. "We'll take care of everything." When the farmer came back, the barn looked like World War III. There was hay all over the ceiling, mud all over the walls. The place was a wreck. He yelled, "What happened? What happened?" Suddenly the two women came out from the back of the barn. They were covered with mud. They looked horrible. And the farmer started apologizing. "I knew I shouldn't have left you here alone with my bull. I knew he'd be too much trouble. I should have known you wouldn't know how to mate him." "Stop apologizing," they said. "Your bull was a perfect gentleman. The problem was with our cow. We had a heck of a time trying to get her to lie on her back."

All right, it's not the funniest joke in the world. It's in questionable taste. And it's not one that I would tell. However, it does make the principal's main point—that education is important. And it was offered in a rural area of the country. It should have been perceived as mildly amusing. Yet the principal who told the joke described the audience reaction as dead silence. They glared at him and looked like they wanted to throw things.

"I can't figure it out," I said. "There are problems with the joke, but it made your point and it should have gotten at least a mild response."

"Oh, there's one thing I forgot to tell you," he said. "Two superintendents in the audience were elderly single women."

Need I say more? He had inadvertently offended two key

members of his audience. As a result the rest of the audience felt embarrassed and uncomfortable. The really sad part was that the offensive reference could have been easily avoided. It wasn't necessary to use "two old-maid English teachers" in the story. The joke would have worked just as well with two people of any sex or occupation that didn't know about animal husbandry. In fact it probably would have been funnier to label the protagonists as two "city slickers."

You've got to keep your radar on at all times in order to detect anything that might offend your audience. That's why audience analysis should continue right up to the moment of your presentation. You never know when you will learn something crucial.

For example I was asked to give a speech at a Valentine's Day meeting of the San Diego Rotary Club. The meeting was a gala affair attended by a few hundred members and their spouses. Seated on the dais with club dignitaries, I chatted with the president until the program began. He noted that the flowers decorating the room had been donated by the widow of a recently deceased florist. The florist had been a popular member of the club, and his widow was in the audience. Those casual remarks averted disaster! My speech had included a joke about a florist who mistakenly ships a memorial wreath instead of a festive floral arrangement. It would have proved extremely offensive and upsetting.

No matter how well you think you know your audience, take an extra moment to eliminate unnecessary assumptions. You'll be glad you did.

RULE 3: THE MORE SPECIFIC, THE MORE EFFECTIVE.

Thorough audience research can also pay off by making your humor more effective. It allows you to create "in-jokes"— humor based on specific references to your audience's interests, values, and foibles.

An in-joke makes you an "insider." It contains information that is thought to be known only by members of a particular group. Using an in-joke communicates that you're "in" on it.

It's the intellectual version of a secret handshake. It creates group bonding and identification with your audience. It also generates a lot of laughter because it's based on surprise. Your audience, which doesn't expect you to possess inside information, will laugh heartily at your revelation.

An item in the show business trade paper *Variety* on February 14, 1986, illustrates this principle:

> Rep. Howard Berman (D-Hollywood Hills, San Fernando Valley) arrived late at yesterday's Motion Picture & TV Assembly luncheon sponsored by the Motion Picture Association. He flew in from the Democratic Party caucus at Greenbrier, W. Va., and his plane was delayed.
>
> "I hope," he told the studio executives gathered to hear his talk, "that the extra time you've had with each other has not led to more than two personnel changes."[1]

The quip was an inside joke referring to the entertainment industry's constant reshuffling of executives from one studio to another. It communicated Berman's knowledge of his audience and made them feel he was one of them. And it made them more receptive to the rest of his speech.

RULE 4: TALK THEIR LANGUAGE.

One of the best ways of developing specific knowledge of your audience is to learn their "language." Humor, like any other form of communication, is most effective when you understand your audience's point of view. However, every person's point of view is unique. Most of us are like the legendary tailor who had an audience with the pope. Afterward a reporter asked, "What's he like?" The tailor replied, "He's a 42 regular."

Each of us looks at things and events through the prism of our own experiences. Perceptual psychologists say that we each invent our own universe. We are what we've experienced. And we reveal our personal universe through language. What does this mean for analyzing an audience? It means that we want to know "where they're coming from." We want to "talk their language." We want our choice of words to reflect the universe of our audience.

How do you ensure that your humor really connects with your audience? The magic word is *jargon*. Jargon refers to the slang, buzzwords, and phrases peculiar to a particular group of people. Like the in-joke, jargon helps establish a bond between speaker and audience. It also sharpens communication.

A good example comes from a speech by A. Wright Elliott, executive vice president of the Chase Manhattan Bank. In an address to advertising executives in Venice, Italy, Elliott used jargon to break the ice:

> Venice! What a city! The perfect meeting site for people like you—hypersensitive to time—to deadlines, to "drop-dead dates." Here in Venice you can't postpone anything by saying, "I'll cross that bridge when I come to it."[2]

In the advertising business the phrase *drop-dead date* refers to an absolute deadline. By using this phrase in his quip, Elliott communicated awareness of his audience's work and built rapport with them.

If a little jargon goes a long way, then a lot of jargon goes even farther. It's like learning to speak a foreign language. You can speak a few words to show you made an effort or you can become fluent. The more jargon that you know and use, the more effective you will be with your audience.

Let's see how this works. A baseball player was having dinner with his wife when their baby started to cry. The wife was tired. She'd spent all day working. So she said, "Change the baby." The husband was taken aback. He said, "I'm a baseball player. I don't know how to change a baby." The wife put her hands on her hips and said, "Look, buster, you lay the diaper out like a diamond, you put second base on home plate, put the baby's bottom on the pitcher's mound, hook up first and third, and slide home underneath. And if it starts to rain, the game ain't called, you start all over again."

Now that's communicating!

While he was president, Ronald Reagan addressed a wide variety of audiences. His efforts to establish a common bond with each of them provide a model worthy of emulation. Here are some classic examples:

The International Association of Chiefs of Police, September 28, 1981: "You and I have a few things in common. Harry Truman once said about the job I have that being president is like riding a tiger: A man has to keep riding or he'll be swallowed. Well, that's a pretty good description of what you do for a living."

Republican party picnic in Utah, September 10, 1982: "You know, this is almost as big a crowd as an Osmond family reunion."

The American Medical Association, June 23, 1983: "I'm delighted to address this annual meeting of the AMA House of Delegates, and I want to congratulate Dr. Jirka and Dr. Boyle on their new positions. I can't help but think what a great place this would be and what a great moment to have a low back pain."

Presidential Awards for Excellence in Science and Math Teaching, October 19, 1983: "Well, it's wonderful to have all of you here today at the White House. We want you to enjoy our little get-together today. So, please, lean back, relax, and stop worrying about what the students are doing to the substitute teachers back home."

Visit to Walt Disney's EPCOT Center, March 8, 1983: "I just watched a program—I don't know just what to call it—a show, a pageant with several hundred of my junior high and high school friends here, and I'm pleased to announce I didn't get hit with one spitball."

Six Rules for Putting Humor into Its Most Powerful Form

A little girl watched as her father the clergyman prepared his sermon. "Daddy," she asked, "does God tell you what to say?" "Of course, child," the father answered. "Why do you ask?"

"Then why," said the little girl, "do you keep scratching some of it out?"

Why indeed! Perhaps because he knows that all good writing is rewriting. That's why editing is essential in the preparation of effective humor. Careful editing ensures that your humor will have maximum impact. It forces you to think about what you're going to say. It makes you evaluate the exact wording of your stories. And it helps you put your quips and anecdotes into their most effective form.

Six simple rules will guide you through the editing process:

1. PUT THE PUNCH LINE AT THE END.

This sounds like common sense, and it is—yet the rule is frequently broken. A good example comes from a compendium of wit and humor:

> A woman was bemoaning the fact that her husband had left her for the sixth time.
> "Never mind," consoled the neighbor. "He'll be back."
> "Not this time," sobbed the wife. "He's taken his golf clubs this time."[3]

Here's a joke from a leading jokebook for speakers and the punch line isn't even at the end. Unfortunately this is typical.

Let's make sure you understand my point. The punch line is "He's taken his golf clubs." That's the joke. The woman knows her husband won't return because he's taken his golf clubs. Yet the joke as written says, "He's taken his golf clubs *this time.*" Why is *this time* tacked on at the end? I don't know. What I do know is that it weakens the joke. (And I admit, the joke is pretty weak to begin with.)

The point is that you never want to continue speaking past the point of surprise in a joke. When the punch line is at the end, your audience is surprised and amused. When it's not, they're surprised and confused. The punch line is a spark that ignites laughter. It doesn't catch fire if you keep speaking.

2. ELIMINATE EXCESS WORDS.

You've probably heard that brevity is the soul of wit. Do you know the corollary? The longer the joke, the funnier it better be.

Audience expectations rise in direct relation to the length of humorous material. And this just makes sense. Most people regard their time as precious. The more you take, the more they expect in return. So your goal should be to chisel away at your quips and anecdotes. Cut out the fat. Make every word count.

When you use personal anecdotes, talk them into a tape recorder. Then make a transcript. Why? Because most people have a tendency to add extra words. When you can see the words in front of you, it's much easier to edit. Cut the story down to essentials. Then practice saying it that way until it comes naturally.

Remember, if you find yourself saying, "To make a long story short," then it's already too long.

3. MAKE IT CONVERSATIONAL.

This rule acknowledges the fact that most speakers get their humor from a written source—jokebooks, newspapers, or magazines. There's nothing wrong with that. The problem occurs if you don't adapt the written humor for oral presentation.

Anecdotes in a magazine are designed to be read silently, not read aloud. So put them into your own words. Remove the tongue twisters. Look for words or phrases that can be replaced by gestures or vocal intonations. Simplify the language as much as possible. And cut out the extra words!

4. CREATE AN IMAGE.

There's a basic rule of writing that applies especially to humor: Specific is terrific. It means that specific, concrete images are more effective than vague, abstract ones. You want your audience to see a picture. A fuzzy image is difficult to see and loses audience attention. So it's your job to make the picture sharp and clear.

Note the difference between the following two opening lines for an anecdote:

* Three guys walked into a bar.
* Woody Allen, Lee Iacocca, and Donald Trump walked into a bar.

The first line is vague and fuzzy. The second line creates a very specific image. It's easy to visualize and it's more interesting.

Replace vague references in quips and anecdotes with specific images. Your humor will become more effective. And your audiences will pay more attention.

5. PUT THE AUDIENCE IN THE PICTURE.

Earlier in this chapter we discussed the importance of learning specific information about your audience. It is during the editing process that such information comes into play. When you sharpen your humor with specific images, try to use local references familiar to your audience. Make their world a part of the anecdote. Put them in the picture. For example, instead of saying, "Someone walked into a store," use the name of a local store. Look for opportunities to insert local references into all your jokes and stories.

After you've identified an opening for a local reference, make the reference as specific as possible. A good example comes from Thomas Labrecque, president of the Chase Manhattan Bank. Here's how he began a speech to a Los Angeles audience in 1984:

> It's a great pleasure to be with you today. I always enjoy coming to California. I've been a big fan of this state ever since Walter O'Malley moved his corporate headquarters to Chavez Ravine. (But please don't tell any of our good Brooklyn customers that.)[4]

Although Labrecque is talking about the Los Angeles Dodgers baseball team, he doesn't mention them. Instead he says,

"...Walter O'Malley moved his corporate headquarters to Chavez Ravine." Walter O'Malley was the Dodgers' owner, and Chavez Ravine was the location of Dodger Stadium. These references are even more specific than "Los Angeles Dodgers" and proportionately more effective with the audience.

6. CHOOSE THE RIGHT WORD.

Ernest Hemingway was once asked why he rewrote *For Whom the Bell Tolls* five times. The questioner wanted to know what was so difficult. Hemingway reportedly replied, "Getting the words right." The story may be apocryphal, but its moral should be taken as gospel: Word choice is critical.

John R. Bonee, a corporate communications expert, has noted that word choice can make the difference between a good speech and a great speech. He cites FDR's declaration of war against Japan as an example. That speech begins with the words "December 7, 1941: A day that will live in infamy." Bonee has observed that the original manuscript began differently. FDR's speech writer had typed, "December 7, 1941: A day that will live in world history." Roosevelt replaced *world history* with *infamy*. By changing one word he created a great speech.[5]

Word choice is even more critical with humorous material. It makes the difference between success and failure. For example I was at a meeting of businesspeople where the speaker used a good joke. He said, "Sign in a workaholic's office: Thank God for Mondays." Surprisingly it didn't get much response.

An instant analysis revealed the problem. The joke was based on the cliché "Thank God it's Friday." The punch line "reversed" the cliché and replaced Friday with Monday. Who would prefer Mondays to Fridays? Only a workaholic. So the speaker made his joke: "Sign in a workaholic's office: Thank God for Mondays." But look closely at the phrasing. The original cliché is "Thank God *it's* Friday." So the joke should have been "Sign in a workaholic's office: Thank God *it's* Monday," not "Thank God *for* Mondays." That minor mistake wrecked the joke. That's what happens when you don't choose the right word.

In short you have to be carefully prepared—like the fourth-grader who had been learning about first aid when a car crashed in front of her house. The next day she told her teacher about the accident. The little girl said, "There was a man with his arm bleeding. But I was prepared." The teacher said, "Did you use first aid?" The girl said, "Yes. I put my head between my legs so I wouldn't faint."

This story teaches us three things. First, first aid, like charity, begins at home. Second, you won't faint if you're prepared. And third, it never hurts to use your head.

If you think about it, these are the keys to developing successful humor. First, begin at home. Do your homework and learn as much as possible about your audience. Second, be fully prepared. If you're prepared, you won't faint. Third, use your head. Edit your humor into its most effective form. And if you have trouble applying these rules—deciding whether a story is appropriate or choosing the right word—just remember Yogi Berra's advice for making tough decisions: "When you come to a fork in the road, take it."

FIVE

Building Yourself Up by Putting Yourself Down

You grow up the day you have your first real laugh—at yourself.

—Ethel Barrymore

I sometimes begin a speech with these lines: "Eight years ago I practiced law with an international corporate law firm in San Francisco. Today I'm a humor consultant. Now, whether or not you think the world needs a humor consultant, I'm sure you'll agree we can use one less attorney." Most people do agree. I can tell by their applause and laughter. The reason these lines work so well is simple: I'm making fun of myself.

Why Self-Effacing Humor Is So Powerful

Self-effacing humor is a leadership trait. It reflects strength and confidence. It shows that you're secure enough to laugh at yourself. It also creates rapport, boosts morale, and makes you more likable.

Perhaps that's why it's frequently used by Miller Communications senior vice president Fred Hoar. A veteran Silicon Valley advertising and public relations executive, Hoar knows that his name has an unfortunate connotation, particularly when linked with his profession. In order to counter the negative meaning and show his sense of humor, he makes fun of the situation. He begins his presentations by saying, "My name is Fred Hoar. That's spelled F, R, E, D." His audience is instantly won over.

Walter Kiechel III, an editor of *Fortune* magazine, terms the self-deprecating jest "the most admirable form of executive humor." His conclusion is based on research about communication between high- and low-status individuals. According to Kiechel, researchers have learned that joking is usually begun by the higher-status person. Therefore when executives poke fun at themselves, they momentarily eliminate the status difference that separates them from subordinates. This creates an opportunity for meaningful communication. The self-effacing humor acts as a bridge across the status gap.[1]

This theory is confirmed by common experience. For example employees of ASK Computer Systems Inc. could easily be intimidated by Sandra Kurtzig, the company's multimillionaire chairman, president, and CEO just by virtue of her status. But she eliminates such fears with large doses of self-effacing humor. Her descriptions of how she built the $200-million company from scratch are typical:

"I'd like to tell you I started in a garage, but I didn't have a garage."

"When I started this company, my long-range planning consisted of figuring out where I'd go to lunch."

"When I told people I was in software, they thought that meant women's lingerie."

Such lines dispel nervousness in subordinates and make Kurtzig very approachable.

Another top executive who pokes fun at himself is Dr. Ronald Cape, chairman of Cetus Corporation and a past president of the Industrial Biotechnology Association. One of his major missions is to improve the public image of biotechnology. "Within the biotechnology field there is a general feeling that we are terribly misunderstood," he explains. "Both scientists and industry people believe that the public would be more supportive of our work if only they were better educated, if only they had all the facts."

Unfortunately it's not as simple as it seems. "The people who are trying to educate the public are scientists," states Cape. "They don't realize that the majority of the public has a blind that goes down as soon as they see science coming at them." In order to solve this problem Cape has been trying to get biotechnology people to put their message into more human, nonscientific terms. And in order to make his point Cape tells a story that pokes fun at his own communication abilities.

"A few years ago I was having a lot of trouble explaining biotechnology to my mother," he says. "So in a talk in my hometown I brought my mother along and directed the talk to her, even though the audience was five hundred engineers. I chose my language very carefully hoping there wouldn't be a single word or phrase that she wouldn't understand. Afterward I was driving her home, confident that I had achieved my goal. So I said, 'Well, Mom, how did you like the talk?' And she said, 'Oh, it was wonderful. I understood everything except the science.'"

The power of self-effacing humor isn't limited to top executives. No matter where you sit on the corporate ladder, you can probably benefit by poking a little fun at yourself. However, you've got to pick your spots.

Dr. Charles Gruner, professor of speech communication at the University of Georgia at Athens, has studied humor and persuasion for more than twenty years. He says, "A little self-deprecating humor shows that a speaker feels strong enough to make fun of himself. It creates audience rapport." The key words are *a little*. Social science research indicates that self-effacing humor operates as a curvilinear function: It's most effective at the top of the curve. This means that the two extremes—no self-effacing humor and too much self-effacing humor—are equally ineffective. Let's examine why. A total lack of self-effacing humor casts you as a stereotypical businessperson—a stuffed shirt. Too much self-effacing humor makes you a "Woody Allen" character—a neurotic type constantly putting yourself down. The most effective approach lies somewhere in between. By offering an occasional self-effacing quip, you obtain the benefits without the backlash.

What if you're talking about very serious matters that affect the lives of hundreds or thousands of people? You're talking about budgets or layoffs or lawsuits. You're talking about marketing plans or cash flow or trade barriers. Can you still use self-effacing humor?

Of course you can, *if* you make an important distinction. *Distinguish yourself from your subject matter.* Learn to take your work seriously without taking yourself so seriously. No matter how serious your work or topic, it's always safe to poke fun at yourself. In addition to creating rapport, self-directed humor offers a strategic competitive advantage: It keeps your ego in check and maintains your perspective.

How Politicians Create Rapport

Politicians have long recognized the value of self-effacing humor in creating a positive image. In fact they have transformed the act of "telling one on yourself" into a veritable art form. Businesspeople can learn a lot by observing their public-sector counterparts in action.

For example Tennessee governor Ned Ray McWherter always acknowledges a glowing introduction with a self-effacing story. He likes to tell about his visit with a constituent who said, "Ned Ray, I've been seeing you a lot in the paper lately. And Ned Ray, I've been seeing you a lot on the tube lately. And Ned Ray, I just want you to remember one thing, the size of your funeral is going to depend a hell of a lot on the weather."

McWherter's story creates instant rapport with his audience. By poking a little fun at himself, he communicates his sense of humor and ability to "take a joke." And most important he humanizes himself after an introduction that makes him sound like a saint. Any manager or executive can use McWherter's technique to advantage.

New York governor Mario Cuomo also uses self-effacing humor to create rapport. A good example is a speech he delivered to the New York Press Club: "As I left Albany to come down here tonight, she [my wife] gave me some last-minute advice. She said, 'I know it's a difficult subject and a tough group. But don't be intimidated. And don't try to be charming, witty, or intellectual. Just be yourself.'"[2]

In addition to creating rapport, self-effacing humor can be used as a diplomacy tool. That's how it's used by former Alaska floor leader Bill Ray to keep debates on track. "I'll stand up and say, 'I hope I'm on the right page, Mr. President,'" says Ray. "This helps the rest of them who may not be on the right page." Ray also finds that self-effacing humor can take the sting out of a caustic remark. "You give someone a jab and then you turn it around to include yourself," he explains. "You imply that you might be as dumb as he is given the same opportunity."

Businesspeople can apply Ray's ideas to the endless meetings that they routinely attend. Self-effacing humor can help rein in irrelevant participants, guide the discussion, and keep the agenda moving along. All that's required is a willingness to laugh at yourself. "If you don't laugh at yourself," observes Ray, "you can't laugh at anyone, in the true sense of the word."

And if you can't laugh at yourself in national politics, you may not be electable. Senator Bob Dole found that out the hard way when he ran for vice president on the Republican ticket in 1976. Known for a sharp tongue and a sharper wit, Dole castigated his opponents unmercifully. According to *Time*, some analysts still believe that Dole's fiery style kept the Republicans out of the White House in 1976.[3]

By the time the presidential primaries of 1988 rolled around, Dole had learned his lesson. He made a conscious effort to aim some of his zingers at himself. In fact one of his self-effacing quips concerned his previous lack of self-effacing humor. "My assignment [in the 1976 campaign] was to go for the jugular, and I did—my own."[4]

How to Defuse Controversial Issues

Although the chief benefit of self-effacing humor is its ability to create a general feeling of goodwill, it can also be used to address specific issues. A classic example comes from the 1960 presidential campaign. Candidate John F. Kennedy had to answer the charge that his family's wealth gave him an unfair advantage. He defused the issue with calculated self-effacing humor. Striding to the podium at a press conference, Kennedy told reporters that he wanted to read a telegram from his father. He read, "Dear Jack, Don't buy one more vote than necessary. I'll be damned if I'll pay for a landslide." The tactic worked, and the wealth issue was laughed out of the campaign.

Twenty years later a similar strategy was used by Ronald Reagan to overcome a negative image about his age. Reagan was sixty-nine years old when he ran for president in 1980. And he won the election despite criticism that he was too old for the job. During his first term he never missed an opportunity to poke fun at his age. A small sampling of his self-effacing age quips include the following:

"And it's with a happy heart that I share with you the honor of this special occasion, the 105th annual meeting of the great American Bar Association. It isn't true that I attended the first meeting."

"Somebody did quite a research job . . . to find a picture of me in the Dixon YMCA band. This should lay to rest the rumor that photography had yet to be invented when I was that age."

"When I was in fifth grade, I'm not sure I knew what a national debt was. Of course when I was in fifth grade, we didn't have one."

"And I want to say that I don't mind at all any of the jokes or remarks about my age, because Thomas Jefferson made a comment about the presidency and age. He said that one should not worry about one's exact chronological age in reference to his ability to perform one's task. And ever since he told me that, I stopped worrying."

The effect of four years of self-effacing age jokes was magical. When Reagan ran for a second term in 1984, the age issue was barely mentioned—yet he was four years older!

Another candidate with an age problem in the 1984 presidential sweepstakes was Colorado senator Gary Hart, who lost the Democratic nomination to Walter Mondale. Reporters checking into Hart's past had discovered a discrepancy about the year of his birth. It appeared that Hart had tried to shave a year off his age.

A solution was offered by Democratic party adviser Frank Mankiewicz. He suggested that Hart could eliminate the age change with self-effacing humor. Hart could start a speech with a statement of fact and then say, "I'm as certain of that as I am of my own age."[5] Unfortunately we'll never know if the tactic would have worked. Rather than defusing the problem with humor, Hart ignored the issue, and it dogged him throughout his campaign.

How to Improve Corporate Image

The power of self-effacing humor to create goodwill and defuse thorny issues is not limited to individuals. It can be applied by corporations to enhance a company's image. Take Intel Corporation, for example. On April Fools' Day the Santa Clara–based semiconductor manufacturer publishes a spoof of its employee newsletter. Parody issues have lampooned topics such as excess inventory, corporate reorganizations, and employee benefits. One cover even sported a photograph of Chairman and CEO Gordon Moore admitting that his economic predictions flopped. (See the excerpt on pages 84–85.) That April Fools' issue reflects Intel's commitment to an open culture. It demonstrates that Intel management is strong enough to laugh at itself. And it boosts employee morale.

Similar benefits were realized by Apple Computer Inc. when the company sent out its 1985 holiday greeting card. According to the *San Francisco Chronicle*, the card's only message was "All Is Calm, All Is Bright." Industry observers commented that the card showed Apple felt secure enough about its future to poke fun at itself—exactly the image Apple wanted to convey after a year of management turmoil.[6]

Perhaps the most conservative organization to harness the power of self-effacing humor was the Moral Majority. Several years ago it sought to counter its image among liberals as a bunch of far-right book burners. Its solution: advertise and sell "Official Moral Majority Book Burning Matches." Moral Majority members distributed them in Washington to anyone who accused the organization of book burning. According to one newspaper, the ad read, "These matches come complete without sulfur heads and an official list of the top ten books to be burned. Only the list is blank, to make a striking impression on everyone. The Moral Majority does not sanction book burning of any description." Dr. Ronald Godwin, a Moral Majority spokesman, was quoted as saying, "People love them. They're a great humor item, and one thing the Moral Majority needs to do is develop a sense of humor."[7]

One thing everyone needs to do is develop a sense of humor. And self-effacing humor is a good way to begin. So poke some fun at yourself. It helps keep things in perspective. It reflects confidence and security. It shows that you're a leader. Go ahead. Admit your minor mistakes and laugh at them. Everyone else will anyway.

Excerpt from Intel April Fools' Employee Newsletter

news

Moore Once Again Says, "Recession Will End."

As he did in the spring of 1981 and 1982, Gordon Moore, chairman and chief executive officer, recently predicted that the recession saddling the semiconductor industry would end soon.

"This time I'm sure I'm right," Gordon said in a meeting with security analysts. "All the signs of a prerecovery period are there: bad pricing, weakening demand, overcapacity, and a general sense of malaise. On the premise that it can't get any worse, I'm predicting it will therefore start getting better."

The recession began in the fourth quarter of 1980, when Intel reported lower quarter-to-quarter results for the first time since the 1974–75 recession. In the spring of 1981 Gordon predicted the first quarter would be the low point, with sequential gains in revenue and earnings during the remainder of the year. The prediction proved half right. Earnings climbed from the first quarter's nickel a share but then dropped back to a dime in Q4. "The problem in 1981," Gordon noted recently, "was that we thought the recession was a V-shaped one, with a sharp drop and a sharp recovery as in 1974–75."

As the recession dragged on into 1982, Intel suddenly saw a strong increase in demand during the spring. While moving ahead with hiring and plant expansion programs in response to the apparent upturn, Gordon sounded a note of caution in his second annual "recession will end" prediction when he said, "Even two robins don't make it spring." As it turned out, the third robin stayed south, and Q3 and Q4 pretax earnings headed in the same direction. "The problem in 1982," Gordon said, "was that we thought the recession was a U-shaped one, with a sharp drop, a long bottom, and then a sharp recovery.

"This year I think we have the shape down. It appears this recession will go down in history as a W-shaped one, with a sharp drop, a little bitty recovery, a little bitty drop and then a sharp recovery. I think we're starting up the last leg of the W now. What's more," he concluded, "I saw four robins in my garden this morning."[8]

Eight Self-Effacing Anecdotes for Any Occasion

John Augustine, a lobbyist for DuPont/Conoco, believes that you can never go wrong with self-effacing humor. "Lobbyists must establish a relationship with senators and representatives," he observes. "And you can't talk to a legislator as if your issue is a matter of life and death. You can't afford to take yourself too seriously." Good advice for anyone.

Practicing what he preaches, Augustine often takes stories he's heard about someone else and switches them to make fun of himself. One of his favorites originally concerned two travelers and a lawyer who stop at an inn. In Augustine's version the lawyer becomes a lobbyist:

> Two travelers and a lobbyist stop at an inn. The innkeeper says, "I've only got two rooms. Someone will have to stay in the barn." One of the travelers volunteers and goes to the barn. A few minutes later there's a knock on the door. The innkeeper says, "What is it?" The traveler says, "I can't stay in the barn. There's a cow out there and I'm Hindu." So the other traveler volunteers. A few minutes later there's a knock on the door. "I can't stay in the barn. There's a pig out there and I'm Jewish." So the lobbyist goes out. A few minutes later there's a knock on the door. The innkeeper opens the door, and there stand the cow and the pig.

You can apply this story to yourself simply by following Augustine's strategy. Just replace *lobbyist* with your own profession or position. If you don't like Augustine's pig story, don't worry. All of the following self-effacing anecdotes are ready-made rapport builders just waiting for the insertion of your occupation.

1. AN HISTORIC EVENT

Three men died and went to heaven on the same day. The first man was the pope, the second man was Billy Graham, the third was a [occupation]. Now, Saint Peter met them at the Pearly Gates to usher them into their new, eternal homes. As Saint Peter led them down the golden streets, he stopped in front of three buildings—two tiny little shacks and one immense mansion. Saint Peter directed the pope and the Reverend Graham to the shacks. Then he told the [occupation] to move his things into the mansion. Immediately both Billy Graham and the pope reverently inquired as to why two great servants like themselves would spend eternity in cozy, but unattractive shacks while a [*occupation*] was spending eternity in such a mansion. Saint Peter replied, "Hey, guys, we've got lots of preachers and popes up here. This is our first [*occupation*]!"

2. BRAINS

A man walked into a store to buy some brains and asked the storekeeper for prices. The storekeeper said, "Bankers' brains are $100 a pound. Doctors' brains are $110 a pound. Engineers' brains are $120 a pound. And [*occupation's*] brains are $500 a pound." The man said, "How come the [*occupation*] brains cost so much more than the other brains?" The storekeeper said, "You know how many [*occupations*] it takes to get a pound of brains?"

3. CHAOS

Three gentlemen arrived together at the Pearly Gates and were informed there was only room for one. They decided that the man with the oldest profession would be the one allowed to come in. The first stepped forward and said, "The Lord made Adam and then created Eve out of a rib from Adam, and that took surgery. I'm a surgeon, so I guess it's me." But before he could move in, the second one said, "Wait. Before the Lord did that, he worked six days. Everything was chaos and he worked six days and created Earth. That makes him an engineer. I'm an engineer, so I guess that calls for me." Then the third one stepped up and said, "Hold on a minute. I'm an [*occupation*]. Who do you think made all that chaos?"

4. TAKE YOUR PICK

Two young women met a frog on the street. "Kiss me," the frog said, "and I'll turn into a [*occupation*]." One of the women picked him up and put him in her purse. "Aren't you going to kiss him?" the other asked. "No. Who needs another [*occupation*]? A *talking* frog is really worth something."

5. DAMAGE CONTROL

Soviet leader Mikhail Gorbachev was reviewing a May Day parade. He asked, "Who are those people marching with the troops?" An aide said, "Those are [occupation]s, sir." Gorbachev said, "Why are they in the ranks with the military?" The aide said, "You'd be surprised at the damage they can do."

6. A TOUGH PROBLEM

God and Saint Peter were talking about problems in heaven. God said, "We're losing money every day. We've got to straighten things out." Saint Peter said, "What should we do?" God said, "Get a [occupation] to straighten things out." Saint Peter said, "Where are we going to find a [occupation] up here?"

7. THEY NEVER LEARN

Three [occupation]s rented an airplane for their annual hunting expedition in Canada, where they stayed in a lodge by a lake. They landed on a tiny landing strip, and the pilot warned them that they'd have to travel light on the return trip to clear the trees at the end of the runway.

When the pilot returned one week later, he found to his dismay that the [occupation]s were waiting for him, each dragging a heavy moose as a trophy of the week's hunting. "There's no way we'll clear those trees," he said. But the [occupation]s begged, cajoled, and finally offered him a thousand-dollar bonus if he'd attempt a takeoff with all the booty. He reluctantly agreed.

The plane sped down the runway, gathering speed, and finally took off into the air. It soared higher and higher, but clipped the trees at the end of the runway and crashed into a field just beyond. The plane and cargo were destroyed, but the [occupation]s and the pilot survived. "Congratulations," the [occupation]s said. "We made it one hundred yards farther than we did last year."

8. BIRDS OF A FEATHER

A doctor, an engineer, and a [*occupation*] go sailing. Their boat springs a leak and starts to sink. Then they notice that sharks are circling the boat. And they begin to panic. Finally the doctor decides to jump in and try to swim for shore. As soon as he gets in the water, the sharks attack and devour him.

The boat continues to sink until the engineer can't stand it anymore. He dives into the ocean and swims frantically for the beach. The sharks attack and devour him too.

By now the boat is nearly under water, and a crowd has gathered on the beach to try to rescue the [*occupation*]. But before they can do anything, the boat sinks and the [*occupation*] is forced to swim to shore.

To the crowd's amazement, the sharks circle the [*occupation*] and guide him safely to the beach. As he steps onto the sand, the bystanders rush up to him, asking why the sharks didn't attack.

He replies, "Professional courtesy."

Telling It Like It Is: Techniques for Effective Delivery

From the silence which prevails I conclude Lauderdale has been making a joke.

—**Richard Sheridan**

An older preacher was talking to a younger preacher. The older preacher said, "You know, sometimes on Sunday morning the congregation begins to nod off. So I've found a way to wake them up. At the point in my sermon when they begin to doze, I say, 'Last night I held in my arms a woman who is the wife of another man.' That wakes them up. Then, when they look at me startled, I say, 'It was my dear mother.' "

A few weeks later the young preacher was giving a sermon and some of his congregation began dozing off. And he remembered what the older preacher had told him. So he said, "Last night I held in my arms a woman who is the wife of another man." The whole congregation looked at him. Everyone was awake. And he said, "I can't remember who it was."

The young preacher had a problem that is shared by many businesspeople around the world: an inability to remember quips, jokes, and anecdotes. The preacher's response is also quite common—he tried to tell his story anyway. It's astounding how many people will attempt to tell a funny story even though they can't remember significant details. They believe that key items such as the setup and the punch line will come back to them as they speak. Unfortunately such optimism is usually misplaced. And as businesspeople stumble around trying to recall how many MBAs it takes to screw in a light bulb, any humor in their tales rapidly disappears.

The memory lapse is only one of several basic mistakes that can derail successful delivery of humorous material. *Mistakes* is the key word. It is fundamental errors in delivery rather than lack of sophisticated comic ability that typically cause problems for business speakers. Although many claim they can't tell a joke, their delivery can be improved just by avoiding a few common mistakes.

The Six Secrets of Successful Delivery

RULE 1: LEARN YOUR LINES.

The first rule for delivering humor successfully is to know your material. This means more than just remembering the punch line. It means practicing the quip or anecdote and knowing what words to emphasize. It means understanding why it's funny. And it means memorizing all the significant details. If you don't take the time to learn your lines, your audience may end up laughing *at* you rather than with you.

RULE 2: BE CONFIDENT AND COMFORTABLE.

An old man was hit by a car. As he lay in the street waiting for an ambulance, an onlooker covered him with a jacket and propped his head up on a pillow. The onlooker asked, "Are you comfortable?" The old man said, "I make a living."

No matter what you do for a living, you must be comfortable with humor in order to deliver it effectively. Humor comes in many forms. If you can't tell a joke, then use one of the simple types of humor discussed in chapter 3. Just make sure that you're comfortable with whatever type you choose.

You must also have confidence in every story you tell. Any uncertainty or hesitation in your delivery will lower your chance of success. It is a basic rule of communication that people tend to respond the way they are expected to respond. Humor is no exception. A delivery without confidence communicates that you don't expect anyone to find your stories funny. In deciding whether to use a particular quip or story, apply the rule of grammar for commas: When in doubt, leave it out.

RULE 3: DON'T ANNOUNCE THAT YOU'RE GOING TO TELL A JOKE.

The single most common mistake in the delivery of humor is announcing that you're going to tell a joke. Business speakers do it all the time. "A funny thing happened to me on the way over here today...." "My secretary just told me a great joke that I want to share with you...." "That reminds me of a funny story...."

What are you doing when you use such lines? First, you take away the surprise that's at the heart of most humor. And second, you say, "Now I'm going to be funny"—which increases audience resistance. Neither outcome is desirable. Besides, resorting to such lines is lazy. It means that you didn't take the time to analogize your humor to one of your presentation points.

The most effective approach is to make your point, say "It's like...," and then tell your story. Listen to the difference between saying "It's like..." and "It reminds me of a funny story." When a speaker says "It's like...," he or she implies that a relevant analogy will follow. In contrast, "It reminds me of a story" produces the horrid anticipation of an irrelevant, unfunny anecdote. As unfair as this reaction may seem, it is a result of long-term social conditioning. Speakers have probably been reminded of funny stories that aren't funny since the Stone Age. So audiences tend to cringe when they hear that phrase.

Of course there are exceptions. The best example comes from the oratory of Sandra Kurtzig, chairman, founder, and CEO of ASK Computer Systems Inc. In a speech to shareholders Kurtzig made a point and then said it reminded her *speech writer* of a joke. When the laughter stopped, she told the joke with absolute confidence, having absolved herself of all responsibility.

RULE 4: PAUSE FOR THE PUNCH LINE AND WAIT FOR THE LAUGH.

If announcing a joke is a mistake because it alerts your audience too soon, then not alerting them at all is equally disastrous. No one will know that they're supposed to laugh.

Does it seem strange that an audience would not know that it's supposed to laugh at humorous material? The explanation lies in the serious nature of business communication. Remember, the great advantage of using humor in a business presentation is that no one expects you to be funny. The down side is that your audience may not be mentally prepared to recognize humor. In order to ensure the correct response, you must signal your intentions.

The proper time to communicate that you expect smiles or laughter is just before the punch line. A short pause will do the job. The pause alerts the audience that a punch line is coming and prepares them to laugh. A good example is an old, self-effacing quip that many speakers use to break the ice: "I noticed a few of you came early to get a good seat... in the back." Punctuating this remark with a pause before the punch line, creates the special rhythm that identifies the remark as a joke.

After you've told the punch line, pause again. This pause gives the audience time to react. It is a further signal that you expect them to laugh or at least chuckle. If you continue immediately without pausing, you inhibit audience reaction and decrease your chance of success. When the audience does laugh, don't continue until they've finished laughing.

The duration of audience laughter depends on the size of your audience, as well as the strength of your anecdote. A small audience usually produces a single, rapid burst of laughter. In contrast a very large audience generates laughter in three waves. The first wave comes from the people sitting up front. The second wave is from almost everyone else. And the third wave comes from the people who laugh because everyone else is laughing. That's why a speech with humor takes longer to deliver to a large crowd. Keep this in mind when planning the length of your presentation.

Finally remember the lesson given by the apocryphal professor of comedy:

Professor to student: "Ask me, what is the secret of comedy?"
Student: "What is the secret of..."
Professor: "Timing!"

RULE 5: ANTICIPATE AND PREPARE.

Now I've got some good news and some bad news. The bad news is that no matter how many rules you follow, it's inevitable that things will sometimes go wrong during your presentations. The microphone will go dead. The lights will go out. A loud noise will disrupt your chain of thought. The good news is that you can anticipate such problems and handle them with humor.

It's a serious mistake to ignore awkward moments that occur when you're making a presentation. When you continue as if nothing happened, then your audience will become distracted. For example let's say you're presenting the latest budget figures and the lights suddenly go out. If you continue without acknowledging the problem, then your audience has two choices. First, they can think that you don't realize that the lights went out. That will lower your credibility. After all, only an extremely unperceptive person could miss such an event. Second, your audience can think that you're aware of the lighting failure but that you're too nervous to acknowledge it. You will appear too stage-frightened to deviate one iota from your prepared presentation. In that event your audience will become extremely uncomfortable because they feel sorry for you. In either case they will stop focusing on the specific content of your presentation. Your points will not be heard or retained. And your communication goals will not be accomplished.

To avert such tragedy, you must put your audience at ease by communicating both an awareness of the embarrassing incident and that you're undaunted by it. These objectives can be accomplished with a humorous acknowledgment—a quick quip that makes light of the situation.

A good example occurred during a White House state dinner honoring Egyptian president Anwar Sadat in 1981. President Ronald Reagan was midway through his remarks when the sound of fire engines filled the room. Without missing a beat the president looked out the window, then looked at his guests and said, "Congress isn't in session, is it?" The guests laughed, and the president continued his speech.

The Ronald Reagan example illustrates an important principle about the humorous acknowledgment. It doesn't have to be very funny. Its purpose is to communicate that you're aware of and undisturbed by an awkward situation. Your audience will laugh at almost anything because your quip will relieve their tension. Most important, a lower standard applies to humor that is spontaneous. People don't expect as much.

Think about your own experience. Have you ever laughed at a line that someone said "off the top of their head"? Part of what makes it funny is its speed. The person who said the line is "quick." We admire rapidly improvised wit and laugh to show our appreciation, even if the line isn't particularly hysterical.

You can take advantage of this phenomenon by making your humorous acknowledgments *appear* spontaneous. Just follow a simple three-step process: Anticipate awkward situations that might arise; write your ad libs in advance; and be ready to use them when the awkward moment occurs. This technique is a time-honored favorite of professional speakers. It changes embarrassing disruptions into opportunities for establishing a reputation as a quick wit. It's a classic example of turning negative events into positive actions.

The power of the canned ad lib was demonstrated perfectly by actor David Niven during the Oscar Award ceremonies of 1974. As Niven prepared to introduce Elizabeth Taylor, he was interrupted by a streaker—a naked man who ran across the stage. Niven reacted instantly. "Isn't it fascinating to think," he said, "that probably the only laugh that man will ever get is by stripping off his clothes and showing his shortcomings?"

An article by John Culhane in *Reader's Digest* later revealed the secret of Niven's instant response. "Viewers were amazed at Niven's quick wit," wrote Culhane. "But streaking was something of a fad then, and the show's producers had prepared the perfect squelch, just in case."[1] You, too, should be prepared—just in case.

RULE 6: KEEP IT BRIEF.

A dignitary visiting a foreign land made an appearance before a large gathering of its peasants. He launched into a long, rambling anecdote that continued for more than thirty minutes. The peasants were respectfully silent. When the speaker was done, his interpreter rose and said four words. Everyone laughed uproariously. The dignitary was stunned. "How could you tell my story so quickly?" he gasped. "Story too long," said the interpreter. "So I say, 'He tell joke. Laugh.'"

Most businesspeople don't have an interpreter to intercede with their audiences. This is unfortunate. It means that no one will order your audience to laugh if you tell a long, drawn-out joke. More important, no one will order them not to groan.

The surest way to turn off an audience and kill the humorous potential of your anecdotes is to drone on too long. The best advice on this subject, and on delivery in general, comes from Franklin D. Roosevelt. When asked to reveal his secrets of public speaking, he said, "Be sincere; be brief; be seated." Enough said.

Great Ad Libs for Awkward Moments

On May 7, 1988, then vice president George Bush made an embarrassing slip of the tongue during a routine campaign appearance. His speech was about being a partner with Ronald Reagan. And he said, "We've had triumphs. We've made mistakes. We've had sex." He meant to say "setbacks." When the crowd stopped laughing, Bush was ready. He said, "I feel like the javelin thrower who won the toss and elected to receive."

That night the story was covered on the *NBC Nightly News*. Anchorwoman Connie Chung reported the story as follows: "Bush got a big laugh, but it was unintentional—a slip of the tongue. But then he made a very good recovery." In fact the line about the javelin thrower was a standard "canned ad lib." Bush had it ready in case of a flub, and it worked perfectly. The results speak for themselves. A potentially negative news story was made positive, or at least neutral, by the fact that "a very good recovery" was made.

The next time you need to recover from an awkward situation, you can use the javelin-thrower line. Or, depending on the situation, you might try some of the following canned ad libs:

1. You're giving a presentation and a slide is upside-down.
   - "I'll get another one, this one must be defective."
   - "It looks good no matter how you look at it."
   - "For those of you standing on your heads."
2. Someone points out a spelling error in your work.
   - "Mark Twain once said he never respected anyone who couldn't spell a word more than one way."
3. You rush into the wrong meeting.
   - "This isn't the Kaplan bar mitzvah?"
4. You're writing on a flipchart and the highlighter runs out of ink.
   - "Obviously I've come to the dry part of my presentation."
5. In the middle of a meeting, you have to hunt through your briefcase for a key document.
   - "Well, as Frankenstein once said, 'Lucky my head's bolted on.'"

SEVEN

Handle Hostile Questions with Humor

He's been that way for years—a born questioner but he hates answers.

—Ring Lardner

An old man had been very religious all his life. But as his end neared, his faith wavered. He began to doubt the existence of God. So he asked God for a sign. He said, "God, I'm going to pray like I've never prayed before. Just give me a sign. Let me win the Irish Sweepstakes within the next year." And then the old man started praying. He prayed sixteen hours a day. All he did was pray.

Eventually a year passed. But the old man didn't win the Irish Sweepstakes. And he was angry. And he cursed the heavens. He said, "God, I've been religious all my life. I've prayed for a whole year. But you couldn't give me a sign. You're not there." All of a sudden the sky turned black. Lightning flashed, and a voice boomed out of the clouds: "Old man, meet me halfway. Buy a ticket."

Unfortunately many of the people you encounter during your career will not be predisposed to meet you halfway. They will be angry. They will be upset. They will have chips on their shoulders. And they will express their anger toward you in a variety of unpleasant ways. One of the most annoying will be the hostile question.

Hostile questions are asked by people who seek a confrontation. Their purpose is to provoke. The questioner is often more interested in venting emotions than in obtaining answers. He wants to get in his licks while you're available as a target. His questions serve as missiles of anger and frustration that can be hurled in your direction. What did you ever do to upset this person so much?

When Hostility Rears Its Ugly Head

You're never immune from a hostile question. It can occur in any setting from one-on-one meetings to formal podium presentations. However, its destructive potential is highest in a group setting. That's when it can unleash the bandwagon effect.

The bandwagon effect comes into play after you've made a successful presentation. The audience may be a few executives in a boardroom or hundreds of prospects at a trade show. Either way their reaction is gratifying. It's clear that you've connected. They're really buying what you're saying. After briefly basking in your glory, you offer to entertain questions. The first few are simple, and your answers confirm the audience's initial impression—you're a genius. Heads nod approval at your every word. Visions of sugarplum bonuses dance in your head. Then suddenly a shrill voice from the back of the room cuts through your fantasy like a Ginzu knife. A hostile question has reared its ugly head.

There is an instant change of atmosphere. The same people who were nodding approval only moments ago have suddenly distanced themselves. They seem to be siding with the questioner. Their attitude, though unspoken, rings loudly in your ears. They're silently screaming "Yeah, what about that? What about this issue the hostile questioner just raised? What do you have to say about that?" A sudden chill fills the room.

It's the bandwagon effect in full force. A whole roomful of supporters have suddenly turned against you just because one person asked a hostile question. What are you going to do?

Several responses are possible. You can ignore the question, refuse to answer it, or pretend to answer by changing the question. But these tactics will decrease your credibility and increase audience hostility. You can also answer the question directly in a serious manner. This is a good response, but there's a better one. You can defuse the question with humor.

For example, consider the telephone company representative at a community-relations event. After delivering an upbeat presentation she throws the meeting open for questions. An angry customer demands to know why long-distance rates keep rising despite record profits. Tension fills the air. The proper response is critical for getting the event back on track.

The phone company representative could launch right into a serious answer. Instead she says, "I've got some good news and some bad news. The bad news is you're absolutely correct—long-distance rates are going up. But the good news is that the continents are drifting closer together."

When the laughter subsides, she offers her serious explanation for rate increases. Even if the hostile questioner doesn't listen, at least the rest of the audience now gives her a fair hearing. The bandwagon effect has been nullified.

Let's analyze what happened. A humorous acknowledgment of a tough question defuses tension and breaks down barriers. It can help change the questioner's mind-set from an antagonistic, prejudged opinion to a more neutral, willing-to-listen attitude. The effect can be described in military terms: Humor takes the sting out of the attack and disarms the questioner. Most important, the humorous acknowledgment ensures that your serious response will not be wasted. It eliminates the highly charged emotions that interfere with the questioner's and your audience's ability to hear your answer.

In our telephone company example the company had carefully constructed a serious response to the question about long-distance rates. And its representative had been specifically trained to present this response. However, if she had launched right into it, some of its impact would have been lost. The audience would not have heard all of it. They were too emotionally charged by the hostile question to pay full attention to the response. The humorous acknowledgment recaptured their attention.

Humorous Acknowledgment Versus Flip Response

A humorous acknowledgment should never be confused with a flip response that laughs away a tough question. The latter tactic is completely inappropriate. You never want to look like you're making fun of the questioner or ignoring his concerns. A humorous acknowledgment should always be followed by a serious explanation.

Businesspeople can take a cue from political leaders, who have a long tradition of defusing hostile questions with humor. As public servants politicians must routinely submit to the unrelenting scrutiny of an antagonistic press. In a business that thrives on confrontation, reporters who *don't* ask tough questions will be dismissed as lightweights by their peers. In this atmosphere of ancient Roman spectacle, humor may be the politician's only protection when he or she is thrown to the media lions.

The questioning can become particularly tough when it's directed toward the chief executive of the United States. As the head of state the president is responsible for the actions of the entire government bureaucracy. And ever since Harry Truman said, "The buck stops here," reporters have been trying to make presidents admit their mistakes. Presidents have been retaliating with humor.

The technique is illustrated by an exchange that occurred during a Ronald Reagan news conference in Washington, D.C., on September 28, 1982:

REPORTER: Mr. President, in talking about the continuing recession tonight, you have blamed mistakes of the past, and you've blamed Congress. Does any of the blame belong to you?

RONALD REAGAN: Yes, because for many years I was a Democrat.

The same technique was used many years earlier by John Kennedy in this memorable exchange with the press:

REPORTER: What is your administration doing for women?
JOHN F. KENNEDY: Whatever we've done, I'm sure it isn't enough.

In both examples the humorous acknowledgment of the tough question elicited some much-needed laughter and bought the president some room to maneuver. It is also interesting to note that both responses were self-effacing. This can be a very effective device for creating humorous acknowledgments.

Perhaps the most famous political use of a humorous acknowledgment occurred during a debate between Ronald Reagan and Walter Mondale in the presidential campaign of 1984. Reagan, running for reelection, thought he had put the issue of his age to rest. Suddenly a reporter asked Reagan if he was too old to serve another term. Reagan responded with these now-immortal lines: "I'm not going to inject the issue of age into this campaign. I am not going to exploit for political gain my opponent's youth and inexperience." The response changed the entire momentum of the debate, and Walter Mondale never recovered. Reagan went on to win reelection in a landslide victory.

One business executive who endorses the humorous acknowledgment technique is Joseph Wahed, senior vice president and chief economist, Wells Fargo Bank. He uses humor to help him communicate complex banking concepts. "In anything as complicated as business economics, it's important to inject two things: experiences that affect everyone in the audience and personally related, light humor," he says. As an example he cites a typical question he receives: "Isn't the dollar very weak?" Wahed's response: "That reminds me of when I went to the doctor and he said, 'You're as sound as the dollar.' " He then offers a serious response.

Wahed points out that humor must be used judiciously. "Since I work for a bank, I have to project an image of conservative bank solidity. However, there's always someone in the audience who hates that, whose checking account is all messed up, or who had a bank loan application turned down." Wahed proceeds with caution when that person asks a hostile question. For example, the disgruntled customer might ask, "Isn't it true that banks all over the world are colluding to control the world?" Wahed says he always responds to those questions in a very serious manner. "I never make fun of them," he explains. "I respect the person very much indeed."[1]

Walt Disney Company Chairman Michael Eisner is another executive who has learned to use the humorous-acknowledgment technique. An awkward question that he fields on a regular basis is "Mr. Eisner, what's your favorite ride?" The question is awkward because Eisner is the chief executive of the company that runs Disneyland and Disney World. He traditionally avoids answering the question because he doesn't want to favor one ride over another. However, Eisner has recently developed a more satisfactory response by using humor. The opportunity to try it out came at a question-and-answer session at the Fuqua School of Business at Duke University. Inevitably a student asked, "Mr. Eisner, what's your favorite ride?" Eisner's new answer: "The stock market."[2]

Gary Ames, president of U.S. West Communications—one of the "baby Bell" telephone companies created by the breakup of AT&T—has developed an all-purpose humorous acknowledgment. He uses it when fielding awkward questions from anyone—customers, legislators, employees, reporters, the general public. After receiving a tough question in an employee meeting Ames replies, "That's a great question. While I generalize for the next thirty seconds, Larry Pinnt, seated in the back of the room, will be thinking about what the answer really is. When I stop talking, Larry is going to say something very specific because I don't have the slightest idea what the answer is."

Ames notes that his approach works well as long as: (a) you have someone else in the room who can answer the question; and (b) the question does get answered. In addition, his response is valuable because it shows that he doesn't have all the answers. "My humorous admission of ignorance encourages people to ask questions," Ames explains. "This is particularly important with lower-level employees. I want to know what's on their minds. And they might not otherwise ask a potentially embarrassing question to a senior executive. Humor is by far the best technique to generate honest dialogue between two people."

How to Develop Humorous Acknowledgments

How can you develop humorous acknowledgments to tough questions? The same way you develop serious responses—anticipate and prepare. Analyze your communication situation and know your audience. Who will you be talking to? What will they ask? What hostile or embarrassing questions would you ask if the roles were reversed?

Make a list of the questions you expect to field. When you develop your serious responses, write some humorous acknowledgments. Try it with a group of managers who must address the same issues. You'll probably come up with forty-nine answers that are flippant and insulting. But then the fiftieth will be a gem that you can use forever.

A good example of this process comes from a seminar I conducted for a group of managers from a state tax authority. As tax collectors they are routinely barraged by a variety of hostile questions when they make public-information appearances in the community. One question that comes up frequently and heatedly is: "Why are tax forms so complicated?"

The traditional answer is that the state legislature dictates the information required on the forms. So the tax collectors tell the public to blame the legislators. Although this may be true, the answer does little to assuage the hostile questioner. A tax collector who offers the traditional answer is perceived as one more finger-pointing bureaucrat who doesn't want to take responsibility.

To generate goodwill, I suggested that they address the question of why tax forms are so complicated with a humorous acknowledgment. Their first attempts included:

"Because they're really a secret government IQ test."

"They're actually simple if you don't earn any income."

"Don't worry, we've got a new one for people like you—you just connect the dots."

Although these responses are arguably amusing, they will not accomplish the goal of building goodwill. Far from defusing the question about tax forms, they will provoke further hostility.

Just as the group was becoming frustrated and wanted to give up, someone had one last idea. "If someone asks me why the tax forms are so complicated," he said, "here's what I'll say: 'They're written by the same people who write instructions for assembling children's toys.'"

Bingo. This response is a winner. It is genuinely funny. It doesn't antagonize the questioner. And it can be used by any tax collector whenever the tax-form question arises. After the tension is defused, the tax collector can explain that the blame for complicated tax forms really lies with the legislature.

Handling Hostility One-on-One

The same principles apply in one-on-one situations—anticipate and prepare. A good example involves a very young-looking woman who was married to a man who looked older than his years. In public places, such as restaurants, she was often taken to be his daughter. After becoming extremely frustrated by this continuous mistake, she developed a humorous acknowledgment. Now when asked to order for her "father" she replies, "He's not my father—but please don't tell my husband."[3]

Although the mistake will continue to be made, the funny response has eliminated the woman's frustration and tension. Her approach makes sense for anyone in a similar situation. When you know that an awkward or embarrassing question is going to recur, anticipate its appearance and be ready with a humorous response.

The technique is particularly useful in dealing with hostile questions from the boss. Los Angeles attorney Steve Katleman offers an example. He tells of two attorneys who were handling a major deal for their law firm. They were in the middle of the deal when the senior attorney surprised the junior attorney. He said, "I'm going on vacation to Australia, you handle the deal." The junior attorney said, "I'm going on vacation too." The senior attorney erupted in rage. "You know I need you in the office when I'm not here," he fumed. "How can you schedule a vacation for the same time as me?" The junior attorney defused the situation with his reply: "I'm just trying to maximize our time together."

A key area of one-on-one business activity that can be improved with humorous acknowledgments is customer service. In today's competitive market the customer is more important than ever. Businesses of every size and type are developing more programs and investing more resources in attempts to please their customers. Unfortunately the effort isn't always successful. Mistakes happen. A product doesn't function properly. A service falls short of its promise. No matter what the specific problem happens to be, the customer will make it known. He or she often does this by asking the businessperson to answer a pointedly hostile question, such as "Why did you drop the ball?" Sometimes the question is phrased a little less delicately.

Once again, an effective way of dealing with these situations is to anticipate the problems and prepare potential responses. A good example involves a waiter in a restaurant that I patronize. Unhappy customers have an immediate impact on an important part of his income—tips. Although he is an excellent waiter, he occasionally goofs up an order. When a customer angrily asks why the main course has been served with spaghetti instead of potatoes, the waiter is prepared. He replies, "I'm terribly sorry. My memory is good—it's just short." The humorous acknowledgment, followed by an immediate correction of the side dish, usually preserves his tip.

Man is by nature a questioning animal. We continually seek to expand the boundaries of our knowledge by poking and probing into the unknown. The question is the instrument of our investigation. We ask questions for many reasons—to learn, to clarify, to explain, as well as to attack. Our capacity to generate new questions is infinite, especially when a speaker has no time for a question-and-answer period.

Despite our endlessly novel inquiries, there are three great questions that we will always ask: What is the meaning of life, what is the nature of God, and what the heck are you talking about? This last inquiry is known as a hostile question. It may take many forms and it will inevitably be asked when you're most vulnerable. Be prepared with a humorous acknowledgment. Its ability to defuse tension is unrivaled, and its return in goodwill is unquestioned.

EIGHT

Crack Jokes, Not Skulls: Managing Conflict with Humor

A diplomat is a person who can tell you to go to hell in such a way that you actually look forward to the trip.

—Caskie Stinnett

Police Officer Adelle Roberts was investigating a routine family-disturbance call—a husband-and-wife fight. As she parked her patrol car in front of the offenders' house, a television flew out of a second-story window. Loud voices argued as she walked to the front door and knocked. An angry man screamed, "Who is it?" Roberts knew that if she said, "Police," it would make things worse. Instead she replied, "TV repairman." The man started laughing and opened the door. A favorable atmosphere had been established for resolving the dispute.

Humor can provide a powerful tool for managing work-related conflicts. It can reduce tension, create rapport, and put things into perspective. You've seen how humor works when you're talking to an audience and handling a hostile question. Now let's explore techniques for using humor to handle conflicts on the job.

It's Not What You Say

One of the prime rules of communication theory is that "over time, the content fades, but the relationship remains." If you have a conversation with someone today, a week from now you won't remember exactly what was said. A year from now you will remember even less. The "content" will fade. What you *will* remember is how you felt about interacting with your conversational partner. Were you friendly? Were you arguing? Did you enjoy talking to the person? The "relationship" will remain. That's why humor is so important: it helps create a positive relationship that will be remembered for a long time. And establishing a positive relationship is one of the keys to managing conflict.

The value of humor in creating a positive relationship was recently confirmed in a study conducted by Dr. Robert Baron, a psychology professor at Rensselaer Polytechnic Institute. The study concluded that confrontations at work often depend on how you say things rather than what you say. Baron hypothesized that most people can't simultaneously entertain incompatible feelings such as anger and amusement. Therefore, he reasoned, if an angry person is made to chuckle with the person who induced the anger, then hostile feelings should lessen.

To test his theory, Baron had students role-play executives of a large company. In pairs they discussed critical business issues under the watchful eye of a researcher. However, one person in each pair was a confederate, secretly instructed to disagree with any position voiced by the other.

After the disagreement subjects were manipulated in one of four ways, one of which was through the use of humor. The confederate showed cartoons to the subject and asked assistance in choosing the funniest for a communications class. Later the subjects completed a questionnaire about their feelings toward the confederates. Among other things the study showed that using humor often reduced anger and produced a more positive encounter. Specifically, humor put the subjects in a better mood, improved their ratings of the confederate, and increased the likelihood that they would choose a constructive approach to resolving conflicts.[1]

Resolving Conflicts with Humor

The Baron study highlights the value of humor as a reframing device. *Reframing* is a psychological term that refers to changing the meaning in a situation. The term is borrowed from the world of art. Changing the frame that surrounds a picture literally changes the way the picture looks. The process works the same way psychologically. When a situation is reframed, the facts remain the same but are viewed in a different way. After you hear a pep talk, the glass of water that looked half empty looks half full. New meaning is attributed to the situation. Humor, because of its ability to put things into perspective, provides an important frame for creating new meanings in conflict situations.

Dr. Paul Watzlawick of the Mental Research Institute in Palo Alto, California, believes that humor defuses conflicts by changing our expectations: "When a conflict is escalating, things seem to be going inexorably in an anticipated direction. But if something completely unexpected happens, then things can't continue that way and a change must occur."

Humor, by its very nature, brings about this type of change, Watzlawick observes. "Jokes have a buildup that creates certain expectations which are destroyed by the punch line," he explains. "When our expectations are shattered, we suddenly see the situation in a different context. This gives the situation a different meaning and, in the case of a joke, causes us to laugh. And once people can laugh about a problem, then it's on the way to resolution."

The workplace provides endless opportunities for using humor as a reframing device. Wherever people meet to conduct business, conflict is the norm. Conflicts of wills, personalities, and ideas. Conflicts of plans and strategies. Conflicts of interest. The world of work is characterized by conflict. And humor thrives in that environment. Jokes are used to relieve tension and change minds. Seasoned managers try to make opponents see the "humor" in a situation. They point out incongruities and exaggerate to the point of absurdity—anything for a laugh that may change an opposing viewpoint and defuse the conflict. Experience has taught them the truth of the old saying "You can't laugh and be angry at the same time."

An excellent example of humor's ability to reframe conflicts involves Roland Michener, a former governor-general of Canada. Michener encountered a group of striking maintenance workers during a ceremonial visit to a public school. His dilemma: Crossing the picket line would place the government in the labor dispute; backing down from the line would diminish his authority. As pickets swarmed around him, Michener reframed the situation by addressing them as friendly constituents. "How very nice of you all to turn out to see me!" he announced. "Thank you. Shall we go in?" By the time the pickets stopped chuckling, Michener had entered the school without incident.[2]

A similar example involves auto executive Eugene Cafiero. When he was president of Chrysler, Cafiero traveled to England to meet with workers at a troubled plant there. Ushered in to meet the burly unionists, he was confronted with a man who loudly proclaimed, "I'm Eddie McClusky and I'm a Communist." The Chrysler executive extended his hand and said, "How do you do. I'm Eugene Cafiero and I'm a Presbyterian." The ensuing laughter defused the potentially explosive situation.[3]

In both situations a few well-chosen words transformed a physically dangerous conflict into a humorous encounter. The reframing occurred because the governor-general and the Chrysler executive didn't respond in a way that the crowds anticipated. When their expectations were shattered, the crowds were forced to view their situation in a new context.

Reframing with humor isn't limited to physical confrontations. It can also be used to change perspectives in conflicts that arise over business strategy. A classic example involves the Ford Motor Company's debate over plant closings as a cost-cutting device during the 1950s. Doom-and-gloom projections by company accountants had controlled Ford's decisions to cut back production. Several plant shutdowns had already occurred, when the accountants demanded another.

Ford president Robert S. McNamara held a meeting of top executives to discuss the proposal for another plant closing. Although everyone was opposed, no one wanted to challenge the accountants. The conclusion looked inevitable, when one old-timer said, "Why don't we close down all the plants and then we'll really start to save money?" When the laughter ended, the executives decided to stop letting accountants run the company. The quip reframed the issue and saved the plant.[4]

Go with the Flow

A different type of reframing is based on the principle of "going with the flow." Its difference lies in the way it handles provocative assumptions. In traditional reframing the underlying assumption is rejected and replaced with a nonprovocative frame. The previously discussed examples of the Canadian governor-general and Chrysler executive Eugene Cafiero illustrate this process. In both of those examples the antagonist's underlying assumption of hostile worker versus authority figure was rejected. The governor-general changed the frame from hostile workers to a gathering of friendly constituents. And Cafiero changed the frame from a labor dispute to a religious discussion.

In contrast, "go with the flow" reframing is based on *accepting* the provocative assumption. Essentially we agree with the person seeking a confrontation. However, the provocative assumption is redirected back toward the antagonist in a way that avoids conflict. The classic example of "going with the flow" reframing is a legendary story about actress Eve Arden. Arden was appearing in a play, when a telephone began ringing beside her. It wasn't supposed to ring. She looked across the stage at her leading man, who wore a barely suppressed smile. He was playing a little joke on her. She couldn't get angry and scream in front of a theater full of people. So she went with the flow. She answered the phone, turned to her leading man, and said, "It's for you!"

By accepting the provocative assumption that there was supposed to be a telephone call, Arden turned the tables on her antagonist. She dumped the problem back in his lap and removed herself from a potentially embarrassing conflict. She also demonstrated her own sense of humor about the situation—and her unfailing wit.

Go-with-the-flow reframing helps us resist our natural inclination for confrontation. This is a deep-seated instinct that appears in the earliest stages of human development. It is typified by the two-year-old who says "no" to every parental request. As adults we retain this predisposition to confront the people around us and expect others to behave in a similar manner. That's why go-with-the-flow reframing is so powerful. It defeats the expectations of your would-be antagonist and gives you the advantage of surprise and laughter.

A perfect example involves an office worker who was frequently late for work. Although he always had good excuses, his supervisor warned him that his next lateness would be his last. Inevitably he was late again. When he arrived at 9:35, a silent tension filled the office. All eyes focused on him as the angry supervisor approached. But before the supervisor could speak, Mr. Late smiled and stuck his hand out. "How do you do," he said. "I'm applying for a job I understand became available just thirty-five minutes ago. Does the early bird get the worm?"[5]

The office exploded in laughter and the supervisor forced a smile. The natural inclination of someone in Mr. Late's position would have been to offer additional excuses. However, that would have placed him in direct conflict with his supervisor. By accepting the provocative assumption that he was fired, Mr. Late went with the flow, surprised his supervisor, and preserved his job—at least until his next lateness.

A simple method for applying go-with-the-flow reframing is to take things literally. An excellent example involves an executive who was asked to reduce her departmental budget and did so—several times. After she had squeezed out the last ounce of fat, she showed the budget to the company president. He ordered her to reduce it more. Her solution was to take the request literally. She went directly to the nearest photo-copying machine, reduced the budget to the size of a postage stamp, and gave it back to the president. He approved it after he stopped laughing.[6]

There are many opportunities every day to engage in go-with-the-flow reframing. Potential conflicts abound. Routine interactions with clients, secretaries, bosses, and competitors are fraught with confrontations. Reframe even a small fraction of those conflicts and your work life will be more pleasant and productive.

Reducing Conflicts with Humor

So far we've examined situations where the use of humor resolved a conflict. However, a more common role for humor involves conflict *reduction* rather than resolution. Humor can buy time until a solution presents itself.

Lieutenant Jim Dachauer, who teaches assertiveness training and conflict management at the San Francisco Police Academy, believes humor can be a valuable tool for cooling confronta-tions. He finds humor particularly useful as an "interrupter"— a message designed to prevent assertive behavior from be-coming aggressive. Much of his training class focuses on this area. He explains, "There are four ways of being assertive. If I ask you to do something more than twice in one of those four ways, then you'll perceive me as aggressive. And then you'll respond aggressively. A humorous interrupter can pre-vent that from happening."

As an example Dachauer poses a situation where someone has disobeyed two direct orders to leave a room. He says, "Now I have a choice. I can give a third order, be perceived as aggressive, and then the person will almost be forced to fight me. But if I back down, I lose my authority. So to break the cycle, I'll say something funny out of left field. Then we can both smile, release some tension, and start over again."

The classic example of a humorous interrupter comes from the U.S. House of Representatives. A debate about the economy grew stormy when specific solutions to halt inflation were proposed. The issue proved so divisive that several congressmen almost came to blows. Just as pandemonium was about to erupt, Congressman Morris Udall took the floor. "I think we should let the Post Office handle the inflation problem," he reportedly said. A stunned silence gripped the House as members tried to comprehend the statement. "They wouldn't solve the problem," Udall continued, "but they'd certainly slow it down." The chamber burst into laughter, and the debate resumed in a more civil tone.

Humorous interrupters offer a marvelous device for handling on-the-job conflicts. When a confrontation with a colleague becomes heated, you can temporarily defuse the argument by making an unexpected joke. Focus on areas of agreement; make a joke about the competition, working conditions, or current events. The ensuing laughter creates a cooling-off period. It prevents the conflict from escalating past the danger point. However, make sure that the joke seems relevant to the confrontation. A joke that appears to be offered solely as a distraction may provoke even greater wrath from your opponent.

Humorous Hints to Avoid Conflict

Humor can also be used to prevent tension *before* it occurs. A prime area where laughter is the best preventative medicine involves the exercise of authority. For example as a manager you have to tell people what to do, yet there is an inherent conflict between you and your staff every time you perform this basic managerial function.

The old school of management relished this kind of conflict. It was an opportunity to show who was boss. The modern manager regards such "brute force" as a last resort and a sign of failure. It means that he or she hasn't successfully motivated the troops. More important, a direct order often creates resistance and resentment, which leads to further problems down the line. Where does humor fit into these situations? It provides a velvet glove around the iron fist of authority. A request for cooperation phrased in a funny way—a humorous hint—can eliminate resistance and resentment caused by a direct order. Humor cushions the blow.

One expert in the humorous-hint school of management is Leslie Czechowicz, former vice president of operations at Designware, Inc., an educational software company. When employees were milling around the water cooler after 9:00 A.M., she cracked the whip—literally! "I had a whip in my office that I cracked loudly when people should have been working," she explains. "They usually started laughing and went back to work." A direct order in that situation would have just caused hard feelings, she adds.

The indirect nature of the humorous hint is a two-edged sword. Its inherent ambiguity reduces potential *compliance*, as well as potential resistance. That's because the people who receive your humorous hint don't have to respond to it. They may think you were just kidding. Or they may be personality types who ignore everything except direct orders. In either case they won't take the hint.

So why bother giving a humorous hint in the first place? The advantage is that some people *will* respond to it. That ultimately translates into less resistance and resentment to you and your authority. In the long run it will help establish your reputation as a superior manager and produce a happier work force. In addition, you always have the option of escalating your authority when dealing with people who ignore a humorous hint. You can repeat your instruction less ambiguously and more forcefully—as a direct request or direct order.

A variation on the humorous hint technique involves upward communication within an organization—lower- and middle-level managers sending a message to the top brass. In that situation humor is necessary due to a *lack* of authority. You can't give orders to the boss, but you can give humorous hints.

However, a message sent upward is substantially riskier than a message sent the other way. If a superior gives a humorous hint that doesn't work and a conflict develops, he or she may have a bad day. If a subordinate gives a humorous hint and a conflict develops, he or she may be looking for a job. The solution: Build in a factor of anonymity.

Let's see how this works. An army office staffed by civilian ballistic-missile engineers was run by a colonel who set an impossible work schedule. After several weeks the staff was demoralized and burned out. They wanted to complain, but the colonel was never available. Working on top-secret documents, he arrived early in the morning, locked himself in his office, and left late at night.

With no relief in sight, the engineers conspired to bare their grievances. Using the "take things literally" technique, they attached an intravenous tube to a turnip and hung it on the colonel's door. When the engineers arrived the next day, the colonel's door was open. A meeting was held and the problems were resolved.

The turnip was effective as a humorous hint because of the anonymity factor. With no one to blame, the colonel was forced to take the turnip in a humorous vein. His only alternative was to penalize the entire office staff. However, that alternative would have reflected poorly on his management abilities.

How to Use Humor in Negotiations

Now let's look at the use of humor in the most common conflict situation in the business world—negotiations. A special, highly structured type of conflict, the negotiation represents an organized interaction of opposing interests. Corporate deals, labor disputes, litigation settlements, and most other types of business activity all involve some form of negotiation. Humor can help establish a constructive climate for negotiations. It can provide a safety valve when talks grow heated and facilitate continued communication. Humor can also act as a catalyst for making people relax and drop their guard.

An ingenious experiment confirmed the value of humor in negotiations. Two groups of students were divided into pairs of sellers and buyers to bargain over the price of a painting. They believed that they would be evaluated for their skill in bargaining. All participants were told to negotiate the best possible price.

However, the buyers were all confederates. Following directions from the researchers, half the buyers made their final offer by saying, "Well, my final offer is x dollars." The other buyers smiled and said, "Well, my final offer is x dollars, and I'll throw in my pet frog." The results: Buyers who offered the frog were able to "buy" the painting for a lower price. In fact a statistical analysis revealed that sellers who laughed at the frog line were particularly likely to grant concessions.[7]

From formal business discussions held with clients to off-the-cuff decisions made with colleagues, the world of work is a world of negotiation. Even going to lunch involves several negotiations: when to go? where to meet? what to eat? The study's results are well worth bearing in mind during the hundreds of routine negotiations that we conduct every day.

Many of the informal negotiations that make up the average workday concern how work will be assigned and performed. One of the most commonly debated issues is when an assignment will be due. This is a frequent subject of negotiation between managers and their secretaries. The manager wants a report typed ASAP. The secretary already has a pile of assignments with that same deadline. Many experienced secretaries have learned to use humor to obtain a more reasonable due date. In fact one secretary I know has prepared for this negotiation by hanging a sign above her desk. It portrays a person laughing hysterically and proclaims, *"You want it when?"*

Humor can also play a useful role in extremely serious negotiations. A good example involved negotiations in a very sensitive legal matter: desegregation of San Francisco public schools. The case occurred several years ago, when George Deukmejian was attorney general of California. Lawyers for all the interested parties met in federal court to coordinate the complex litigation. The plaintiff, local school district, amicus curiae, and the state each had representatives at the conference table. The room was packed with attorneys, and the atmosphere was extremely tense. Everyone wanted more time to prepare, but the judge wanted the case resolved before the new school term began.

The judge directed his first remarks to Deputy Attorney General Asher Rubin: "I understand the state wants to make a motion in this case. Is that correct?"

"Yes, Your Honor," said Rubin.

"How much time will you need?" asked the judge.

All eyes turned toward Rubin as the tension crackled through the room.

"Well, Your Honor," he said, "this is a very complicated case. We'd like sixty days."

"Sixty days!" the judge exploded. "I don't give anybody sixty days! What the hell do you people do in the attorney general's office anyway?"

"Well," replied Rubin, "we spend most of our time trying to spell Deukmejian."

The judge's laughter filled the room and the tension was broken. The state received forty-five days to make its motion.

The deputy attorney general's quip about his spelling problem was particularly effective because it was self-effacing. By poking fun at himself, he established a foundation for agreement with the judge. In effect, the deputy attorney general was saying, "I'm dumb"—a proposition with which the angry judge could readily agree. Once this initial "agreement" was established, the conflict was on its way to resolution. Self-effacing humor offers a common ground in conflict situations. It guarantees that your most hostile, antagonistic opponent can always agree with you on at least one thing—your shortcomings.

Caveats

If you look back over this chapter, you'll notice a pattern. A conflict was resolved, reduced, or prevented through the *intentional* use of humor. Angry voices dissolved into laughter and the protagonists lived happily ever after. Does that seem a bit unrealistic? Common sense tells us that purposeful humor won't make every conflict magically disappear. Common experience tells us that many conflicts are resolved without the slightest bit of humor. And still other conflicts involve totally unintentional humor.

For example, attorney and negotiation expert Gerard Nierenberg recalls a negotiation where one side displayed its anger by using a strategy called apparent withdrawal. "That's where the leader of the negotiating team leaves, but the rest of the team stays," explains Nierenberg. "Unfortunately, the leader wasn't familiar with the room. When he got up to leave, he walked into a closet and closed the door behind him. Everyone knew it was a closet and we waited to see what he would do. Three minutes went by. Five minutes went by. Ten minutes went by. Slowly the door opened. And at that point everyone was just rolling on the floor, because they understood exactly what happened to him and how he felt. And from that moment on the tension was relieved. He came over and sat down, and we continued the negotiation to a successful conclusion."

Although unintentional humor can be very effective, it is outside the scope of our discussion. Unintentional humor is, by definition, unintentional. You can't plan it, control it, or develop a skill for using it. View it as a bonus. When it pops up and helps defuse a conflict, consider yourself fortunate. But don't sit around waiting for it to happen. Put your efforts into mastering the humor techniques that are within your conscious control.

As a humor consultant I'd be guilty of gross negligence if I didn't acknowledge that humor can backfire in a conflict situation. However, such cases can usually be attributed to lack of preparation. When you use humor during a conflict, it's essential that you have some knowledge of the players involved. You must assess their personalities. You must decide what they may or may not find offensive, how they relate to you, and what type of humor is appropriate for them.

Although using humor always involves some degree of risk,

the same can be said for just opening your mouth. After all, you don't have to use humor to be perceived as inappropriate or offensive. Every type of communication engenders some risk. But despite the risks associated with humor, a carefully prepared attempt at humor during a conflict situation is worth the effort. The fact remains, as demonstrated by the Baron study, that the way we say things *does* make a difference. And humor, if used appropriately, provides a powerful tool for diplomacy.

It's like the executive who was traveling in Europe when his butler called to say his pet cat had died. The executive was very upset. "You spoiled my entire trip," he complained. "You should have been more diplomatic."

"What do you mean?" asked the butler.

"Well, you could have sent a telegram that the cat was on the roof. Then a few days later you could send a telegram that the cat fell off the roof. Then a telegram that the cat was in the hospital. And finally a telegram that the cat had died. That way I would have been emotionally prepared."

The butler apologized, and the executive continued his trip. A few weeks later he got a telegram from the butler: "Your mother is on the roof."

The butler had the right idea, but the wrong technique. His attempt at diplomacy showed a lack of common sense. By blindly applying the solution for dealing with a dead cat, he ignored an important difference in the new situation. He made no distinction between his employer's cat and his mother. The two situations required very different diplomatic approaches.

Although the butler's blunder was extreme, the principle it illustrates is general: Every situation is unique. Each interaction with other people requires you to assess the situation from a fresh perspective. You must recognize individual nuances, make adjustments, and use good judgment.

That's the bad news: Common sense is a prerequisite for using humor successfully. The good news is that you don't have to be a comic genius to manage conflicts with humor. Manuel Gallegos, a vice president at Eureka Federal Savings

& Loan Association, doesn't consider himself to be a particularly funny person. But he does use his sense of humor to defuse potential conflicts. When branch managers call with complaints, Gallegos begins return calls by saying, "How did we destroy your morning?"[8] This simple question gets the conversation off to a light and constructive start. Any manager can use a similar approach.

Humor and Debt Collection

Can a punch line improve the bottom line? The answer is yes, according to Chic Thompson, president of the Creative Media Group. His Virginia-based advertising agency uses cartoons to motivate delinquent accounts into paying up. Thompson believes that his collection cartoons work because they're unexpected and they command attention from the secretary to the president. "A letter might go ignored," he explains. "But a cartoon grabs the eye and can be even more guilt-provoking and persuasive than the written word."

Thompson's four-cartoon set allows companies to induce increasing amounts of guilt in their debtors. The first cartoon, when a bill is 30 days overdue, depicts a dog asking for a payment. After 60 days the dog is depressed over the bill. At 90 days the debtee is crushed under a pile of bills. Finally, at 120 days, comes the one that never fails—a tearful man kneeling in a pool of blood with a knife in his back. Its caption reads, "Please pay the money you owe. I trusted you."

Thompson developed the cartoons after some of his clients failed to cough up. "We tried the usual methods—invoices, letters, pleading phone calls—but the cartoons got the results," he recalls. In fact he says that payment of his company's overdue bills has increased by 17 percent since he began sending the cartoons.

The cartoons are particularly useful for sensitive collection situations where more forceful methods aren't appropriate; for example, when the debtor client is a personal friend or when the client has a good payment history but has become delinquent on a certain invoice. Though it may sound like a strange way to collect money, the cartoons actually provide an excellent tool for resolving conflict. Each payment received represents one less potential court battle. And if the cartoons don't work, so sue.

N I N E

The Carrot and the Shtick

Laughter is the shortest distance between two people.
—Victor Borge

A woman joined a nunnery where the nuns took a vow of silence. She was allowed to say only two words a year. At the end of the first year she had an audience with the mother superior. She said, "Hard work." Another year went by and she had another audience. She said, "Lousy food." The third year passed. She saw the mother superior again. This time she shook her fist, threw her robes on the floor, and said, "I quit." The mother superior said, "I knew you would. Since you got here, all you've done is complain."

The story was told by Monte Lorenzet, editorial services manager at Raychem Corporation of Menlo Park, California. He used it to prevent a department meeting from turning into a gripe session. "When employees get together in a group, they usually discuss problems," he observes. "After a while it can turn into a lot of moaning and groaning. And that can send the whole meeting into a negative spiral." Lorenzet used the nun story to restore positive momentum. "Humor makes people step back and say, 'It ain't so bad. We may have problems in our work, but we can handle them.'"

Humor is a powerful tool for improving morale and motivation in the workplace. It keeps people loose and productive. Each shared laugh helps build the team spirit prized by successful executives. And when top management leads the laughter, a bonding occurs that inspires employees to greater heights. This view is echoed by Renn Zaphiropoulos, founder of Versatec Inc., a computer-printer manufacturer. He says that humor helps him produce an informal atmosphere conducive to communication. "A person who doesn't laugh may be a ruler, but he would get only what he asked for—nothing more," states Zaphiropoulos. "In high-tech companies you can't survive by having people do merely what you ask them to do. You hope for pleasant surprises."[1]

Zaphiropoulos's observation really applies to any type of company or organization. People will speak up, offer ideas, and make suggestions when they know that such activity will not be penalized. The trust necessary to elicit such participation can be built through humor. An environment that tolerates humor will tolerate other employee communications. And if a job requires a smooth flow of communication for successful performance, humor can play a critical role in keeping channels open.

Humor as a Motivational Tool

Jim Kiehm, a seasoned financial executive, agrees that humor opens lines of communication. In fact, he finds that communication improved by humor increases productivity and saves time. As an example he cites a messy auditing job that he monitored when he was a supervising partner with Arthur Andersen & Co. As a senior accountant from another office was running the fieldwork. Kiehm went to see her for a status report. A senior accountant, she was typically nervous about having her work reviewed by a partner—particularly one from another office. She described the problems she had uncovered and how the client had gotten into them. Kiehm sat back and said, "Well, that's pretty much state-of-the-art stupid." The comment was designed to communicate Kiehm's sense of humor.

"It lightened things up," he recalls. "The senior thought, 'Oh, this guy is real.' The humor helped create a nonthreatening environment. The senior relaxed and reviewed all the details I needed to know about the audit."

Kiehm is quick to note that his staff wouldn't consciously try to hide details from him. His point is that an environment perceived as threatening is not conducive to a free flow of information. "If my staff is on pins and needles when I ask a question, they're going to focus on not making mistakes," he explains. "If they're not worried about that, then the exchange of information is much freer and much more valuable. It's also a lot more comprehensive and concise. So, contrary to popular opinion, humor doesn't waste time. It can actually speed things up."

Many businesspeople refrain from using humor because they believe it's a time waster. The stereotype is the tough executive who comes to a meeting with a set of objectives and plows through the agenda until they're completed. Or the hard-nosed auditor who wants to complete an audit in a certain number of hours.

Kiehm believes that this narrow approach loses sight of the real objectives. "The objective is not just to get through the agenda or the audit," he states. "The objective for a meeting is either imparting or receiving information and perhaps agreeing on an action plan. The objective for an audit is really information gathering, analysis, and conclusion. These are the real objectives, not just getting through the number of hours." According to Kiehm, a lot of people fail to make this distinction. But once you acknowledge the real objectives, humor's role becomes apparent. "If humor is used in a fashion that makes more efficient or more free-flowing the information," he states, "it helps accomplish the real objectives. It makes the process more productive."

The proposition that humor can improve group productivity is supported by an experiment conducted by Howard R. Pollio, professor of psychology, University of Tennessee at Knoxville. Pollio had observed that humor could strengthen group bonds and relieve anxiety. But it could also distract from the task at hand. Puzzled by this apparent contradiction, he wanted to know: Do joking and laughing facilitate or interfere with group problem solving?

In order to answer this question, Pollio had six-person groups work on two tasks for ten minutes each. The NASA Task required the groups to rank the importance of fifteen items needed for a trip across the moon. The Anagrams Task required the groups to create as many anagrams as possible out of the letters ACDEFGINORST. In both cases, humor was limited to spontaneous remarks and behavior that arose from the interaction of people in each group. Observers, who watched videotapes of the groups at work, rated them for frequency and duration of occurrences of laughter. The results: Group performance of the NASA Task was not significantly affected by humor. With the Anagrams Task, significantly more anagrams were created by groups that produced more laughter.[2]

Pollio draws several conclusions from these results. "Groups that are having fun do better when it's a straight production task like how many units you can turn out," he states. "The anagrams were basically a production task. The number you get depends on how long you stick with it. If you're having a good time, you'll stick with it longer, and that creates the possibility for a greater output. In the case of more complicated group-problem-solving activities, such as the NASA Task, humor doesn't get in the way. The results suggest that the notion that laughter interferes with group performance is a myth."

The experiment yields an important implication for managers. It suggests that anyone managing a production task should consider encouraging laughter within the work group. For example, let's say you have a group of "temps" stuffing envelopes. This is exactly the kind of routine task that will be facilitated by laughter. But how do you start them laughing? The secret lies in not putting excessive restraints on the people engaged in the task. Create an informal atmosphere. Give them permission to banter with each other. Once they start chatting, laughter will probably occur as a natural by-product of normal group interaction. If you want to be really Machiavellian, have one of your own clerical people infiltrate the group. The "ringer" can then start the laughter flowing.

What about managing higher-level tasks? Pollio's results indicate that group productivity for such tasks is not affected by fun and laughter. Does that mean that managers should not encourage laughter in groups performing those tasks? Not exactly. Despite his own findings, Pollio believes that laughter can serve a useful purpose for a group engaged in a higher-level activity. "There's no reason not to encourage them to laugh," he explains. "It doesn't get in the way and it probably makes people feel better about what they're doing. We just didn't measure that."

Pollio didn't measure those feelings because they wouldn't fit into the mainstream of publishable research—a fact that he readily acknowledges. "Humor research is preoccupied with narrow measures," he states. "When you focus too narrowly on a single measure, you miss the fact that you've got a complicated human being in a complicated socioeconomic system. What's not being assessed is how much group members identify with their coworkers, how much they identify with their company, how much they like coming to work. It's unfortunate that items like job satisfaction aren't measured. I think we would find that humor facilitates the comfort or happiness of group members with their jobs."

Group Cohesion and Team Spirit

One of the intangible items that Pollio implies may be facilitated by humor is group cohesion. If people enjoy their jobs, have fun, and laugh together, they'll probably form a tightly knit group that works well together. In business jargon this is referred to as team spirit. It is an axiom of management theory that an effective manager is someone who can transform a group of people into a team. While a group is merely a collection of individuals, a team is a group of people who work together toward a common goal. Their efforts are coordinated. They share a sense of camaraderie. Teamwork expresses one of our greatest potentials as human beings—our ability to work together.

The idea that a team is superior to a mere group is reflected throughout our language. Would anyone go to a basketball game and yell, "Go group go"? Would you root for a football "group"? Would any manager go to a seminar in "group building"? Would any leader exhort the troops on the importance of "groupwork"? Do annual reports ever talk about a company's well-seasoned executive "group"? The underlying assumption is that a team can accomplish more than a group. Perhaps the ultimate expression of this distinction is a popular toothpaste ad: A *group* had 21 percent fewer cavities with Crest. But Crest was invented by a *team* of researchers.

If humor does make a group more cohesive, then it has important implications for the workplace. It would mean that humor helps create the bond between people that distinguishes a team from a group. But how do we know if humor plays a role in group cohesion? An answer comes from the research of W. Jack Duncan, professor and University Scholar in Management at the Graduate School of Management, University of Alabama at Birmingham.

According to Duncan, a discussion of humor and group cohesion must begin by challenging the assumption that a cohesive group is more productive. "The cohesive group has never been shown to be more or less productive than a noncohesive group," he states. "There's an intervening factor—the performance norm. A performance norm is an informal group objective. A cohesive group with a high performance norm will be more productive than a cohesive group without a high performance norm."

Here's why. In a highly cohesive group the group members have great influence over each other's behavior. If the group has a high performance norm, its members will influence each other to be more productive. However, without a high performance norm, group members will not influence each other to improve productivity. In fact they may influence each other to be less productive.

The lesson for managers is simple: Establish a high performance norm for your group. If your group has a high performance norm, then making it more cohesive should make it more productive. And that returns us to the main question: Can humor help improve group cohesion? Duncan believes it can. "Managers can use humor to become closer to the group by joking with people and breaking down that natural distance between bosses and subordinates," he states. "The effective manager can use humor in a motivational sense by using it to become more integrated into the total social network or group."

In a recent study of twenty-five work groups, Duncan examined the relationship between humor and the social network of the groups. His finding: Managers who were accepted as friends engaged in the humor network in the same proportion as other members of the group. In other words when subordinates regard the manager as a friend rather than "the boss," the manager initiates jokes and is the target of jokes as much as anyone else.[3]

This finding is consistent with research about joke targeting and group identity. According to Pollio, humor draws a boundary that establishes group membership. "When A, B, and C make jokes to and about each other, it creates a group identity," he explains. "Their joking simultaneously draws a line and forms a bond. The jokes say who or what is on which side of the boundary. In fact you get offended when you don't feel included in the group that's doing the targeting."

Pollio's comments about group identity become particularly significant when coupled with Duncan's study. In his research Duncan identified two types of managers who remain outside the humor boundaries of the groups they supervise: the arrogant executive and the benign bureaucrat. The arrogant executive has a lot of authority and uses it to get things done. Despite his competence, he is generally disliked. Work-group members never joke about him in his presence, and he rarely jokes about them. If the arrogant executive does joke about a group member, it's considered offensive. It's automatically interpreted as a put-down, even if it's not intended that way. The benign bureaucrat is incompetent and gets no respect. He is the butt of a lot of jokes. However, the group is insulted if he makes jokes about them.

Practical Applications

The work of Duncan and Pollio shows that humor can provide an extremely valuable tool for improving productivity, particularly by facilitating teamwork. But as academics, they operate in the realm of theory and experimentation. Let's look at some "real world" examples that support their ideas.

One executive who applies their lessons is Kip Witter, former vice president of finance and treasurer at Amdahl Corporation. Does he encourage the people he manages to use humor? "Absolutely," he states. "If people are laughing, they're generally too busy to do other, more destructive things." Witter particularly dislikes management philosophies that glorify intragroup conflict. He finds little value in the "butting heads" approach to problem solving. "When there's conflict, all kinds of artificial barriers go up," he states. "People don't think properly. They don't behave normally. Individually, and as a group, people operate far below potential, whether the conflict is overt yelling and screaming or whether it's subtle hidden agendas waltzing back and forth."

In order to discourage such conflict, Witter uses humor to set a proper tone for group interaction. "You can use humor to start a meeting instead of preaching the gospel about how we're all here for some noble corporate purpose," he states. "You can break the ice and get everyone on the same team." One of Witter's favorite techniques for developing team spirit is to tell a joke at his own expense. "By doing this you say, 'Hey, I'm one of you guys,'" he explains. "'I'm not here to beat my own agenda to death. I'm really part of the group.' You express some vulnerability. People appreciate that."

Witter's enthusiasm for humor in meetings is shared by John Joseph, a veteran insurance industry executive. As manager of national health sales with the CNA Insurance Companies, he used humor to promote a relaxed atmosphere, and it must have worked. In his first year in that position, sales under his control increased from $10 million to $16 million. One of his secrets: He opened quarterly staff meetings with magic tricks related to his agenda.

For example at one meeting Joseph wanted to discuss a problem: Everyone working on a particular project had been pulling in different directions. To introduce the topic, Joseph took a piece of rope and cut it into three unequal pieces. He then announced that all three pieces were of equal length and they all played an important role in the project. Naturally his audience disagreed. They protested that the rope consisted of three *unequal* pieces. "That's only because they're different people," Joseph replied. "When I put them all together and get them to work in the same direction, they become equal." As he spoke, he manipulated the ropes so that they appeared to be of equal size and length. He then tied them together into a circle. "Then I untied a knot and stretched the rope out again," Joseph recalls. "Suddenly it appeared to be back in one piece, which was our goal—to get moving in one direction."

Jim Kiehm is another executive who uses humor to encourage teamwork. "My objective is to break down whatever artificial barriers exist between a person of less experience and the managers and partners," he states. "So I try to use humor, not to make a buffoon out of myself but to humanize. I can listen to a joke. I can tell one or two. If you don't get the teamwork, it becomes them against me."

When Kiehm was with Arthur Andersen & Co., he searched for targets that would create a bond of shared laughter with his staff. "I looked for common targets," he states. "We could laugh about a mutual situation. We could call a third party dumb. We could find some humor in some of the situations that our clients get themselves into." One of Kiehm's favorite targets was the company's internal bureaucracy. "The focus should be on our clients, not on our own administrative non-sense," he states. "I'd much rather be out talking to clients about their business than dealing with internal paperwork."

Kiehm cautions that his approach requires careful monitoring of the image it creates. "You don't want to send a message that all the rules are baloney," he explains. "That's wrong. But if another memo comes out and you say, 'Oh great, another report to complete, another checklist to fill out,' and you roll your eyes upward with a 'why me' look, that's okay. Hopefully it puts into focus what I think is and isn't important. It provides an example for my staff people who are looking for an example." In other words Kiehm is using his sense of humor to emphasize that the top priority should be the client.

Humor in Critical Situations and Disasters

Humor's ability to lighten things up is particularly important in work situations that involve morale-sapping communications. The classic example is working in "customer service"— better known as the complaint department. Listening to people air grievances all day is not conducive to achieving a state of ecstasy on the job. And without a good feeling for your work, performance inevitably suffers.

You don't have to work in a complaint department to experience the depressing effect of negative communications. Anyone who deals with customers or clients in any capacity eventually lands on the wrong end of a noncomplimentary remark. Similar morale deflation is shared by people who must spend a lot of time listening to someone bark orders—an experience not limited to menial positions. Many high-level jobs entail submission to an even higher authority. This can become demotivating during critical situations, when the orders become a major source of annoyance.

A good example involves the tense communications between commercial pilots and the air traffic controllers who issue their orders. Humor often lubricates the situation. Typical is the following exchange between an air traffic controller and the captain of a Continental jetliner, who identified his flight as Yellowbird, the airline's trade name:

> "Continental, that's a nonstandard call sign," the controller replied.
> "But Pan Am is 'Clipper,'" the pilot complained.
> "Yes, but you're not approved to use 'Yellowbird,'" the controller admonished.
> Then, out of the blue, another voice chimed in: "Besides, you look more like a yellowbellied sapsucker to me."[4]

The joking banter helps to clear away minor irritations that occur during peak travel periods. And the majority of the humor involves quick one-liners that defuse absurd situations.

A conversation between a Kennedy International Airport air traffic controller and a British Airways pilot during a peak travel time is typical. As the jetliner approached, the controller asked if the pilot could "both slow down and reduce his altitude in a very short interval—an almost impossible maneuver. After a pause, a crisp British voice responded: 'I can comply, sir, but only if I leave the aircraft.'"[5]

By providing a way of dealing with ridiculous orders, humor plays a vital role in maintaining the pilots' morale. Instead of becoming frustrated or angry, they laugh. The humor helps them maintain a productive attitude. And by keeping the pilots focused on flying, the humor helps avert potential disasters.

Humor can also play an important role when disaster does strike. In a "laugh or cry" situation, choosing to laugh helps maintain morale during the recovery period. It puts the disaster into perspective and enables people to be productive. Joking about the disaster also provides a form of mutual support among coworkers during troubled times.

The commercial real estate industry in Santa Clara County, California, better known as Silicon Valley, provides an excellent illustration. A major slump in the electronics industry in 1985 had produced a corresponding slump in real estate business. The goose that laid the golden egg had been cooked. Stories of millionaire developers going broke were common. From the point of view of real estate salespeople, it was a disaster of titanic proportions.

An article in the *San Jose Mercury News* revealed how real estate insiders were coping with the crisis. They were laughing. They were making fun of their problems with jokes such as:

Two developers met on a golf course one Sunday afternoon, and the first one asked the second one what he'd been doing lately. "Not much," he replied. "What with this overbuilt market and the lack of tenants, I've been spending a lot of time working on my golf game. How about you?" The second developer preened with pride. "I'm building a $40 million church," he said. "It's going to have marble floors from the same quarry as the marble in St. Peter's, stained glass from Stuttgart, West Germany, and the pews are made of inlaid wood from the Far East." The first developer gasped in awe and admiration. "That's incredible," he said. "What's the denomination?" And the second developer said, "I'm not sure yet. It's on spec."

"I've never been closer to my lender," boasted a local developer. "He calls me every day to make sure my phone hasn't been disconnected."

Three mayors, Ed Koch of New York City, Tom Bradley of Los Angeles and Tom McEnerny of San Jose, were called up to heaven. God granted each of them one wish. Koch asked God to rid his city of crime. God agreed, but said it was a big job. He wouldn't be able to finish it until 1990. "I'll be gone (from office) by then," Koch wailed. Next was Bradley's turn. He asked God to help Los Angeles clean up its air pollution. God agreed but said it was a big job. He wouldn't be able to finish it until 1995. "I'll be gone by then," Bradley wailed. Then God turned to McEnery and asked him what he wanted for San Jose. McEnery asked God to help him lease the vacant office and industrial space. "I'll be gone by then," God wailed.

Why all the jokes during such a bleak time? An explanation came from Drew Arvay, a senior consultant with Caldwell

Banker Commercial Real Estate and president of the Association of South Bay Brokers. "We're trying to find humor in ourselves," he said. "We're putting a difficult situation in perspective. We're trying to put it in a positive light and keep our wits about us."[6]

Arvay's comments highlight the motivational power of humor. In laughing at disaster, he and his fellow real estate brokers took a first step toward asserting control over the situation. They didn't allow themselves to become paralyzed by the slump. They energized themselves with humor and prepared for the future. When the slump ended, they were much better prepared for the new cycle than their colleagues who had done nothing but whine.

Smoothing a Merger

Perhaps the most fascinating example of humor used to maintain morale during a critical period involves the merger between Allied Corporation and Bendix Corporation. Mergers always create a certain amount of fear and anxiety. People worry about layoffs. They worry about changes in management style. They worry about culture clash. A sense of foreboding permeates the atmosphere. The Allied-Bendix merger featured all of these concerns and more.

Allied acquired Bendix in early 1983 after a takeover battle involving Bendix and two other companies. William C. Purple, the head of the Aerospace and Electronics Group and a veteran Bendix executive, became one of five operating group vice presidents reporting to Allied chairman Edward L. Hennessy. Purple tried to lighten the postmerger atmosphere by poking fun at sacred cows. For example, here's the way he introduced Hennessy at Bendix management meetings: "This is Ed Hennessy. He has had six jobs in seventeen years. If his resume had come across my desk, I wouldn't even have interviewed him." And his description of Hennessy's background as a Catholic seminarian: "They gave him a dollar on weekends and told him to have a big time. Now you know what his idea of a big time is."

Purple didn't limit his quips to Hennessy. He fired his good-natured barbs directly at the differences between the corporate cultures of the two merged companies. For example despite the fact that both companies employed many engineers, the Allied people were much more formal. *The Wall Street Journal* reported that the Bendix people perceived them as a "reserved bunch, given to wearing dark business suits and keeping a watchful eye on one another." As a result Bendix engineers shed their sports coats and started wearing business suits. This change did not escape Purple. At one meeting he quipped that lingering over dinner wasn't a good idea because rented outfits had to be returned by 9:00 P.M.[7]

Did Purple's antics have any effect? The *Journal* reported that Allied's "starchy corporate culture" had been loosened up a bit by Bendix's "self-confident informality," and that intangibles such as Purple's humor were "helping along what Mr. Hennessy says is the smoothest of the roughly 20 mergers he has been through in his career."[8]

According to the *Journal* the humor was welcomed by Hennessy. He was quoted as saying that he wants his people to feel "comfortable about speaking up and not to worry about retribution later on." But Purple had the final word. He was quoted as saying that if Hennessy "couldn't take it, I wouldn't want to work for him."[9]

Euphemisms

Many of the examples we have looked at thus far have featured managers who have a ready wit and know how to use it. They motivate people by saying the right funny thing at the right time. But what if you're not a natural wit? What if you don't know any good jokes? What if you can't perform clever magic tricks? What if you're uncomfortable poking fun at yourself? Is there a *simple* technique for consciously using humor to

138 MALCOLM L. KUSHNER

build morale and motivation on the job? Is there a technique that *anyone* can use?

Fortunately there is. It's called the euphemism. Designed to minimize interpersonal friction, a euphemism is a word or phrase that makes an uncomfortable topic sound better. It helps us say things that we find difficult to say directly. When used appropriately euphemisms help maintain morale by taking the sting out of irritating messages and by communicating that you cared enough to make the effort.

An elaborate example of a euphemism recently appeared in Herb Caen's column in the *San Francisco Chronicle*. A rejection slip sent to a writer by a Chinese economic journal was delicately phrased as follows:

> We have read your manuscript with boundless delight. If we were to publish your paper, it would be impossible for us to publish any work of a lower standard. And as it is unthinkable that, in the next 1,000 years, we shall see its equal, we are, to our regret, compelled to return your divine composition and beg you a thousand times to overlook our short sight and timidity.

Caen's translation: "Don't ever send us this kind of garbage again."[10]

Although few people routinely offer such flowery prose in the name of diplomacy, most of us do employ euphemisms on a regular basis. Have you ever said that a friend was pleasingly plump? Do you refer to a graveyard as a memorial park? Who removes the refuse from your home—a garbageman or a sanitation engineer?

Euphemisms represent an overlap between humor and motivation. We create euphemisms in order to motivate people to view particular topics in a more positive light. Yet if you stop to think about them, they're funny. Comedian George Carlin acknowledged the inherent humor of euphemisms in a routine about looking for a small box of laundry detergent in the supermarket. He found "king size," "family size," and "economy size." "King size" really meant small. My own experience confirms Carlin's observation. A delicatessen that I frequent offers sandwiches in two sizes, medium or large. What if you want a small sandwich? Hint: Order a medium.

Although euphemisms can be amusing, we often use them for a serious purpose: to define the world in our own terms. This notion is aptly summarized by the psychiatrist Thomas Szasz: "In the animal kingdom, the rule is eat or be eaten; in the human kingdom, define or be defined." Szasz views life as a struggle for definition, with language as the primary weapon. If Szasz is correct, then euphemisms represent a major part of the arsenal.

Szasz's theory is well illustrated by our legal system. Attorneys function as professional warriors engaged in a war of words. With the courtroom as battlefield, they fight for judicial acceptance of their definition of events. And euphemisms figure heavily in their skirmishes. For example:

"My client may be a medical professional who abuses drugs and alcohol, but he is not a drunk doctor—he's an impaired physician."

"My client hangs out with a group of rowdy teenagers who wreak havoc in their neighborhood, but he has never been a member of a gang—it's a youth organization."

These legal euphemisms would elicit gales of laughter if cited by comedian George Carlin in a routine. Yet they are offered by no-nonsense lawyers for the serious purpose of motivating judges and juries to accept a certain view of events. They are perfect examples of the humor-motivation overlap.

If euphemisms are so simple and so powerful, why are they overlooked as a method of building morale in the workplace? After all, they serve an inherently morale-building function: putting a positive spin on a negative message.

The answer lies in the double-edged nature of the euphemism. Although it can put a positive face on minor irritations, a euphemism can also be employed to obscure major truths. Unfortunately years of the latter use have given euphemisms a bad reputation. They are commonly perceived as Orwellian devices used by business and government to divert attention from mistakes and bad news. For example, you go to a hospital to visit a sick uncle. You arrive and ask a nurse about his status. She says, "Well, we've had a little negative patient-care outcome." Do you know what that means? He's dead!

It is precisely this type of use that has given euphemisms a bad name. Big business is one of the biggest offenders. When the boss calls you into his office and says there will be some "reductions in force," you're fired. Price increases are "upward adjustments." Business losses are "net-profit revenue deficiencies." And one telephone company subsidiary talks about internal and external profitability. External is revenues. Internal is cutting costs—such as jobs.

My all-time favorite business euphemism occurred in the annual report of an airline company. Required to explain millions of dollars in income from an insurance payment, the company attributed its windfall to the "involuntary conversion of a 747." Translation: One of its planes crashed.

The government also produces more than its fair share of Orwellian euphemisms. Tax increases are "revenue enhancers." Material that leaked to the press is "unclassified controlled information." Military equipment never explodes—it's just subject to an occasional "energetic disassembly." And then there's the most famous government euphemism of all: "strategic misrepresentations," better known as lies.

One last example: Did you know that there's no smog in Los Angeles? There are "atmospheric conditions that occur during certain times of the year." That's how the Los Angeles 1984 Olympics volunteers guidebook instructed them to refer to smog.

In light of such Orwellian usage, it's not surprising that euphemisms have a bad reputation. However, there is a positive side to the story. The euphemism's inherent humor and its ability to make an uncomfortable topic sound better *can* be used to boost morale in the workplace.

The key to using euphemisms as a management tool is applying them to appropriate subjects. Used properly, euphemisms are a social lubricant. Obscuring petty annoyances that no one wants to confront is the essence of diplomacy. In contrast, obscuring more serious topics with euphemisms will earn you a reputation as devious and manipulative. So how do you decide which topics are proper subjects for euphemisms? How do you get labeled as a diplomat rather than a liar? By following a basic principle of good management: Know your people.

In order to determine if a particular topic is appropriate for euphemism, look at two factors: your relationship with the people at whom the euphemism is directed, and their ego involvement in the topic. The critical variable is ego involvement. If a person is highly ego-involved and takes a subject very seriously, then euphemisms are inappropriate. However, if the topic is irritating but not ego-involving, then euphemisms will build morale. The person will appreciate your effort to reduce the irritation.

Consider a few examples. Several years ago, while conducting a series of seminars for the San Francisco Sheriff's Department, I learned that deputies must rewrite reports that are unclear and ungrammatical. Most deputies do not view themselves as great writers. They are not insulted by a rewrite order, but view it as a minor irritation because it means extra work. So the order is an appropriate candidate for euphemism.

How could a supervisor handle the situation? Instead of saying, "Jones, rewrite this report," the supervisor might say "Jones, I'm going to give you an opportunity to win the Pulitzer Prize." The deputy might say, "Huh?" And the supervisor would then explain that the report needs to be rewritten. Of course if a particular deputy thought he or she was a great writer, then the euphemism would be inappropriate. That's why "knowing your people" is essential.

Three primary benefits result from the euphemism technique. First, it takes the sting out of minor irritations and helps people maintain a positive frame of mind. Second, it improves communication by forcing people to learn what's ego-involving to their coworkers. Third, it shows that you care about your colleagues. Even if your euphemism isn't hilarious, it communicates that you've made an extra effort on their behalf. All of this helps improve motivation and morale.

Euphemisms can be easily constructed as good-news/bad-news jokes. One example was developed by the deputy sheriffs in my seminar. Their problem concerned the occasional overflow of all the toilets in the county jail—a minor, yet annoying problem that agitated prisoners and made work more difficult. Whenever a "flood" occurred, the deputies going off duty had to report the problem to the next shift. Here's how the deputies decided to euphemize the news: "We've got some good news and some bad news. The good news is that they finally installed a swimming pool in the jail. The bad news is it's connected to the sewer."

Is it really worth the effort to create and use such euphemisms? Will a single euphemism really change anything? The answers to these questions are yes and maybe.

It is definitely worth trying to take the sting out of minor bad news by coating it with a humorous euphemism. Self-interest dictates the attempt. It helps protect you against the negative reaction that the news will produce in your audience. In ancient times a messenger who brought bad news to the king would be put to death—an extremely negative reaction. We're a little more enlightened today, but we still tend to confuse the message with the messenger.

The effect of a single euphemism is potentially great. The euphemism about the toilets in the jail is a good example. A deputy who comes to work and immediately hears about clogged toilets may fall into a bad mood. The bad mood may affect job performance. The deputy, on a short fuse because of his mood, may lose patience with a prisoner and ignite a riot. In contrast, if the deputy is greeted by the swimming-pool euphemism, he may laugh and start work in a good, or at least neutral, mood.

Is a single euphemism really going to prevent a prison riot? You never know. But more important, even if a particular euphemism isn't funny, it contributes toward a cumulative effect. If everyone in a workplace looks for opportunities to euphemize minor bad news, then the work environment is more pleasant, upbeat, and motivating. And that translates into improved productivity.

The positive power of euphemisms is best summed up by three managers who were talking about their work. The first one said, "I'm so great, the boss sent me to headquarters for executive training." The third manager said, "Incredible." The second one said, "I'm so great, the boss sent me to Harvard for advanced business classes." The third manager said, "Incredible." Then the first two asked the third manager, "What's the boss done for you?" He said, "The boss sent me to charm school." They said, "Charm school? What could you learn at charm school?" "Well," he replied, "now I say 'Incredible' instead of 'Bull.' "

YHTBT Humor

Let me guess what you're thinking. Maybe euphemisms can improve morale, but you don't think the examples we've discussed would work. They don't seem particularly funny. You're absolutely correct. The euphemisms involving deputy sheriffs are not especially hysterical—now. But they may have been sidesplitters when originally used. That's true of much on-the-job humor. It often doesn't translate beyond its immediate context.

I call such humor YHTBT—You Had to Be There. This is probably the most common type of humor in the workplace. It includes all the little quips, comments, observations, and repartee that pepper the interaction of people in an office or factory. It's the stuff that never seems funny later when you tell it to someone who wasn't there.

Much YHTBT humor derives its funniness from the relationships between the people in a workplace. For example, when Jim Kiehm was an audit partner at Arthur Andersen & Co., he had a running gag with a young accountant on his staff. "One kid I called Guido," he explains. "His name was Bill, but I always called him Guido. He'd come up to me and say, 'Read my lips. My name is Bill.' And I'd keep calling him Guido." It sounds silly, but this is exactly the type of humor that can keep a workplace running smoothly. While not hilarious, Kiehm's running gag creates rapport with his staff. It breaks down barriers and helps establish an atmosphere of esprit de corps. "If the young staff people enjoy what they're doing, you get terrific quality work," Kiehm states. "You've got to establish teamwork."

Kiehm's relationship with his secretary was also maintained with large doses of YHTBT humor. A typical example is the time he went on a four-week business trip. He wanted to make sure his secretary watered his plants. So he wrote a list of things that he wanted her to follow up on in his absence. "There were letters that had to go out and documents that had to be filed," he recalls. "But every other item on the list was 'Water my plants.'" When Kiehm returned from his trip, the plants were in good shape. However, there were a dozen five-gallon buckets of water lying about his office. "I asked my secretary what are all these buckets of water doing here?" he states. "She said, 'I didn't want to forget to water your plants.'"

Jim Kiehm and his secretary will not be appearing on the *Tonight Show* anytime soon. They will not become luminaries in the pantheon of immortal comedy teams. They will not even be considered funny by most people. But none of that really matters. Because most people *weren't there*. The YHTBT humor practiced by Kiehm and his secretary is funny to them. And it helps them express an essential part of their relationship.

YHTBT humor is perhaps the least amusing but most powerful form of humor in the world of work. It is humor stripped to the bare bones. Its amusement value is so weak that it has no shelf life. Its funniness cannot be brought to those who were absent when it occurred. Yet it is a powerful force in building positive relationships between people in a work environment. One "Hey Guido" from Jim Kiehm was probably more motivating to a young accountant at Arthur Andersen & Co. than a million hilarious anecdotes. The power of YHTBT humor comes from its emphasis on establishing direct relationships between people. In place of hilarity, it provides a wink and a nod. It creates an atmosphere of conspiracy. The participants are "in" on something.

In the final analysis YHTBT humor reveals the engine that makes humor such an effective motivational device—the act of sharing a personal experience. Shared experiences are the building blocks of personal relationships. Laughing at a quip or anecdote is a form of shared experience that brings people together. YHTBT humor yields the same effect but more intensely. It provides a more personal and direct connection. That's why it's not funny if you weren't there. And that's why it's so meaningful if you were.

Whatever Form It Takes, Humor Is a Prime Motivator

What's my motivation? The question is a Hollywood cliché associated with actors trying to understand their roles. But the question is as old as humans' attempts to influence each other. It is particularly applicable to the workplace. People are not moved to action without reasons.

It's like the man who became chairman of the charity committee of his local hospital. He reviewed all the fund-raising records. And he discovered that the richest person in town had never made a donation. So he went to visit him. He said, "Our records show that you're the richest person in town, but you've never contributed to the hospital." And the rich man said, "Do your records also show that my widowed mother was left absolutely destitute? Do they show that my brother is totally disabled? Do they show that my sister was abandoned with four young children?" By now the chairman felt really ashamed. He said, "Well, no, our records didn't show that." And the rich man said, "Well, I don't do anything for them, so why should I do anything for you?"

Using humor in the workplace doesn't guarantee that people will want to do anything for you. But it does increase the odds. It can make people more productive. It can boost morale. And it can transform a group into a team. Although motivation must ultimately come from within the individual, you can use humor to influence that process. As an ancient Etruscan philosopher once said, "Laugh and the world laughs with you. Cry and you may not cry alone, but you'll never get a group discount."

How to Use Physical Humor to Motivate People

Many successful managers and executives occasionally use physical humor to motivate people. Their devices range from unusual props and attire to unexpected actions, such as dancing. Here are a few examples.

Balloons

Insurance executive John Joseph blows up balloons, twists them into animal shapes, and leaves them on the desks of colleagues and customers. He uses the balloons to break the ice in initial meetings and to get a smile out of people who are having a bad day. Earlier in his sales career the balloon sculptures served as a great door opener that helped him get past secretaries.

Masks

Martin Gonzales, manufacturing program manager for Hewlett-Packard Company, uses masks to win people over to his point of view. A good example occurred at a budget meeting he had to attend with several fellow managers. The goal was to divide up funds for the coming year. Each manager wanted as much as possible. Gonzales scored points by putting on a pig-snout mask.

Hats

Michael Smith, former deputy U.S. trade representative, used to get laughs by suddenly whipping out and donning baseball caps during negotiations with the Japanese. His approach must have worked. It produced an agreement that eliminated Japanese quotas on U.S. beef.

Dances

Sam Walton, chairman and founder of Wal-Mart, has used dance as a motivational device. He promised to dance a hula at dawn on Wall Street if his company achieved its performance goals. The goals were met and the promise was kept—hula skirt and all. It is this type of management that consistently lands Wal-Mart on *Fortune*'s most-admired companies list.

TEN

Use Humor Without Saying a Word

It was so quiet you could hear a pun drop.
—Arthur Baer

A movie actor had a disturbing secret and asked his agent for advice. The actor said, "If I tell the producer my secret before filming begins, he may not hire me. If I tell him after filming begins, he may fire me. What should I do? My secret is that I have false teeth." The agent thought for a moment and replied, "Keep your mouth shut."

If you're uncomfortable using oral humor, it may be wise to follow the agent's advice. Does this mean you have to become a stuffed shirt? No way. The workplace offers a myriad of opportunities for expressing your sense of humor without ever uttering a word. Just the objects that you choose to have around you carry a powerful message.

A case in point was the office of the late G. Robert Truex, Jr., former chairman of Rainier Bancorp. in Seattle. Truex described his office as "traditional, handsome, and overlarge"—the normal habitat of a high-powered executive. In order to counteract that image, Truex used a "Beware of Owner" door-mat to greet visitors who entered his office. The atmosphere was further softened by numerous windup toys strategically placed on Truex's bookcase and credenza. The crowning touch was a plush gorilla wearing a red T-shirt and a paper crown. It peered out at office proceedings from the leaves of a potted palm tree. Truex believed that his doormat, toys, and gorilla encouraged people to relax. *The Wall Street Journal* quoted him as saying, "Please don't get the impression that because I have these toys that I come to work in a clown hat. We conduct business here."[1]

A similar approach is taken by John J. Creedon, chairman of the executive committee of Metropolitan Life Insurance Co. Creedon has tempered the imposing atmosphere of his mammoth, walnut-paneled office by seating two Snoopy dolls dressed in business suits in front of his huge desk. They put people at ease and create a more comfortable environment.[2]

Placing toys in an office is only one of many ways to silently reveal a healthy sense of humor. There are others—even if you don't happen to inhabit a plush office.

Signs and Posters

One of the simplest ways of communicating your sense of humor without saying a word is to hang up a funny sign, poster, or cartoon on your office wall. It immediately sends an important message to the world. It demonstrates that you have made a conscious decision to display something humorous. It shows that you appreciate humor.

The power of a funny sign or poster should not be underestimated. Visitors to your workspace make assumptions about your character and attitudes based on your choice of wall decorations. That's why job seekers are always advised to scrutinize the walls of an interviewer's office. Pictures, signs, and posters provide clues to the interviewer's personality and interests. They enable the job seeker to make quick, educated guesses about the best way to handle the interview. Let's face it, a person with a *Far Side* cartoon on his wall projects a different image from a person who displays a poster of company work rules.

In addition to communicating your sense of humor, signs

and posters can be used to address specific problems. I spotted a good example at a secretary's desk in Digital Equipment Corporation's Field Service Logistics facility in Woburn, Massachusetts. Two signs graced the secretary's cubicle wall:

"YOU MAY KNOW WHERE YOU'RE GOING. GOD MAY KNOW WHERE YOU'RE GOING. DOES YOUR SECRETARY KNOW WHERE YOU'RE GOING?"

"LACK OF PLANNING BY YOU DOES NOT CONSTITUTE AN EMERGENCY FOR ME!!!"

Although coated in humor, the signs contain serious messages about two of the biggest problems commonly faced by secretaries around the world: the boss's failure to communicate his or her whereabouts and work flow. By posting the signs the secretary reminds her boss to keep her informed. Contrast the signs with the secretary's other option for handling the problems: constant oral reminders to the boss. This would probably be perceived as nagging and provoke unnecessary friction. The signs are acceptable because they are amusing.

A similar device was employed in the office kitchen of Harris Data Services in Ashland, Virginia. Harris vice president Duane Klevgard got tired of people leaving dirty cups and dishes in the sink. After several discussions failed to produce results, he solved the problem with a sign: "PLEASE DON'T LEAVE DISHES IN THE SINK. WHO DO YOU THINK I AM—YOUR MOTHER?" "People grinned when they saw the sign," recalls Klevgard. "It didn't offend anybody and it brought the problem to everyone's attention. It was about 95 percent effective."

The taxonomy of workplace signs also includes an entire class devoted to the prevention of potential customer hostility. Such signs assume that the wheels of commerce will not always turn smoothly. Examples include:

Sign in a local bank: "MISTAKES MADE WHILE YOU WAIT."

Sign on a restaurant manager's office door: "I'M TAK-
ING COMPLAINTS BETWEEN 6:00 AND 6:30—SUNDAY MORNING."

Sign above the cash register in a photocopying store:
"PRICES SUBJECT TO CHANGE BASED ON CUSTOMER ATTI-
TUDE."

These signs offer humor as a temporary lubricant for reducing friction until the underlying problem can be resolved.
They act as a safety valve for slowing the buildup of customer
anger. They help ensure that the problem doesn't get blown
out of proportion. They also help diagnose the depth of the
problem—if a customer doesn't even smile at the sign, then
you *know* you're in trouble!

Even extremely sensitive situations can be addressed by
humorous signs if they are handled properly. A good example involves a set of posters displayed prior to a union-
representation election at Lawrence Livermore National Lab-
oratory in 1983. Management was convinced that a large voter
turnout would defeat the union. In order to encourage voting,
management waged a humorous poster campaign reminding
employees to vote. The posters, all designed around a patriotic
theme, were not knee-slapping, sidesplitting, or rib-tickling by
any stretch of the imagination. However, they were effective.
They gained attention by treating patriotic themes in a mildly
amusing way that didn't distract from the main message—get
out and vote.

Each poster featured a picture of an American patriot ac-
companied by a slogan that tied into the upcoming election.
Examples include the following:

- Betsy Ross sewing a flag: "DON'T FORGET TO VOTE—THE
  ELECTION ISN'T SEWN UP."

- Paul Revere: "THE BALLOTS ARE COMING! THE BALLOTS ARE COMING! VOTE IN THE REPRESENTATION ELECTION."
- Teddy Roosevelt: "SPEAK SOFTLY AND CARRY A BIG VOTE. VOTE 'NO REPRESENTATION.'"
- Franklin D. Roosevelt: "THERE'S NOTHING TO FEAR BUT FORGETTING TO VOTE. VOTE 'NO REPRESENTATION.'"
- George Washington on a dollar bill: "DON'T PASS THE BUCK—VOTE! VOTE 'NO REPRESENTATION.'"
- Ben Franklin flying a kite: "IT WOULD BE SHOCKING NOT TO VOTE. VOTE 'NO REPRESENTATION.'"

According to Lew Reed, one of the posters' creators, the humorous poster campaign culminated a lengthy, very serious campaign. "The posters were a way of building awareness without being heavy-handed," he explains. "They helped the voters to remember our message, as well as the time to vote." The response proved rewarding. More than 90 percent of eligible voters participated in the election. Reed notes that this was an outstanding turnout, especially for an election in which votes were cast by mail-in ballots. The final tally: 75 percent of the voters voted against the unions. Reed attributes the voter response to the posters. "The voters appreciated the humor," he states. "In comparison to other, serious campaigns that we've conducted, the humorous posters were much more effective."

Humorous office signs also provide an excellent vehicle for advertising a product or service. A good example can be found hanging on the cubicle wall of Brenda Schaeffer, a purchaser at Spectra-Physics Construction & Agricultural Division in Dayton, Ohio. The sign reads as follows:

AN ENGINEER IS SOMEONE WHO KNOWS A GREAT DEAL ABOUT A VERY LITTLE SUBJECT AREA. AS HE PROGRESSES IN HIS CAREER HE LEARNS MORE AND MORE ABOUT LESS AND LESS. HE ENDS UP KNOWING EVERYTHING ABOUT PRACTICALLY NOTHING.

A SALESMAN IS SOMEONE WHO KNOWS A LITTLE BIT ABOUT PRACTICALLY EVERYTHING. AS HE PROGRESSES IN HIS CAREER HE KNOWS LESS AND

LESS ABOUT MORE AND MORE UNTIL HE KNOWS ALMOST NOTHING ABOUT PRACTICALLY EVERYTHING.

A PURCHASING AGENT IS SOMEONE WHO STARTS OUT KNOWING EVERYTHING ABOUT EVERYTHING BUT HE ENDS UP KNOWING NOTHING ABOUT ANYTHING BECAUSE OF HIS LONG ASSOCIATION WITH ENGINEERS AND SALESMEN.

The name "W. H. Brady Co. Industrial Products Division" appears on the bottom of the sign, along with the company's address and logo.

Every time Brenda Schaeffer looks at that sign, her awareness of the W. H. Brady Company increases. In fact every time one of Schaeffer's fellow purchasers walks by her cubicle, awareness of the company increases. That one simple sign is doing a lot of hard work. It's keeping the W. H. Brady Company in the forefront of its customers' minds. You can bet it was worth the small expense required to print it.

Bulletin Boards

One simple way to institutionalize "silent" humor in your workplace is to provide a bulletin board devoted to funny material. This gives people an outlet to express their sense of humor. The bulletin board can include sections for graffiti and a joke of the day, as well as funny news clippings, cartoons, and photographs. And don't worry about finding material. Once the bulletin board is established, you'll find that it will fill up rather quickly.

You don't believe me? Stop worrying. Here are a few tried-and-true methods for filling up a humor bulletin board:

- Ask vacationing coworkers to send outrageous postcards back to the office. You know the kind I mean—a chimpanzee dressed in overalls riding a tricycle, a picture of a wax-museum statue of Elvis, a "Wish You Were Here" card from Lompoc Federal Penitentiary.
- Shoot photographs of company activities outside the office

and add funny captions or talk bubbles. Hint: Events such as Halloween and Christmas parties contain two major sources of funny photos—costumes and gifts.

- Ask everyone in your workplace to bring in a baby picture of himself or herself. The fun begins when everyone tries to guess who's who.
- Ask everyone in your workplace to bring in a 1960s photo of themselves. This is a variation of the baby-photo request, and it can produce even better results. Sure, baby pictures are cute, but they don't really tell you much about the person. Sixties photos often reveal youthful life-style choices. There's just something about seeing a college photo of your CEO wearing tie-dyed pants and love beads that's good for morale.

If the prospect of a good laugh isn't enough motivation to elicit contributions from your coworkers, try holding a contest. The possibilities are endless. You can arrange prizes for the cutest baby photo, the wildest postcard, or the funniest photo caption. You can create awards for the funniest news clipping of the week or month. Whatever method you choose, be sure to take some time to spread the word throughout your workplace. The larger the number of participants, the funnier and more successful the contest will be.

Letters and Memos

Another area of opportunity for using humor without saying a word is the written business communication. Letters and memos, those traditional bearers of corporate content, have fallen prey to the great evil of our information age—uncontrolled growth. Computer-generated communications threaten to engulf us. Whether distributed as electronic mail or in the traditional paper format, letters and memos are bombarding us in greater numbers than ever before. And they're just as boring as ever.

In the past it was possible to get away with bland, vapid

memos, but that changed forever with the advent of personal computers. Today anyone can fire off a memo at the drop of a keyboard. With so many written communications competing for attention, the extra edge of a humorous touch is essential. Put simply, you want your letter or memo to stand out in the crowd. How can you accomplish this task? You can make your written communications shine in the spotlight of humor.

The good news is that you don't have to be a great comic writer to give your business writing a humorous edge. The better news is that most business writing is so dull that even the slightest humorous touch will make your work stand out. A good example is the following excerpt from a letter sent from one physician to another: "On examination, Christopher looked like a million dollars (1980 dollars). He was active, alert, playful, and in no distress." The addition of "(1980 dollars)" made the letter stand out in a stack of routine correspondence.

Adding a comic touch to a memo is also an easy way of communicating your sense of humor. A good example is a memo from David Sohm, vice president and general manager of ASK Computer Systems' Data 3 division.

Other Items: We will have a managers' kickoff meeting in July. New product release training will be one stop per region in July. New sales rep training will be in July prior to release training.

Action Required: July is crowded—prepare a proposal to fit all this in (extending July to 65 days is not an option).

The line about extending July isn't hilarious, but it doesn't have to be. It's effective when viewed in context. The line communicates Sohm's sense of humor and puts the July workload into perspective.

Memo mirth also proved effective for Joe DiNucci, when he was U.S. workstation sales manager for Digital Equipment Corporation. When organizing his workstation sales force in 1986,

DiNucci issued a weekly motivational message. Many of the messages began with a humorous quotation that led into the subject of the memo. Typical examples include:

> Weekly worksystems message #2: "'Ninety percent of success is showing up'—Woody Allen."

> Worksystems message #5: "'We have met the enemy and he is us.'—*Pogo*."

Did the quotes have any real effect? DiNucci knows they did. "I got notes from people commenting about the quotes," he explains. "They said my messages were the only things in their electronic mail systems that they didn't flush."

A particularly interesting approach to memo humor is employed by Gerry Bowden, one of the city attorneys for Santa Cruz, California. He uses a set of special rubber stamps to communicate his sense of humor while also getting his message across concisely. His stamp collection offers messages such as "Hallelujah!" "Wanna Bet?!" "Baloney!" "Bull!" "Amen!" "Go for It!" and "Excuses, Excuses!"

"Much of our work for the city involves reviewing letters and documents produced by the various municipal departments," Bowden explains. "They want our blessing. Is this letter okay? Do I need to make any changes in this resolution?" When no changes are required, instead of writing an approval memo, Bowden uses one of his rubber stamps. "When the document comes back stamped 'Amen!' or 'Go for It!' the administrators who sent it know it's all right," he says. They also know that Bowden is "all right"—that he's not a stuffy attorney.

Now, before we get carried away, let's remember that there are limits to using humor in business letters and memos. As with all other uses of humor, the limits are dictated by common sense and good judgment. Overstepping the bounds of good taste creates an invitation for disaster.

That's what happened at a company flooded with memos by its president. In response, a senior executive wrote a parody memo warning about the dangers of " 'memo-itis, a corporate sickness whose main symptom is mental incontinence.' The only cure: Do time in a 'memo re-education camp.' " Unfortunately the company president was not amused. Upon discovering the parody memo, he crumpled it up and flew into a rage at its author.[3]

Obviously a memo insulting the boss is not going to be a big hit under any circumstances. Laughing at, rather than with, a superior is never likely to be a brilliant career move. And performing such an action in writing is downright idiotic. However, don't let an extreme example dissuade you from injecting a little humor into your memos. Just the mildest touch can add an invaluable sparkle.

Newsletters

An additional outlet for using humor in written business communications is provided by the company newsletter. Whether aimed at customers or employees, any newsletter can benefit from the insertion of a short, regular humor feature, particularly if it's placed on an inside page. Many newsletters routinely use cartoons.

Here's why. Company newsletters are notoriously bland affairs. They usually receive a cursory glance prior to being deposited in a circular file. This is not surprising when one considers typical newsletter content: a mix of warmed-over product announcements, financial results, and optimistic projections for the future. Important company announcements don't originate in company newsletters. They just end up there three months later.

A stark contrast to ho-hum company propaganda is offered by a humor feature. It holds out the promise of entertainment and amusement. It gives the employee or customer a motivation to look at the newsletter. And if placed on an inside page, a humor feature provides a powerful incentive for opening the newsletter before throwing it away. It literally hooks the audience.

An excellent example of a humor hook can be found in *Letter from the Lion*, a quarterly customer newsletter published by Dreyfus Service Corporation. Each issue features seven entertaining quotes of the "pearls of wisdom" variety. Past entries include:

"Spare no expense to make everything as economical as possible."—Sam Goldwyn

"One of life's small satisfactions is copping first place on a newly opened checkout line."—Libbie Fudim

"Be careful about reading health books. You may die of a misprint."—Mark Twain

"I am a very good housekeeper. Each time I get a divorce I keep the house."—Zsa Zsa Gabor

The quotes appear in a horizontal strip that runs along the bottom of two inside pages of the newsletter. This strategic placement ensures that fans of the feature must open the newsletter in order to read the quotes.[4]

Has the feature proved successful? Here's the editor's assessment as it appeared in the spring 1983 issue of *Letter from the Lion*:

Our various polls and inquiries, and especially our incoming mail, reveal to our astonishment (and joy) that our modest horizontal enclave of simple human statements in *Letter from the Lion* . . . is the best read and most inspiring feature of this newsletter.[5]

Believe me, it's not so astonishing. Which would you prefer to read, funny quotes or company propaganda? The point is that the quotes force the reader to open the newsletter. Then there's at least a possibility that some of the articles may be read. (See the excerpt from the Adia Personnel Services newsletter on page 163 for another excellent example of the use of humor.)

Annual Reports

One final area of written business communication that should be considered as a candidate for humor is the annual report. Yes, even this most conservative of corporate documents can be enhanced with a judiciously applied light touch. Although more formal than a newsletter, the annual report shares many of the same traits. It's packed full of old news. It's boring. And it's totally self-serving.

Annual reports are usually read in one of three ways. Financial analysts skip right to the "numbers section" of the report. Shareholders look at the photos and maybe read a caption or two. Executives responsible for the report read the entire thing, from "Serving Our Customers" to "Making Quality Products." They think it's fascinating.

Let's talk reality. No matter what you do, it's doubtful that anyone will purchase the movie rights to your annual report. However, you can increase reader interest by adding a touch of humor. A good example comes from the 1987 annual report of ASK Computer Systems Inc. The Mountain View, California-based software company began its award-winning report as follows:

> One of America's greatest management philosophers once said "If you don't know where you're going you might end up somewhere else." Casey Stengel may have mangled the language, but he didn't mince words. He understood the importance of strategy and planning in the achievement of ultimate goals. And ASK agrees with his philosophy—that's why the company has a comprehensive strategy to maintain its leadership position into the next decade and beyond.[6]

This opening is effective for three reasons. First, it's amusing. It stands out in the boring world of annual reports. Second, it's relevant. It leads directly into the theme of the report—strategy. Third, it hooks the reader. Even if no additional humor is used, readers will look through the entire report hoping to find some.

An extreme example of annual-report humor can be found in the 1983 Annual Report for Max & Erma's Restaurants Inc. of Columbus, Ohio. Despite heavy losses the company's 1983 annual featured cartoons that mocked everyone connected with the operation. The report pictured executives sleeping at their desks, shareholders throwing paper airplanes, and people holding a pot containing a ledger book over a campfire. An explanation was offered by Terri Purcell-Lynch, Max & Erma's director of advertising and promotions. "We take our company seriously," she said. "But we wanted to show that we are a light-hearted company running fun restaurants."[7]

In this case the humor was well intentioned but inappropriate. Although the executives were attempting to laugh at themselves, the annual report could have been interpreted as laughing at the shareholders. Put yourself in the shoes of a shareholder. You've invested in a company that is not doing well. Suddenly an annual report appears that seems to celebrate the company's poor performance. And the report was prepared by the very people who have caused the company's problems. You would probably think they were mocking you. They're rubbing your nose in the fact that you made the mistake of investing in a company that they managed. This is a case where less is more. Less-exaggerated humor in a less-visible setting would have been more effective. They should have used their self-effacing humor at the annual shareholders meeting or in a special letter to shareholders.

Gag Gifts

An often overlooked method of using humor without saying a word is the gag gift. In addition to communicating your sense of humor, gag gifts can keep coworkers loose and show that you're thinking about them. For example, when a gorilla barges into an office to sing birthday greetings to a secretary, it gives everyone a lift. And the secretary is flattered by the attention. It's truly the thought that counts.

Gag gifts need not be elaborate. They can be as simple as a "Rush Job Calendar" (the days are numbered backward so that you can order something on the seventh and receive it on the first) or a coffee mug inscribed with a funny slogan (e.g., "I'm not deaf, I'm just ignoring you."). Granted, these are not hysterical, guffaw-producing items. But that isn't their function. The idea is simply to elicit a smile from a coworker who will recognize and appreciate your efforts and attention.

The power of gag gifts was recently illustrated in an Associated Press article that appeared in the *San Jose Mercury News*. Headlined "IDAHO POLICE KEEP SENSE OF HUMOR IN WAKE OF HOAX," the article described a massive search in Twin Lakes, Idaho. Eighty police officers, paramedics, and ambulance crew members spent a night in the woods looking for a stack of bodies. The search was prompted by a man who claimed that motorcycle gangs had engaged in a wild shoot-out. Nothing was ever found to support the story.

Disappointment and frustration over the wild-goose chase were dispelled with a gag gift—a T-shirt bearing the slogan "I Survived the Twin Lakes Massacre." "It's been a big hit, it really has," said Jason Felton, a Hayden Lake police officer. By exaggerating the situation, the T-shirt transformed a night of lost sleep into a funny incident that will produce smiles for a long time.[8]

There's a story about an executive who hated procrastination. So he hung up a sign that said, "Do It Now." Within twenty-four hours his sales force quit, his secretary took a vacation, and his assistant stole the office computer. Despite such risks, I'm going to advise you to "do it now"—start communicating your sense of humor without saying a word today. Hang a cartoon on your office wall. Give a coworker a gag gift. Organize a humor bulletin board. Start looking for opportunities to institutionalize humor in your workplace. Make humor a habit. It will make you a better manager. And that's no joke!

The Sympathy Clause

Quick, think of something fun and amusing. Did the topic of insurance leap to mind? If not, then you're probably one of the millions of people who are less than enthralled with the subject. And it's precisely this joyless image of insurance that often proves troublesome to the people who have to sell it.

"It's real hard to find humorous things in delivering an insurance policy," states Tom Kelly, president of Wm. W. Kelly & Company. "It's like going to an attorney for a divorce. People just don't like it. People don't like insurance and they don't like to pay for it."

In order to remedy this problem, Kelly occasionally inserts the following clause into his customers' policies:

SYMPATHY CLAUSE

Attached to and forming part of Policy No. _____

Of the _____
NAME OF INSURANCE COMPANY

issued at its _____ Agency.
CITY OR TOWN

Date _____   _____ Agent

In consideration of the premium for which this policy is written, and subject to the terms and conditions in the policy to which this clause is attached, it is hereby expressly stipulated and agreed that, in the event of occurrence of loss and/or damage to the property insured hereunder as a result of perils not covered under this policy, or in the event of occurrence of loss and/or damage to other property of the insured not insured hereunder, the Company does hereby extend its deepest sympathy and regret in respect to all such losses and/or damages.

_____ Agent[9]

To prevent misinterpretation of his intent, Kelly only uses the Sympathy Clause with customers whom he has known awhile. "It lightens up the renewal process," he observes. "It's an icebreaker that creates a much more amiable relationship between customer and salesperson. If you've had a few laughs together, it's easier to work together."

Excerpt from Adia Employee Newsletter

A particularly effective use of humor in a newsletter can be found in a 1984 issue of *Adia Ink*, the employee newsletter of Adia Personnel Services. It came to my attention when I judged a competition sponsored by the International Association of Business Communicators.

Today Adia is a leading temporary and permanent personnel placement service with over 550 offices throughout the United States. In 1984 the company was about to go public. In order to prepare for that event it issued a special edition of its employee newsletter. According to Marcia Pear, associate director of communication at Adia, the objective was to educate employees about what going public entailed.

"Prior to going public, we had been a wholly-owned subsidiary of a Swiss corporation," she recalls. "So there was some confusion among employees. They wanted to know exactly what going public meant and how they would be affected." The bulk of the newsletter answered these questions in serious interviews with company executives. However, a sidebar guide to financial terminology featured a host of humorous definitions.

Pear decided to insert the amusing definitions to counteract the inherently boring nature of financial jargon. "The terminology was important to a basic understanding of what it meant to go public," she recalls. "Yet the terms were extremely dry. We felt they had a much better chance of being read and retained if we added a bit of humor. Then the information would be colorful and make an impression." Reaction to the feature was extremely positive. In addition to kudos from Adia employees, the humorous glossary won an award from the International Association of Business Communicators.

"WHAT DOES IT ALL MEAN?"

A Glossary for Going Public

Going public involves more than selling stock—it means learning a whole new lexicon of often bewildering terminology. The following definitions should help you understand what it is they do on Wall Street each day.

Blue Sky   (1) what one wishes for each weekend; (2) in stock talk, refers to laws designed to protect the public from securities offerings which are not "fair, just and equitable."

Book, The   a stockbroker's Bible. Signifies a preliminary indication of interest in a new stock issue.

Going Public   a variation on the "Yours, Mine and Ours" theme. Adia S.A. had previously owned 100% of Adia U.S.. Now, our Swiss parent company retains 70% ownership of the U.S. operation; individual investors own the remaining 30%, which amounts to 1.2 million shares of stock. "To go public" means that there is now a public market in Adia stock.

OTC   (1) alphabetical listing after OTB, but bearing no relation to off-track betting; (2) Over-the-Counter, a method for selling nonprescription drugs; (3) Over-the-Counter, a method for trading stock. Adia's stock transactions take place directly between buyers and sellers. There is no organized securities exchange involved.

Pot   (1) a "high" priority; (2) portion of an offering not distributed by the underwriters, but set aside for discretionary distribution by the manager running the books.

Prospectus   (1) a Roman Account Manager during the days of Julius Caesar; (2) the formal summary of a proposed stock venture. Everyone who purchases Adia stock receives a prospectus describing the offering.

Red Herring   (1) a salty sardine; (2) an act of deception; (3) a preliminary prospectus which was issued up to the date of our initial stock offering, on October 2, 1984.

Road Show   (1) a performance never seen on Broadway; (2) a series of meetings between institutional investors in major financial centers and the management of a company that intends to go public. Usually conducted by CEO.

Run the Books   (1) to manage an off-track betting operation; (2) to be in charge of the marketing, allocation, payment, and delivery of a stock offering.

SEC   (1) a dry champagne; (2) Securities and Exchange Commission. Agency created by Congress to enforce laws for the protection of investors in security transactions.

Tombstone   (1) usually connotes a grave situation; (2) the formal advertisement of a company's stock offering that states terms, underwriters, and where a prospectus can be obtained. Does not constitute an offer to buy or sell securities.

Underwrite   (1) to sign below the dotted line; (2) to agree to purchase securities on a fixed date at a fixed price from a company with the intent to publicly distribute stock. Our underwriting group, comanaged by First Boston Corporation and Kidder, Peabody and Company, bought 30% of Adia U.S., or 1.2 million shares at a price of $12.75 a share. An Underwriting Agreement, or Underwriting the Risk, means that our institutional investors have formally guaranteed their financial support.[10]

Five Great Signs and Memos for Your Office

Each of the following five signs is an example of "off the wall" humor that you can use without saying a word. They are just a few of the examples that I've accumulated in my travels throughout corporate America. They were posted on a wall or were sitting on a desk as I passed through a particular company.

Just reproduce the messages on the paper or posterboard of your choice. Then post them as signs in your work area. Or send them around the office via in-baskets. If you've already seen them in your office, you probably work with people who have a good sense of humor. So go out and find some new signs and memos.

STRESS DIET

Breakfast
½ grapefruit
1 slice whole wheat toast
8 oz. skim milk

Lunch
4 oz. lean broiled chicken breast
1 cup steamed zucchini
1 Oreo cookie
Herb tea

Midafternoon Snack
Rest of the package of Oreos
1 quart Rocky Road ice cream
1 jar hot fudge

Dinner
2 loaves garlic bread
Large pepperoni and mushroom pizza
Large pitcher of beer
3 Milky Way candy bars
Entire frozen cheesecake eaten directly from the freezer

Diet Tips

1. If no one sees you eat it, it has no calories.
2. If you drink a diet soda with a candy bar, they cancel each other out.
3. When eating with someone else, calories don't count if you both eat the same amount.
4. Food used for medicinal purposes NEVER counts, such as: hot chocolate, brandy, toast, and Sara Lee cheesecake.
5. If you fatten up everyone else around you, you look thinner.
6. Movie-related foods don't count because they are simply part of the entertainment experience and not a part of one's personal fuel, such as Milk Duds, popcorn with butter, and Junior Mints.

Enjoy Your Diet!!!!![11]

SIX PHASES OF A PROJECT

1. ENTHUSIASM
2. DISILLUSIONMENT
3. PANIC
4. SEARCH FOR THE GUILTY
5. PUNISHMENT OF THE INNOCENT
6. PRAISE AND HONORS FOR THE NONPARTICIPANTS[12]

****
ANSWER PRICE LIST
****

ANSWERS	$ .75
ANSWERS (requiring thought)	1.25
ANSWERS (correct)	2.50

****
DUMB LOOKS ARE STILL FREE!!!!![13]
****

WHOSE JOB IS IT?

THIS IS A STORY ABOUT FOUR PEOPLE NAMED EVERYBODY, SOMEBODY, ANYBODY, AND NOBODY. THERE WAS AN IMPORTANT JOB TO BE DONE AND EVERYBODY WAS SURE SOMEBODY WOULD DO IT. ANYBODY COULD HAVE DONE IT, BUT NOBODY DID IT. SOMEBODY GOT ANGRY ABOUT THAT, BECAUSE IT WAS EVERYBODY'S JOB. EVERYBODY THOUGHT THAT ANYBODY COULD DO IT BUT NOBODY REALIZED THAT EVERYBODY WOULDN'T DO IT. IT ENDED UP THAT EVERYBODY BLAMED SOMEBODY WHEN NOBODY DID WHAT ANYBODY COULD HAVE DONE.[14]

NEW SICK-LEAVE POLICY

SICKNESS: No excuse. We will no longer accept your doctor's statement as proof, since we believe that if you are able to go to the doctor, you are able to come to work.

LEAVE OF ABSENCE (for an Operation): We are no longer allowing this practice. We wish to discourage any thought that you may have about needing an operation. We believe that as long as you are employed here, you will need all of whatever you have and should not consider having anything removed. We hired you as you are and to have anything removed would certainly make you less than we bargained for.

DEATH (Other Than Your Own): This is no excuse. There is nothing you can do for them, and we are sure that someone else in a lesser position can attend to the arrangements. However, if the funeral can be held in late afternoon, we will be glad to let you off one hour early, provided that your share of work is ahead enough to keep the job going in your absence.

DEATH (Your Own): This will be accepted as an excuse, but we would like a two-week notice, as we feel it is your duty to teach someone else your job.[15]

ELEVEN

Adding Humor and Measuring Mirth in the Corporate Culture

A person reveals his character by nothing so clearly as the joke he resents.
—G. C. Lichtenberg

During the 1985 U.S./Soviet summit meeting in Geneva, Ronald Reagan told Mikhail Gorbachev the following joke:

> An American and a Soviet citizen were having a discussion about who had more freedom. The American said, "I can march into the Oval Office in the White House and say, 'Mr. President, I don't like the way you're running our country.'" And the Soviet citizen said, "Well, I can do that too. I can walk into General-Secretary Gorbachev's office in the Kremlin and say, 'Mr. Secretary, I don't like the way President Reagan's running his country.'"

After the summit Reagan offered a comment about Gorbachev's reaction to the joke: "Thank goodness he laughed."[1]

Reagan's comment highlights the serious role of humor in assessing the nature of different cultures. By telling the joke and gauging the reaction, Reagan gained valuable insights into what is or isn't funny by Soviet standards. Why were these insights valuable? Because knowledge of a culture's sense of humor provides a guide to the basic values and fundamental relationships that comprise that culture.

The business world, like the political world, is made up of entities that represent a vast array of cultures. In the business world the entities are corporations instead of nations. Each corporation has its own set of values, relationships, and ways of conducting business—its own "culture." By examining how people use and react to humor within specific business organizations, we can learn a lot about their cultures.

Business Fad or Fundamental?

A buzzword throughout the 1980s, *corporate culture* refers to the internal social environment of a business organization—the values, attitudes, and beliefs of its employees, the leadership style of its management, and the manner in which the company conducts its business. Like the cultures of different nations, corporate cultures exhibit differences in language, costume, and ritual. From the button-down world of an IBM to the informal style of the early Apple Computer Inc., corporate culture exerts a continuing and significant influence on the way people work.

Today it has become fashionable, if not required, for executives to assess and explore fully the implications of corporate culture in their companies. High-paid consultants conduct anthropological surveys of employee behavior. Corporate culture is included as an action item in company planning sessions. Executive bookshelves are lined with volumes addressing the problems of managing cultural change. However, corporate culture's exalted status in the executive suite is a relatively recent development. Traditionally corporate culture served as a backdrop. Its effects went unnoticed. Nobody thought about it. And it didn't have a fancy label. Culture? That was art, literature, or opera.

Corporate culture might have languished in the backwaters of business awareness forever. But three things occurred that thrust it into the forefront of corporate consciousness. First, an army of academics discovered the area and promptly created a cottage industry in the study of organizational culture.

They examined the effect of corporate culture on everything from decision making and leadership style to market share and productivity. No variable was left unturned. They quickly compiled an arsenal of observations. And their findings were unleashed in an unrelenting flood of reports, statistics, surveys, and studies.

Second, Japan emerged as an economic superpower in an increasingly global marketplace. The American business community, fascinated and obsessed with Japan's success, searched for its source. How could a country known for producing junk suddenly become a world leader in electronics, autos, and computers? What was the secret?

The search produced a wealth of trendy concepts and catch phrases: "total quality control," "statistical process control," "zero-defects," "customer-driven." Eventually researchers realized that all of these items shared one common root—Japanese corporate culture. This discovery moved the search in a new direction. Attention rapidly shifted to Japanese management techniques, motivational processes, and training methodologies. Consultants ran seminars on quality circles, the relationship between managers and workers, company loyalty, and corporate culture as a strategic competency.

The third, and most important, factor that transformed corporate culture into an executive agenda item was merger mania. Obsessed with cutting costs in order to compete with Japan, American companies went into a feeding frenzy—on each other. Large companies gobbled up small ones. Small ones gobbled up large ones. A parade of "white knights," "sharks," and "poison pills" marched across the pages of the business press. And Wall Street rocked as takeovers took over.

"Lean and mean" became the battle cry as merger mania swept America. But after the companies involved in a merger or acquisition had "slimmed down" and "cut out the fat," they had to face the culture problem. Workers from two different organizations were now part of the same team. Their different values, beliefs, and ways of doing things had to be harmonized if the new company was to function successfully. Corporate culture was no longer just a psychobabble concept spouted by self-serving management consultants. It was a real issue that had to be dealt with.

Today as merger mania and global competition continue to dominate the news, business organizations can no longer afford to take culture for granted. Management must take an active role in identifying, understanding, and influencing corporate culture. Although total control of a company's culture may remain elusive, management must move toward that ultimate objective.

Humor Yields Insight into Corporate Culture

Anthropologists have long regarded humor as an important tool for illuminating the inner workings of a culture. Foremost among such scholars is Alan Dundes, professor of anthropology and folklore at the University of California at Berkeley. As the author of numerous books and articles about humor and culture, Dundes has spent much of his professional life studying humor around the world.

Dundes's reliance on humor as a cultural indicator is well established. "Jokes are direct statements that people make about their world," he states. "They are much more authentic statements of values and world view than you get from social scientists conducting surveys." According to Dundes, the jokes, games, and stories that constitute a society's folklore can reveal more about a people than its literature or scholarly works. "Folklore gives a picture of a people drawn by themselves," he observes. "It provides the most reliable reflection of a culture."

Dundes's observations also apply in the context of *corporate* culture. In a business world ruled by sanitized press releases, "Cover Your Posterior" memos, and carefully worded annual reports, humor can play a major role in identifying an organization's real values. Analyzing the jokes and stories used by workers, managers, and executives throughout a corporation can reveal the hidden assumptions that define the culture.

Their humor provides a direct, uncensored view of their shared beliefs.

Uncovering hidden assumptions provides the key to unlocking the mysteries of a corporate culture. It is the hidden assumptions that guide the actions and shape the behavior of the culture's members. How do employees of a particular company view the world? What are their underlying values and beliefs? How do they see themselves, their company, and their competitors? Unfortunately this type of information is not spelled out in policy and procedure manuals. Hidden cultural assumptions must be pieced together by carefully observing the behavior of a corporation's employees.

An excellent starting point is the interaction of new employees with veteran employees. The new employee, faced with the task of learning how to behave in the organization, will look to the veteran employee for guidance. In response the veteran will "show the ropes" to the newcomer. During this learning process, also known as enculturation, the veteran employee will pass along knowledge of the hidden assumptions.

The transfer of this knowledge is a very informal process. It often occurs when a new employee, unfamiliar with the culture, violates one of the assumptions. In correcting the "mistake," veteran employees will tacitly reveal the existence of the assumption. For example new employees who joke about a taboo topic will quickly learn of their error. The reaction of veteran employees will communicate and correct the mistake. A direct correction might involve telling the new employee not to make jokes about the topic. An indirect correction might be a reaction of disgust, pity, head-shaking, or equivalent display of negative reinforcement. In either case the new employee will learn about the hidden assumption.

By observing how veteran employees interact with new employees, particularly in the area of jokes and humor, we can begin to detect the hidden assumptions. What do people in the company laugh at? What are they supposed to laugh at? What aren't they supposed to laugh at? When a veteran employee tells a funny "war" story, what is the point of the story? Does it poke fun at a superior? At a competitor? What actions make someone a target of ridicule in the company? Humor exposes the shared beliefs and values assumed by a culture because knowledge of those assumptions is required to "get" the joke.

Humor's Role in Corporate Culture

Even more important than humor's role in identifying the nature of a culture is humor's role in shaping the culture. A company in which laughter is encouraged is a very different place to work than one in which humor is discouraged or merely tolerated. A workplace stimulated by laughter tends to score higher marks in job satisfaction and productivity. Communication, creativity, and morale are all affected by the amount and type of humor sanctioned by an organization.

A corporate culture with a "sense of humor" is likely to be more open and responsive. By breaking down barriers and making people more approachable, humor promotes a healthy exchange of ideas within a corporation. A good laugh cuts across organizational boundaries. It fosters communication between different levels of management and different functional areas of the company. Humor helps create and maintain the vast internal network of communication channels that ties an organization together. Most important, it provides a common ground. The phrase "Heard any good jokes lately?" can bridge the gulf between people of the most divergent backgrounds. It has even been known to initiate civil communication between marketers and engineers.

A corporation's view of humor also affects the way a company relates to outsiders. For example, what is the company's attitude toward customers? Is it service with a smile? Or is the customer a clown? The prevailing metaphor will have a very direct impact on customer satisfaction. Similar considerations will influence behavior toward vendors, shareholders, community groups, and government officials.

By consciously influencing the type and amount of humor used, top management can nudge the culture in a particular direction. Its two main types of influence are personal example and formal decree. Personal example is simple. By using humor in their work, executives send a message to the entire organization. They communicate that humor is okay. Their leadership serves as a model that legitimizes and encourages similar activity by subordinates. In the case of formal decree, executives can establish programs that officially reward and promote the use of humor. For example, sense of humor can be treated as a formal evaluation item in annual job-performance reviews. In addition, humor can be institutionalized as a formal part of the company's communication rituals. Examples include an annual "roast" of executives by the troops, funny telegrams on people's birthdays, and tongue-in-cheek employee newsletters on April Fools' Day.

Despite the benefits to be gained by encouraging humor in a corporate culture, few executives make the effort. Several reasons may account for this state of affairs. Executives may feel that humor is alien to their personal style. They may believe it would diminish, rather than enhance, their image. They may doubt that efforts to promote humor would produce any tangible results. This last attitude highlights the main reason that executives ignore humor as a management tool: Its effects haven't been rigorously measured.

The Bottom Line for Humor

A fellow who barely got through business school became a multimillionaire manufacturer. At a school reunion his surprised former classmates asked the secret of his success. "Well," he said, "after we graduated, I started making tailpipes for trucks. Soon I was selling to General Motors. It cost me $3.00 to make each tailpipe and I sold them for $6.00. You know, it's amazing how those three percents add up." Amazing indeed. What's not amazing is that he had measured his business, albeit incorrectly. His profit percentage was 50, not 3.

Since the dawn of commerce, businesspeople have had a fascination with measurement. "What's the bottom line?" The question echoes from the smallest mom-and-pop shop to the largest industrial complex, from the boardroom to the shop floor. Inquiring minds want to know: what's the bottom line? It is the central question in the world of business. It's how we keep score. Yet the question's importance derives not from the numbers that provide its answer but from the fact that it can be answered with numbers.

"What's the bottom line?" is really a question of measurement. It asks for a summary of results and assumes they can be quantified. And therein lies the problem for humor in the workplace—how can it be measured? How do you quantify a smile or a chuckle? How do you measure a good laugh?

Absence of measurement has given humor a special status in the business world. It has joined mom and apple pie as an icon beyond dispute. "Humor—we need more of it," say executives. "Laughter—it's good for morale," say personnel directors. "A little levity improves productivity," say managers. But after all is said and done, much is said and little done. Humor remains the subject of little more than lip service. It's called important and then ignored. That's the paradox: Businesspeople don't take humor seriously.

The situation is not likely to change until the effects of humor can be represented numerically. Common sense tells us that humor is an important force in corporate culture. Gut reaction reinforces this feeling. But common sense and gut reaction are not enough. In a world that plays by the numbers, investment in humor will be ignored until quantifiable results are demonstrated. Unfortunately modern accounting systems, with their bias against intangibles, will not provide the solution. New measurements will have to be devised if humor and other important intangibles are ever to receive the serious attention they deserve.

The problem can be traced to deficiencies inherent in traditional accounting methods. According to traditional wisdom, a company should evaluate expenditures for new programs and equipment based on potential return-on-investment. However, the traditional formula looks only at how rapidly the investment will pay for itself. The formula assumes that a new program or piece of equipment will cut costs. It doesn't account for investments that pay for themselves by helping to create and attract new business. As a result the traditional formula doesn't account for "intangibles"—items such as improved product quality, faster delivery of goods and services, and greater customer satisfaction.

There may be no accounting for taste, but no accounting for other intangibles is a serious problem for American business. Better quality, more flexibility, and quicker response time are considered essential if America is to compete successfully in the global marketplace. But how do managers justify an investment that will improve such intangibles? The answer is they don't, unless they can show that the investment will also cut costs. Traditional return-on-investment accounting is strangling America's ability to compete.

The key question that traditional return-on-investment accounting fails to ask is, What is the cost of *not* making the investment? The answer to that question can be very enlightening. For example let's assume that a company produces widgets. But the widgets have a problem: Their screws rapidly become loose. Sales have begun to decline due to the widgets' reputation for poor quality. To solve the problem, the company is thinking about purchasing a screw-tightening machine for $1 million. The sales department forecasts $10 million in new business over the next three years if the screw problem is solved. The machine won't cut costs, but it will solve the problem. Should the company purchase the machine?

Under return-on-investment accounting methods, you ask how long it would take for the machine to pay for itself out of savings it would generate. The answer is never because the machine produces no savings. So traditional accounting would veto the machine as an unnecessary $1 million expense. A very different result occurs if you look at the cost of not making the investment. Sales continue to decline. And you also lose the $10 million in new business that the improved widget would have attracted. The bottom line is that the cost of not making the investment is very expensive.

Identical considerations should apply when evaluating investments in humor. What is the cost of not investing in a program that adds humor to your workplace? What are the lost opportunity costs? For example how much more motivated would your company's employees be if humor was built into their work environment? How much more productive would they be? How many more highly qualified employees would your company attract if it had a reputation as a fun place to work?

The gut reaction to these questions is that investment in humor deserves serious corporate consideration. Like improvement in quality, flexibility, and response time, improvement in the use of humor is essential if American business is to compete successfully. Here's why. A company is only as good as the people who work for it. However, attracting good people is no simple matter. The American work force, influenced by the baby-boomers, no longer judges a job's desirability solely by how much it pays. Today's workers also want responsibility, control over their work, opportunities to exercise creativity, and a positive work environment.

A positive environment is particularly important and represents one of the greatest changes in the baby-boom generation's attitude toward work. Going to work should be fun. Given a choice, baby-boomers will not accept a job that must be performed in a mind-numbing, highly regimented atmosphere. The days of the mental sweatshop are numbered. In order to recruit and retain the best people, companies must offer a work environment that is pleasant, supportive, and fun. Humor plays a key role in creating that environment.

Unfortunately investment in humor, like investment in quality, flexibility, and response time, is not easily justified by traditional accounting methods. Yet investment in these areas is essential. Prospective customers demand higher quality. And prospective employees demand a fun work environment. Companies that ignore these demands risk following in the footsteps of the dinosaurs. But the question remains, how do you justify the investment?

Recognition of the deficiencies inherent in traditional accounting techniques has resulted in a call for new accounting methods. And the call has been heeded. A task force that includes the Pentagon, National Association of Accountants, many large manufacturers, and seven of the Big Eight accounting firms is now developing solutions. Their goal is to account for intangibles.

According to *Business Week*, intangibles such as quality, response time, and flexibility may never be as accountable as traditional "manage-by-the-numbers-people" would like.[2] However, this prediction should not inspire undue concern. Accounting numbers are not really as crucial as widely believed. Wayne Morse, professor of accounting at Clarkson University, explains why: "Accounting numbers, like quality costs, won't give you answers," he states. "They won't tell you what to do. All they will do is suggest where you might look first."[3]

The search for new accounting methods should apply with equal force to humor. Like quality, response time, and other intangibles, humor may never be totally accountable in numeric form. However, the logic underlying accounting numbers suggests that their true value is diagnostic: They spotlight problems and tell you where to look for answers. That's why the ultimate solution to accounting for humor may be the humor audit.

What Is a Humor Audit?

A humor audit is a measurement tool designed to provide insight into the way humor is used within an organization. It is primarily a diagnostic device for discovering areas of humor strengths, weaknesses, and problems. How does humor flow within the organization? Who uses it successfully? Who misuses it? How does it help or hinder the accomplishment of organizational goals and objectives? These are just a few of the questions that a humor audit can address.

The main purpose of the audit is to help managers and executives identify, understand, and control the use of humor in their organizations. By analyzing the answers to audit questions, managers can gain a broad perspective on the patterns of humor use in their departments, divisions, and companies. Armed with this "big picture," managers can quickly discern any problem areas that require special attention. Audit findings, while not prescriptive, also suggest starting points for taking corrective actions.

Basic Features of the Humor Audit

Humor audits can range from in-depth, comprehensive investigations to a couple of questions about a single issue. They can cover humor use by an entire organization or by just a department or an individual.

Two examples will illustrate potential applications of a humor audit. Let's start with a very simple one: The Humor Survey that tracks the general attitude of a company's employees. The survey can consist of ten statements that describe the use of humor within the organization. Sample statements include:

- The company encourages employees to use humor.
- The company is a fun place to work.
- Most people at the company take themselves too seriously.

Employees taking the survey indicate the degree to which each statement applies to them by choosing one of five options: (1) strongly agree; (2) agree; (3) undecided; (4) disagree; (5) strongly disagree. When the results are totaled, the survey produces a numerical snapshot of employee attitudes about humor in their workplace. By administering the survey at regular intervals—every three or four months—you can monitor changes in attitude and take appropriate actions.

A second type of audit, the Humor Disparity Test, is geared toward the individual. It measures the discrepancies between a manager's self-assessment of his or her use of humor and the assessments of his or her subordinates. In other words if you think you've got a great sense of humor but your employees disagree, this audit will show it.

Like the Humor Survey, the Humor Disparity Test consists of a series of statements with which test takers can register (1) strongly agree; (2) agree; (3) undecided; (4) disagree; or (5) strongly disagree. Sample statements include:

- He or she interrupts with his or her own story before others can finish a joke.
- He or she tends to be sarcastic.
- He or she goes out of his or her way to find humor relevant to the work unit.

(The word *I* is substituted for *He or she* at the beginning of each question when the test is given to the manager of the work unit.)

The test is interpreted by totaling the employee responses for each question and computing an average. Each average employee response can then be compared with the corresponding response by the manager. When the numbers are identical, it means that the manager and his or her subordinates agree on how they view the manager's use of humor. When the numbers are different, a disagreement exists.

Let's work through an example. Assume that a Humor Disparity Test is given to a work unit consisting of one manager and three subordinates. Assume that the first statement on the test is, "He interrupts with his own story before others can finish a joke." The first subordinate responds (1) strongly agree. The second subordinate responds (2) agree. The third subordinate responds (3) undecided. The average employee response is 2 (1 + 2 + 3 divided by 3). If the manager responds (3) undecided, then there is a disparity of 1. If the manager responds (4) disagree, then the disparity is 2. If the manager responds (5) strongly disagree, the disparity is 3.

The greater the disparity, the greater the gap in perception between manager and subordinates.

It is important to note that this test does *not* measure the manager's actual humor performance. It only measures how he thinks he performs in contrast to how his subordinates think he performs. The value of this measurement is summed up by an old saying: The truth is as perceived. If your subordinates believe that you behave in a certain way, they will act on that belief even if it's not true. The Humor Disparity Test allows managers to find out what their subordinates are thinking. By observing disparities, managers can gain insights into their humor behavior as well as their abilities as communicators. Most important, the test alerts managers to the need for corrective action when they are out of touch with their subordinates.

The Wave of the Future: Evaluation by Subordinates

Humor Disparity tests and similar subordinate-based audits may sound highly theoretical, but they represent the wave of the future. Although subordinate critiquing of managers is not yet widespread, the concept is gaining in popularity. It is an evaluation technique just coming into its own. In fact a recent article in *Industry Week* identifies subordinate appraisals as a trend for the 1990s. In the article, entitled "Performance Appraisals," writer Joani Nelson-Horchler describes the logic of this prediction:

> What does my boss think of me? That's probably *the* critical question to a manager confronting a performance appraisal. But, in the more team- and service-oriented corporation of the 1990s the more significant questions are likely to be: What do my *employees* think of me? And how do my company's *customers* rate the service I give them?...
>
> Indeed, subordinates may be better judges than are bosses of several aspects of managers' performance: How well one interacts with subordinates, manages work teams, delegates job

duties, corrects inadequate performance, communicates organizational goals, and gives performance feedback.[4]

The article cites Johnson & Johnson, General Electric, and
IBM as companies that already use subordinate appraisals in
the executive/manager evaluation process. For example managers headed for IBM's management school receive feedback
from a questionnaire distributed to their subordinates. The
questionnaire assesses how well the managers communicate,
delegate, and make decisions. The article concludes that the
1990s will herald an increasing use of subordinate appraisals
as a method of judging managers.

The 1990s may also witness an increasing number of humor
audits conducted for a wide variety of purposes. In addition
to auditing employee attitudes and individual performance,
humor audits can be used to identify and measure subcultures
within an organization. Questions addressed might include:
What are the differences in the types of humor used by different
departments? What are the differences in the way humor functions in different departments? How do different departments
define appropriate humor? The patterns uncovered by such
audits can be invaluable in understanding the relationships
and communication flow within and between departments.

The Numbers Game

One company was interviewing accountants. They asked the
first one, "How much is two and two?" He said, "Four." They
said, "Thank you," and called in the next applicant. They asked
her, "How much is two and two?" She said, "Four-point-zero."
They said, "Thank you" and called in the next applicant. They
asked him, "How much is two and two?" He said, "How much
do you want it to be?" They said, "You're hired."

While it's true that people can play games with numbers,
without numbers there is no game. That has been the major
stumbling block to acceptance of humor by the corporate
world—no numbers, no playing time. A humor audit solves

this problem. It provides a first step toward quantifying the effects of humor within an organization. It also allows an organization to examine humor's role in the corporate culture systematically.

Although humor is an "intangible," it has a direct impact on communication flow, work environment, and productivity. That's why establishing a proper role for humor in your corporate culture is crucial if your organization wants to compete successfully. The audit offers a snapshot of your organization's humor strengths, weaknesses, and problems. By administering the audit on a regular basis you can monitor changes and take appropriate actions. As Yogi Berra once said, "Don't make the wrong mistakes." The knowledge gained from a humor audit will enable you to follow his immortal advice.

Humor Disparity Test

Give this test to a manager and his or her subordinates. Subordinates answer the questions as they appear. The manager answers the questions as he or she thinks the subordinates will answer. The greater the disparity, the more a problem is indicated.

Directions: Fill in the number of the most appropriate response for each question as it applies to your manager.

> 1 = Always
> 2 = Most of the time
> 3 = Once in a while
> 4 = Almost never
> 5 = Never
>
> *He* = your manager
> (male or female)

_____ 1. He interrupts with his own story before others can finish theirs.

_____ 2. He chooses his anecdotes carefully.

____ 3. He goes out of his way to find humor that may be relevant to his work responsibilities.

____ 4. He tells ethnic or racist jokes.

____ 5. He gives positive feedback to ethnic or racist jokes.

____ 6. He tends to be sarcastic.

____ 7. He smiles when people tell him a joke.

____ 8. He takes a lot of words to tell a joke that could be said in a few words.

____ 9. He ridicules people.

____10. He stops you if he's heard your joke before.

____11. He displays a sense of humor.

____12. He discourages other people from using humor.

____13. He encourages other people to use humor.

____14. He tells sexist jokes.

____15. He gives positive feedback to sexist jokes.

____16. His humor is sophisticated.

____17. His humor is inappropriate.

____18. His humor boosts the morale of the people around him.

____19. He uses humor in memos.

____20. He points out the absurdities in a situation.

TWELVE

Turning the Tables on Inappropriate Humor

A sharp tongue is the only edged tool that grows keener with constant use.

—Washington Irving

When Howard Klein was a project manager at Software Publishing Corporation (SPC), he had to make a presentation at a company meeting. The company was in transition at the time and had experienced significant employee turnover—a subject avoided by SPC executives. Klein was scheduled to talk about the need for standards and consistency in software. However, he couldn't resist mentioning the numerous employee departures.

"Consistency means we can't have one thing having different meanings," he began. "Here's an example at SPC: *Exit* is the term we use to get out of our software program. It's also the sign above the doors leading to the outside. And lately it's been the most common type of interview." The audience reaction was funnier than the joke. "No one laughed, and some people went 'Ooooooooo,'" Klein recalls.

Was Klein's humor appropriate? I put the question to Nancy Hauge, director of human resources for operations at Sun Microsystems. She is particularly qualified to comment. In addition to extensive experience in human resources, she has worked as a professional comedy writer. "Although the joke is funny in the abstract," she observed, "it runs the risk that management can be perceived as callous. The subject of exit interviews is very frightening to most employees. The fact that no one laughed indicates that it wasn't funny to the people who might be affected. The joke makes management seem arrogant. In the work situation you must avoid the temptation to let your own sense of humor take precedence over other people's feelings. You must know your audience."

Hauge noted that her reaction might have been different if SPC had talked freely about the issue of exit interviews. In that case the joke would not have been upsetting and might have got a tension-relieving laugh. "The problem is the way humor is built," she said. "You build a tense situation and release the tension with a laugh. Unfortunately the joke contributed to the tension rather than the release." She also noted that the joke could have been improved if it had referred to *management* exit interviews. Then it would have had an element of self-effacement.

My own analysis labels the joke as borderline inappropriate. It was not blatantly offensive, but it may have made some people uncomfortable. Also the joke teller's underlying intention was of dubious merit. He appeared to be a wiseguy purposely voicing a taboo topic in order to shock people and show off. Despite this intention the joke did serve a useful purpose by raising the issue for discussion.

The key question in evaluating the exit interview joke, or any other humor, is how do you define "inappropriate"? Al Pozos, manager of career development systems at Pacific Bell, has a simple test. He believes that humor is inappropriate when it's offensive to the individuals involved. His test: How would the humor appear if it was written up on the front page of your local newspaper? How would you be portrayed? How would you feel?

Pozos's test is a good start but not definitive. Determining whether humor is inappropriate is not always so simple. Appearances can be deceiving. Words and behavior that seem offensive to outside observers may actually be forms of bonding. You have to understand the relationship among the participants. Studies have shown that the more intimate and enduring the relationship among participants in a group, the more likely they are to target each other with hostile humor. This is particularly true for groups that perform dangerous jobs or work under pressure.

My attempt to define inappropriate humor begins with the concept of what is considered "offensive." Humor that legitimately offends a reasonable person is probably inappropriate. (How's that for hedging?) However, my definition goes further. I believe that humor can also be inappropriate if it is embarrassing—either to the person sending it or to the person receiving it. For example, listening to people make fun of themselves can be very uncomfortable if they go into great detail. Have you ever listened to someone savagely joke about his or her impending bankruptcy, divorce, or similar personal matters? It is extremely discomforting.

Where does that leave us in our quest for a definition of inappropriate humor? Probably a little confused. Inappropriate humor is like pornography. Most people think they know it when they see it. Yet trying to define it is like trying to nail Jell-O to a wall. Inappropriate humor escapes easy definition because it depends on a variety of very specific circumstances. It depends on who originates the humor and at whom it's directed, as well as where and when it is uttered. These considerations defy the formation of simple general rules.

Despite such difficulties certain generic types of humor have achieved a reputation as inappropriate. These include racist, sexist, and ethnic humor; sarcasm; and practical jokes. Is their reputation deserved? Are they always inappropriate? Or can they serve any constructive purpose? Let's explore the nature of these types of humor, their effects, and how to deal with them in the workplace.

Are Racist, Sexist, and Ethnic Jokes Inappropriate?

It's Monday morning. People slowly troop into the office and try to prepare for another week of work. Cups of coffee are poured. Cries of "Good morning" and "How was your weekend?" sound in the corridors. Coworkers wake each other up with a spirited exchange of banter. A great new restaurant was discovered over the weekend. Sunday's football game was a travesty. Someone heard a new ethnic joke. And naturally the joke is told.

Is this inappropriate? The joke teller doesn't "mean anything" by telling the joke. He's just trying to inject some laughter into a Monday morning. Anyone who might be offended must be overly sensitive. Is telling a couple of ethnic jokes at work really such a big deal? Yes—for several reasons.

The Threat of a Lawsuit

A primary reason to discourage racist, sexist, and ethnic jokes in the workplace is that they can run afoul of the law. The basic law dealing with such jokes in the workplace is derived from Title VII of the Civil Rights Act of 1964. As stated in federal regulations issued by the Equal Employment Opportunity Commission (EEOC), the law reads as follows:

> Ethnic slurs and other verbal or physical conduct relating to an individual's national origin constitute harassment when this conduct: (1) Has the purpose or effect of creating an intimidating, hostile or offensive working environment; (2) has the purpose or effect of unreasonably interfering with an individual's work performance; or (3) otherwise adversely affects an individual's employment opportunities. (29 CFR § 1606.8(b))

> Harassment on the basis of sex is a violation of Sec. 703 of Title VII. Unwelcome sexual advances, requests for sexual favors, and other verbal or physical conduct of a sexual nature constitute harassment when . . . (3) such conduct has the purpose or effect of unreasonably interfering with an individual's work performance or creating an intimidating, hostile, or offensive working environment. (29 CFR § 1604.11(a))

Over the years the law has evolved to include three basic principles. First, an employer has a duty to maintain a workplace free of harassment and intimidation based on race, sex, color, or national origin. Second, an employer who knows about racist, sexist, or ethnic jokes being told by managers, *or nonmanagers*, has a duty to take corrective action. Third, isolated racist, sexist, or ethnic jokes do not, by themselves, create the offensive environment prohibited by Title VII.

The third principle is a little misleading. In certain circumstances an isolated racist, sexist, or ethnic joke *can* lead to legal liability for an employer. Here's why. Even though it can't serve as the basis for a Title VII claim, an isolated joke can be used as evidence in evaluating such a claim. For example let's say I file a claim that you didn't promote me because of my racial or ethnic identity. Among other things I'm going to point out will be the fact that you once told a joke about my racial or ethnic group. That may prove to be very important in my attempt to show that you discriminated against me.

The potential importance of a single joke is underscored by the decision in *Carter v. Duncan-Huggins, Ltd.* (1984 U.S. Court of Appeals, District of Columbia). In that case an employer wanted the trial judge to instruct the jury that a single racial joke could not be evidence of the employer's alleged discrimination. The trial judge refused. His decision was upheld by the U.S. Court of Appeals. It noted that when a single racial joke is presented along with numerous other pieces of circumstantial evidence, its meaning becomes a matter for the jury to evaluate.

Special Problems for Managers

If the threat of a lawsuit doesn't provide sufficient motivation to eliminate racist, sexist, and ethnic jokes from the workplace, then consider such jokes strictly from a management-theory perspective. They undermine credibility and interfere with effective management by eroding the manager's image of objectivity and professionalism every time they're told or tolerated.

A manager's effectiveness is threatened even if members of

the subject ethnic group are absent when the jokes are told. Al Pozos verifies this from experience; it is part of his job to deal with such jokes. "Let's say you have managers telling black jokes in a nonblack environment," he states. "No one complains until the managers have to put one of the black non-managers on a job-performance improvement program because he's not cutting it. So the guy picks up the phone and calls us internally or files a complaint with the government. He'll say, 'Hey, my manager is prejudiced. Why else would he allow these types of jokes to go on?' So whether or not there's a member of the affected group present when the jokes are told, the jokes create a problem."

Allowing such jokes to be told essentially creates a time bomb that can explode a manager's career. It also puts control of the bomb in the hands of other people. "When managers tell these jokes, whether or not anyone of the affected class is present, they parcel up their careers and hand them out to everyone listening to the jokes," states Pozos. "In effect the manager is saying, 'Anytime you want to give my career a shot in the head, all you have to do is file a complaint against me.'"

An additional point to note is that a person does not have to be a member of a particular racial or ethnic group to be offended by jokes about that group. Many people are offended by any racist, sexist, or ethnic joke.

Effects of Inappropriate Humor

Perhaps the most compelling reason to halt such jokes in the workplace is simple human compassion for the victims. Even when the jokes are told by coworkers rather than by managers, the effects can be devastating. The jokes can impact relationships and behavior both at work and at home. This is particularly true when management ignores the situation.

"Most people derive a lot of their sense of self-worth from their jobs," states Pozos. "If your coworkers make jokes implying you're deficient because of your race, sex, color, or national origin, it cuts right to the heart of your self-image.

And if a manager ignores this situation, it tells you that the boss really doesn't think very much of you. Your problem is not considered to be an important issue. It means that you as an employee and especially as a human being are regarded less highly than others." The effects of such treatment can range from anger and hostility to stress and depression. Extreme cases can result in disability. It is the rare person who does not experience some form of suffering.

Particularly illustrative is the physical and mental anguish that can result from sexist humor. These effects have been observed by Sheva Feld, a clinical psychologist with extensive experience preparing women for positions in predominantly male work groups. She currently works in the employee assistance program at a major utility, where she counsels employees for personal and work-related issues. "Women who are harassed with sexist jokes face a dilemma about telling management," Feld explains, "because often there's pressure to take it and be 'one of the guys' or to joke back and be 'a good sport' about it. So they don't know if they'll get management's support or be laughed at and alienated even further. Even when they get the technical support from management, it may cause further alienation from coworkers."

The effect of this dilemma is unfortunately quite predictable. "It can make the whole environment stressful and make it very difficult to go to work," states Feld. "A woman harassed by sexist jokes has a right to be upset. But instead of having her feelings acknowledged and respected, she may get a lot of 'Oh, you're too sensitive' or 'We're just joking.' Such comments are discounting her experience or feelings and can be seen as another form of harassment."

As a result the woman victimized by sexist jokes often loses self-confidence. She may wonder if there's something wrong with her because the jokes bother her so much. She may become totally intimidated by the person or people who are harassing her. Or she may become totally introverted. "No person is an island," states Feld. "If you're isolated and alienated, the stress can become disabling. There have been workers' compensation cases stemming from harassment."

Victims of racist and ethnic jokes face similar threats to their well-being. Whether the effect is isolation, rage, self-doubt, or withdrawal, a constant diet of such jokes acts as a poison that slowly engulfs people's lives. Put simply, inappropriate humor can be extremely harmful to one's health—both mental and physical.

Dealing with Humor Harassment

Human relations exist in a fragile balance, under the best of circumstances. When that balance includes considerations of race, sex, or ethnicity, people become extremely sensitive. Add some criticism of their sense of humor and you've got a recipe for potential disaster. Given the touchy attitudes that govern human relations, how does one manage a person who tells racist, sexist, or ethnic jokes? What's the best approach? At Pacific Bell, managers are instructed to tell the individual that such humor is inappropriate and must stop. "That's known as 'first-step counseling,'" explains Pozos. "The individual is told that if he or she continues to tell the jokes, disciplinary action will follow."

A common response from a person rebuked for using racist, sexist, or ethnic humor is, "I was only kidding." Or "It was only a joke." How can a manager respond to this defense? Pozos believes it's quite simple. "The manager can say, 'Fine. If you have a real need to tell those jokes, tell them at home.'"

A more challenging situation arises when one employee tells jokes in the presence of other employees but not in the presence of the manager. Pozos handles this problem with a flexible approach. "It depends on how severe the jokes are and what evidence there is to support that they actually occurred," he states. "We recommend that the manager call us and let us handle the investigation. That leaves the manager neutral and out of the middle. Then, after we investigate, if discipline is called for, we make our recommendation in the presence of the manager."

Feld suggests a slightly different approach. She says that the manager should tell the person complaining that the jokes will not be tolerated in the work group. In addition the manager should address the whole group and review the rules about what constitutes discrimination and harassment in general. The manager should state that it won't be tolerated in the workplace. The manager should also say that if it does occur, disciplinary action will take place. The manager should then ask the joke victim if that action feels sufficient. If it doesn't, the manager should offer to confront the joke teller directly. According to Feld this approach addresses the problem while minimizing confrontations and diffusing a company's liability.

The best approach to handling humor harassment is eliminating the problem before it occurs. This can be accomplished with educational programs that build respect among coworkers and inform them about appropriate workplace conduct. "There is a fine line between harassment and joking," explains Feld. "Employees need to know what their rights are, what they're expected to do if they're offended, and what consequences will be suffered by the offenders."

At Pacific Bell all new employees learn about inappropriate humor under Equal Employment Opportunity (EEO) policies and practices. Training includes a general orientation as to what kinds of things are prohibited in the workplace and specifically addresses racist, sexist, and ethnic slurs and jokes. Annual follow-up training reminds employees of their EEO and affirmative action responsibilities. In addition all employees—managers and nonmanagers alike—receive an annual appraisal of how well they've honored their EEO affirmative action commitments. It's considered an integral part of their job-performance evaluation.

Preemptive strikes at racist, sexist, and ethnic jokes need not be limited to formal programs. A very effective education effort can be as simple as a manager communicating his or her displeasure with such humor. Pozos notes that people typically avoid engaging in behavior that generates disapproval from the person in charge. "You'll get a few exceptions," he states.

"But most people will eliminate the racial jokes if they know they won't be tolerated."

Making Good Use of Ethnic Wit and Wisdom

Tolerance of racial, ethnic, and sexual differences is a basic requirement for living in a democratic and pluralistic society. Race, ethnicity, and gender play a major role in establishing our identities. They are the primary ways that most of us define ourselves. Must we really banish such fundamental aspects of existence from our humor? Are all references to race, ethnicity, and sex inappropriate?

Of course not. Ethnic humor has a long and celebrated tradition in the cultures and civilizations of mankind. From the wit and wisdom of Confucius to the stories of Shalom Aleichem, ethnic humor occupies a cherished place in world history. It is only quite recently that "ethnic humor" has come to mean slurs and rude barbs. For centuries ethnic humor served as an expression of one of mankind's noblest traits— the ability to laugh at ourselves.

Can ethnic humor still serve its rich historical function today? Most definitely. One positive way of using ethnic humor is to quote jokes and stories by famous people of your own ethnic extraction. For example Ali Selvi, a Turkish-American systems engineer with Baltimore Specialty Steels, likes to tell stories of Nasraddin Hodja, a fifteenth-century Turkish humorist. In fact, on at least one occasion Selvi used a Hodja story to alleviate an awkward situation.

Selvi's immediate manager and his manager's manager were having a disagreement. Selvi was caught in the middle as each looked to him for support—a classic no-win situation. Pressed to agree with one of them, Selvi told them the following Hodja story:

> Hodja was asked to resolve a dispute. The first person gave his side of the story. Hodja said, "You're right." The second person gave his side of the story. Hodja said, "You're right." A third

person, observing these transactions, said, "What happened to your integrity? One person said, 'X'; you said, 'Right.' The other person said, 'Y'; you said, 'Right.' You can't say they're both right." Hodja said, "You're right too."

Selvi's point was made. Everyone laughed. And Selvi was off the hook.

Every race, ethnic group, and nationality has its famous wits and humorists. Much of their material is timeless or easily adapted to modern circumstances. By using this type of "ethnic humor," you celebrate humankind's rich cultural diversity rather than attacking it. You also come across as knowledgeable and sophisticated. After all, who sounds smarter, the person quoting Confucius from a Chinese text or the person quoting Polish jokes from a bathroom wall?

Another way ethnic humor can be used appropriately is by replacing the ethnic group with a job category. For example, "Did you hear about the engineer who won a gold medal in the company marathon? He had it bronzed." That joke originally featured a member of an ethnic group as the gold-medal winner. In its original form the joke was inappropriate. It labeled all members of an ethnic group as idiots. In its revised form it labels all engineers as idiots. Why is the revised joke appropriate and the original joke offensive? The distinction can be summarized in one word—*choice.* You can choose your occupation. You can't choose your race, ethnicity, or national origin.

Ethnic jokes are based on feelings of superiority. You're supposed to laugh because you feel superior to the group that is the butt of the joke. By converting the ethnic group into a work group, you retain the feeling of superiority without the high degree of viciousness. The conversion also retains the underlying spirit of competition. Ethnic jokes reflect the competition among ethnic groups for resources and prestige in a society. Work-group jokes transfer that competition to a corporate setting. Instead of ethnic rivalries you get work-group rivalries. Marketing versus research and development. Finance versus sales. Purchasing versus everybody.

Of course there is one important difference. Competition among ethnic groups serves no constructive purpose. It brings out the worst in people. In contrast, competition among work groups can provide a healthy stimulus for a business organization. Theoretically it brings out the best in people.

Converting ethnic jokes to work-group jokes is a simple procedure. Although some ethnic jokes refer to specific stereotypical traits, the vast majority focus on the "dumbness" of the target group. Dumbness is a universal trait that can be alleged of any work group. For example:

How can you tell when an executive is using a word processor? He's the one with Wite-Out on the screen.

Did you hear about the technical-writer firing squad? They stand in a circle.

Do you know why ethnic jokes are so short? So engineers can understand them.

One word of caution: Don't use this type of humor if it's too close to the truth. If members of a work group really are performing poorly, don't make a joke about their stupidity. It will not be appreciated. It will hurt a lot of feelings and precipitate a tidal wave of negative repercussions.

What about jokes based on specific ethnic stereotypes? Can they be adapted to the work-group format? Yes, to a limited extent. You can construct similar jokes using occupational, rather than ethnic, stereotypes. "Engineers are nerds." "Sales and marketing people are full of hot air." "Doctors are rich." You get the idea. The following joke illustrates the process:

Why is Saturday morning the best time to be on the Los Angeles freeways? . . .

The rock stars are still asleep.
The doctors are in Palm Springs.

The salespeople are faking their expenses.
The engineers are watching cartoons.
The executives are playing golf.
The mailroom clerks can't get their cars started.

Today's workplace reflects the growing influence of the new global economy. It is an amalgam of cultures, races, religions, and nationalities. Look at the people working next to you. They probably have a background significantly different from your own; and if not your coworkers, then probably your vendors and your customers. As business increasingly transcends national boundaries, understanding and respect for cultural differences become more important than ever before. Ethnic humor can help bridge the gap between people if it's used to celebrate rather than insult their differences.

The Danger of Sarcasm

An explorer was in the jungle when he ran into a tribe of cannibals just sitting down to eat. The head of the tribe told the explorer that he had attended college in the United States. "Do you mean to say," asked the amazed explorer, "that you went to college and that you still eat human beings?" "Oh, yes," said the chief, "but now I use a knife and fork."

Unfortunately that's the way a lot of business and professional people approach humor in the workplace. After learning that humor is a valuable management tool, they misapply the lesson. They immediately dispense large doses of their favorite type of humor—sarcasm. Sarcasm cuts people up and puts them down. Using it on colleagues is like cannibalizing people with a knife and fork. It's uncivilized. Sarcasm is a favorite of executives and professionals because it allows them to flash their wit. It's a big ego exhibit. And it's generally inappropriate because it lowers morale and dissipates team spirit.

"Sarcasm is a very dangerous thing," states Kip Witter, former vice president and treasurer at Amdahl Corporation. "Once it's out there, you have no idea how people are going to react to it and who is going to take it personally. Sarcasm may alienate the victim from the group and thus vitiate the group's effectiveness. You've either lost that person for the duration or, worse, created an antagonist who will work *against* group objectives. That person is going to hate you for the next hour, day, week, month, year, or who knows how long. Sure, sarcasm is easy. And yes, managers can show that they're bright by engaging in these intellectual put-downs. But they have to learn to control that to be good managers."

When Jim Kiehm worked at Arthur Andersen & Co., he learned about sarcasm the hard way. He dished it out on a regular basis until it undermined his entire management style. "When I was a senior accountant, I tended to be very sarcastic," he recalls. "It was a real demotivator for the people I supervised." A typical example is the way Kiehm reviewed staff work. "Reviewing the work of a rookie can be excruciatingly dull and tedious," he explains. "But as a senior I was required to write review points. I used to write things like, 'What is this besides wrong?' It wasn't real motivating for the rookie."

Kiehm changed his style before becoming a partner. And the transformation didn't come a moment too soon. "Sarcasm as a senior is bad enough," he explains. "But sarcasm as a partner is a killer. You will blow these kids right out of the firm. Because here is this semiomnipotent god called a partner who is making sarcastic remarks about the poor staff person and his work. It can be devastating. The staff person figures he's chosen the wrong career and thinks, 'I've got to get out of here.'"

Managing the Sarcastic Employee

Eliminating sarcasm from your management style is often a tough job. But at least you can control your own behavior. What about the people you manage? How do you handle a sarcastic employee? How do you stem a tide of cutting remarks?

A person who directs a steady stream of sarcastic put-downs at a coworker must be controlled. If a manager is lucky, that person will be "set straight" by other members of the work group. Unfortunately, you can't count on this solution. Workgroup members may resist taking such action for fear of drawing sarcastic fire on themselves. In that case the manager must intercede and tell the offender to cease and desist. The alternative is to allow the sarcasm to continue until it completely undermines morale and productivity. After all, it's difficult to be a peak performer if you're always on pins and needles hoping not to become the target of a petty verbal tyrant.

A different sort of problem is presented by the person who directs sarcastic remarks at the company in general. This person believes that the company doesn't pay its employees enough; that its executives are incompetent; and that it's just an all-around inferior place to work. After listening to such people one wonders why they don't seek employment elsewhere. Unfortunately, instead of sending out their resumes, they spread their cynical views by telling jokes such as the following:

What's the difference between a pigeon and a Company A employee? The pigeon can make a deposit on a new car.

How can Company A beat its archrival, Company B? Trade executives.

What's the difference between Company A and a day-care center? A day-care center has adult supervision.

How many Company A executives does it take to make a decision? Nobody knows.

A rich Texas oilman told his sons they could have anything they wanted. The first wanted a few office buildings. So the oilman gave him downtown Houston. The second wanted a fleet of Porsches. So the oilman gave him a few 911s and 944s. The third and youngest son said, "I want a Mickey Mouse outfit." So the oilman gave him Company A.

While they may be funny at first, continuous exposure to such jokes can become extremely annoying. They can be particularly harmful to new employees who have not yet become comfortable with the company. So what's the solution? Do you ban all company-related jokes? Not at all, according to Kip Witter. "It's perfectly acceptable to take shots at upper management, but there's a boundary," he states. "If someone crosses that boundary and poisons other people's minds about executive decision making and company policy, then you have to take action."

His recommendation: Have a one-on-one talk with the offender. Point out the negative impact that the sarcasm is having on the work group. "Tell him that he's not helping the other people and he's not helping himself," states Witter. "You can also point out that he's entitled to his opinions but he may not have all the facts. If he's smart, he'll tumble to it."

Sarcasm as a Positive Force

An exception to the general rule of avoiding sarcasm is offered by Raymond W. Gibbs, Jr., associate professor of psychology at the University of California at Santa Cruz. He believes that sarcasm can play a positive role in the workplace. "We tend to think of sarcasm as a person being bitter or hostile to somebody," he explains. "But in many cases it's actually producing the opposite effect. It's bringing the speaker and listener together, making them more intimate acquaintances."

According to Gibbs, when people are being sarcastic, they often assume that their listeners will understand what they mean. "They assume that you know certain things about the situation at hand," he explains. "Otherwise you won't 'get' the sarcasm. This may mean that sarcasm demands a particular kind of link between a speaker and a hearer. So sarcasm isn't necessarily a bad thing."

As an example Gibbs describes a situation where two people are working with a computer that keeps fouling up. One says, "This is really a terrific piece of equipment here." The other person smiles and nods in agreement. It's clear that the remark was sarcastic, yet no one is hurt by it. "In this case there is no victim of the sarcasm," explains Gibbs. "Nobody is insulted. You're only insulting an object—'I know that you know what I'm talking about'—and it brings us together. It's like we have a secret code."

If you extend Gibbs's logic, sarcasm can be used as a diagnostic tool to discover gaps in employee knowledge. A coworker who doesn't "get" a sarcastic joke about some work-related matter probably needs more information. The lack of response alerts a manager to that need. It gives the manager an opportunity to bring the person up to speed. This is important because the information needed to "get" the joke may also be the information needed to perform the work.

So what's the bottom line? Should sarcasm be shunned or encouraged? The answer depends on the target. When aimed at a person, sarcasm is offensive and does little to enhance interpersonal relations. But a sarcastic remark about an object or situation is potentially useful. It can pull people together.

Handling the Prime Cut

What should you do when you're the victim of sarcasm? How can you handle the situation without losing your cool? Let's say you've just purchased some new clothes and you wear them to work. You're walking down the hall when you encounter the office wiseguy. He takes one look at you and says, "Great-looking outfit." But his tone of voice and facial expressions clearly indicate that he means the opposite. This sarcastic jerk is insulting you. How are you going to respond?

Several approaches are possible. Gibbs suggests playing a little dumb. "Don't immediately accept the remark as a sarcastic attack," he states. "Ask, 'What do you mean by that?' It gives your attacker a chance to back down. Then you can discuss it." A second approach is to play a little dumber. Respond with a cheerful "Thank you," as if the remark were a legitimate compliment. By interpreting the sarcastic remark literally, you subvert the attacker's attempt to embarrass you.

A third possibility is to fire back in kind. Sarcasm is a totally legitimate response *if you're attacked first*. The classic example involves an exchange between George Bernard Shaw and Winston Churchill. Shaw, ever the sarcastic wit, sent a telegram to Churchill. It read, "Here are two tickets to the opening night of my new play. Bring a friend if you have one."

Shaw's attack was uncalled for. He was just showing off, and his sarcasm was mean-spirited. However, Churchill's equally sarcastic reply was hailed as a perfectly justified response. He wired back, "Can't make opening night. I'll come the second night if there is one."

No matter which approach you take toward handling sarcasm, remember to proceed cautiously—especially if you intend to fire back in kind. A slight miscalculation can be extremely harmful. And the damage may take a long time to repair. The word *sarcasm* originated with the ancient Greeks. Its literal meaning was, "making wounds in the flesh by tearing it apart." Today the wounds occur in the ego and psyche. That's why sarcasm is such a dangerous form of humor. It can be used appropriately, but like a porcupine, it must be handled with care.

Evaluating Practical Jokes

The third generic type of humor with a reputation for being inappropriate is the practical joke. The phrase *practical joke* carries a strong negative stereotype. It immediately conjures up an image of exploding cigars, hand buzzers, and strategically placed banana peels. To be labeled as a real practical joker is a career-demolishing fate. It brands one as a lowbrow possessing a lampshade-on-the-head sensibility—someone to be avoided at all costs.

Despite its poor reputation the practical joke is not entirely without a useful role in the world of work. Not every practical joke is of the whoopee-cushion-on-the-chair variety. Practical jokes can be elaborate, highly creative acts that build morale, foster team spirit, and enhance corporate culture. But it's not always obvious whether a practical joke is appropriate.

For example a vice president of a San Francisco insurance company was dying to go to a particular football game in Los Angeles. The president of the company had five pairs of tickets. The vice president dropped a lot of hints but came up dry. On the morning after the game one of the vice president's colleagues went to the office at 6:00 A.M. He filled out a pink telephone message slip as follows: "We'll pick you up at the airport at 5:00. The game starts at 7:00. The limousine will be there. Hope you can get the airline tickets straightened out. Sorry for the short notice." He signed the president's name. Then he put the message at the bottom of a stack of messages on the vice president's desk. Later in the morning the vice president went through his messages and eventually came to the one on the bottom. He read it and became unglued. After calming down he called the president to apologize. The president said, "What the hell are you talking about? Are you out of your mind?" When the vice president learned what really happened, he was ready to kill. But he never found out who did it. The vice president was a stuffed-shirt type who was a frequent victim of such pranks.

Was the prank appropriate? In order to make that determination we have to answer four key questions: How dangerous was the prank? What was the intent of the prankster? How creative was the prank? Did the prank have any special redeeming features? All of these factors work together to determine whether a practical joke is appropriate. Let's examine each of them in detail and then evaluate the insurance company prank.

THE DANGER FACTOR

This is the factor that carries the most weight. Any practical joke that compromises a person's safety is inappropriate. This is dictated by common sense as well as workers' compensation laws. Under those laws employers are financially responsible for injuries resulting from "horseplay" among employees.

Cases awarding compensation to the victims of on-the-job pranks come from all across the United States. In California a factory worker who received a playful bear hug from a co-worker suffered a ruptured spleen. In Louisiana a watchman died of a heart attack after being "kidnapped" by coworkers as a joke. In Florida a trench digger threw a vine at a coworker and screamed, "Snake!" The coworker got scared and had a heart attack. In New York one worker gave another worker a drink of carbon tetrachloride from a bottle labeled gin. These practical jokes were extremely harmful, costly, and clearly inappropriate.

Even the potential for a minor injury should be more than enough to render a practical joke inappropriate. "Let's say someone sprains his ankle," explains Al Pozos of Pacific Bell. "That might not seem like a big deal. But it creates a tremendous amount of paperwork. Who was present? How did it happen? You have to get statements from all the witnesses. The accident report has to go all over the organization."

The danger posed by a practical joke is not limited to physical injury. Potential harm can include everything from ruined business relationships to arrest and conviction for criminal activity. Pozos recalls an example from his days working with AT&T International in Iran. "There was a manager that the staff just absolutely hated, a classic ugly American," he states. "And he had to catch a plane. So somebody called in and said he had a bomb in his suitcase. The authorities pulled the manager and his luggage off the plane. I can't prove it but I'm pretty sure one of his subordinates made the call."

Even though the situation was eventually straightened out, the fake bomb threat was an extremely dangerous prank. It subjected the manager to hostile legal action in a foreign country, harmed his reputation with the authorities, and delayed a planeload of passengers. It was clearly inappropriate.

THE INTENT FACTOR

The bomb threat "prank" also illustrates the role of intent in determining the appropriateness of a practical joke. In fact intent is such an important factor, it often defines whether a set of behaviors even constitutes a joke. For example if the bomb threat had been made by a good friend of the manager, it would be viewed as a joke in extremely poor taste. In Pozos's example the threat was made by someone who "absolutely hated" the manager. In such circumstances it's difficult to view the threat as a "joke." The obviously malicious intent coupled with the potential danger transforms the threat from a joke to a form of harassment.

Intent often plays a key role in the evaluation of practical jokes involved in Title VII harassment cases. In *Butler v. Coral Volkswagen* (1986 U.S. District Court, Southern District of Florida) a mechanic's apprentice was subjected to a hostile work environment because he was black. One example of harassment cited by the court is particularly pertinent. During a rainstorm the apprentice's coworkers sent him out to a parking lot to bring in cars for service. However, the cars didn't exist. The purpose of sending him outside was solely to make him get wet running around the parking lot. In other circumstances such behavior might be viewed as a pretty good practical joke. A little rain never hurt anyone. However, given the clearly malicious intent behind the prank, the court labeled the behavior harassment.

In contrast, when a practical joke is well intentioned, it can build a sense of camaraderie among the participants. Pozos fondly recalls working in an environment that encouraged such joking. "I used to travel a lot and I'd get messages from all over the company," he recalls. "Once I got a message from a Mr. Lion. Well, I didn't know a Mr. Lion. And of course when I returned the call, it was the zoo. We used to do stuff like that all the time. It's not vicious. It doesn't hurt anybody. And it creates a bond between people. It creates a tremendous sense of team spirit."

One additional item to consider when evaluating intent is the victim's feelings. Some people like having jokes played on them. Some don't. To the extent that these feelings are known to the prankster, they can help determine whether a prank was well intentioned.

THE CREATIVITY FACTOR

The third factor is creativity: How much imagination and work are required to create the practical joke? This factor is closely related to intent. Pouring a bucket of water over the head of a coworker is not very creative. It doesn't require a large commitment of time or cerebral effort. Although the prankster doesn't necessarily harbor a malicious intent, nothing about the prank suggests otherwise. In contrast, taking apart an executive's office and reassembling it afloat on a nearby fish pond suggests that the prankster thinks enough of the victim to devote a lot of time and energy to the prank.

The office-on-the-fishpond prank occurred at Sun Microsystems, Inc., on April 1, 1985. The office belonged to Eric Schmidt, vice president and general manager of Sun's Software Products Division. The prank was conceived and executed by a group of engineers led by Jonathan Feiber, Sun's director of programming technologies, and Rob Gingell, a top staff engineer. It was widely hailed as a brilliant expression of the company's corporate spirit. And it spawned an April Fools' Day tradition at Sun.

In 1986, the group purchased an old Volkswagen bug, took it apart, and reassembled it in Schmidt's office. In 1987 the group turned its attention to Bill Joy, one of Sun's cofounders. A bumper sticker reading "I Brake for Pink Flamingos" was placed on Joy's Ferrari. His Ferrari was placed afloat in the middle of the fish pond, and four artificial pink flamingos were placed on shore. In 1988 it was Sun CEO Scott McNealy's turn. An avid golfer, McNealy arrived at work to find his office had been turned into a one-hole, par-four, miniature golf course. Hazards included two sand traps and a birdbath.

In acknowledging the fine line between a malicious prank and an appropriate prank, Feiber defends his practical jokes by invoking the creativity factor. "The pranks were really seen as a creative diversion," he explains. "They weren't pranks in the sense of 'let's spray-paint graffiti on the wall.' They were pranks in terms of 'let's see if we can be creative.' People recognized that there was a lot of engineering involved. The VW bug in the office was completely dismantled and reassembled. For the Ferrari in the pond we built a bridge to move the car from the road to the pond. It wouldn't have been any good to drive the Ferrari across the lawn and leave tire tracks. We wanted people to wonder how it got there. The cleverness and creativity were half the fun."

The elaborate nature of the pranks and the hard work needed to execute them helped make them acceptable. The VW-bug-in-the-office gag is a good example. It required Feiber, Gingell, and eight other engineers to meet every Monday for two months. Feiber drew up a nine-page, final-development plan that assigned a task to each person. After purchasing the bug the group worked for two weeks to take it apart piece by piece. Then on April Fools' Eve they moved it to Schmidt's office and reassembled it. Their task was further complicated because they had to disconnect Schmidt's office computer terminal to make room for the car. Schmidt sometimes accesses the computer by telephone from his home. In order to avoid alerting him lookouts had to be posted at his house to send word when he went to sleep. Early on April Fools' Day morning two people in giraffe suits appeared at Schmidt's home and asked him to sign for his new car kit. He figured that that was the prank—until he showed up at his office.

"There were people who we didn't think would find it funny if they were the victims," states Feiber. "So we didn't do it to them. The pranks were never done in a mean-spirited way. They were seen as a positive way of channeling creativity, consistent with our corporate culture."

OTHER REDEEMING FEATURES

In addition to danger, intent, and creativity, other miscellaneous factors can sometimes play a role in determining whether a practical joke is appropriate. These factors will vary depending upon the individual circumstances of a particular prank. However, they can be identified by looking at the purposes served by the prank. The Sun pranks illustrate three of these factors: team building, company image, and morale.

Team building was promoted by the fact that a small group of people shared a common, intense experience over a period of several weeks. The creative conspiracy pulled the pranksters together. New bonds were formed. Feiber likened the experience to a crash engineering project or an "all-nighter" study session during college days. "We just really had a good time working with each other," he explains.

The pranks also enhanced the company's image both internally and externally. Top-management support of the pranks showed that Sun executives have a good sense of humor and that they encourage initiative. This sent a message to Sun employees about the company's culture. It showed that the company supports creativity and freedom. It showed that the company rewards people who do things differently. And it showed employees at other companies that Sun is a place where you can do something different and have fun.

Most important, the pranks were good for company morale. "Sun is run right at the limit," explains Feiber. "People work incredibly hard. They're incredibly bright. And everybody looks for release. The people who run Sun recognize how hard the company is driven and see the pranks as a relief. The pranks bring some levity to a place where there's an enormous amount of pressure."

And if imitation is the sincerest form of flattery, then Feiber and Gingell can be proud of the new pranksters at Sun whom they have inspired. These include a group of people who put live animals in a vice president's office, as well as a group who moved an executive's office onto an elevator. In fact Feiber himself has become a target. One April Fools' Day, after pulling his own prank on an executive, Feiber returned to his office to find it completely filled—floor to ceiling—with old newspapers.

But Feiber takes it all in stride. He recognizes that the jokes,

210 MALCOLM L. KUSHNER

even those played on him, are a fundamental strength of the company. "The fact that a lot of other people are now doing pranks is really great," he states. "It reinforces the idea that Sun wants people to have a good time, take a look at themselves, and laugh. The fact that I can do these things is one of the reasons I like working here."

THE FINAL ANALYSIS

Now let's return to the insurance company prank. A stuffed-shirt vice president received a fake telephone message inviting him to a football game with the company president. When the vice president responded to the fake message, the president questioned his sanity. Was the joke appropriate? Let's evaluate it based on the criteria of danger, intent, creativity, and other redeeming features.

The first criterion is danger. From the standpoint of physical harm, there was nothing inherently dangerous about the prank. It didn't hurt anyone. Perhaps the vice president suffered a blow to his ego, but it may have needed deflating. The only significant negative consequence was that he was made to appear foolish to his boss. This cannot be dismissed lightly. The fact that the president had cause to inquire whether the vice president was "out of his mind" must be deemed significant harm. The prank called the vice president's competence into question. It also humiliated him in front of his superior.

The intent criterion reveals additional problems with the prank. The vice president was a stuffed shirt who was the frequent victim of practical jokes. Whoever pulled the prank was laughing at, rather than with, him. Unlike the practical jokes pulled on Sun Microsystems executives, this one did not send a message of affection and admiration. Its intent was to cause embarrassment.

The third criterion is creativity. Although the fake telephone message was not the world's most creative prank, there was a modicum of thought behind it. It required the prankster to learn about the vice president's efforts to attend the football game. By tailoring the prank specifically to its victim, the prankster demonstrated a slight amount of effort.

Were there any other redeeming features? Not really. The prank did not promote teamwork or improve morale. It did nothing to enhance the company's image. One might argue that the prank served as a vehicle for communicating the ill will of the staff toward the vice president. However, that message would have been more effectively conveyed through less indirect channels.

Based on these criteria, the prank must be judged inappropriate. It was not particularly creative and it intentionally humiliated its victim.

Inappropriate humor is for the birds... like the parrot for sale at a pet store. A man walked in and wondered why the price was so low. The storekeeper replied, "The parrot is sarcastic. It tells ethnic jokes. And it's totally inappropriate. But if you discipline it properly, you could have a nice pet." The man decided to try and he took the bird home. A few days later the parrot started telling ethnic jokes. The man didn't know what to do. So he opened his refrigerator freezer and stuck the parrot next to a frozen turkey for five minutes. When he pulled it out, the parrot was cold and silent. A few days later the parrot started telling ethnic jokes again. So the man stuck it next to the turkey for ten minutes. When he pulled it out, the parrot was very cold and silent. A few days later the parrot started telling ethnic jokes again. So the man stuck it next to the turkey for fifteen minutes. When he pulled it out, the parrot was covered with frost and shaking. After regaining its composure, the parrot said, "You win. I'm not going to tell those jokes anymore. But I've got one question: What jokes did the turkey tell?"

Although the story does not record an answer to the parrot's question, it's easy to provide one. That's because there's only one kind of humor that turkeys use—inappropriate. Whether it's ethnic, racist, and sexist jokes or unwarranted sarcasm or mean-spirited practical jokes, inappropriate humor is the province of turkeys. So the next time you're tempted to use such humor, think about its effect on the people around you. Don't be a turkey and get left in the cold.

A Judgment Call

The following is an excerpt from a "dictionary" that was circulated by employees via electronic mail at a Fortune 500 company. The name of the company has been changed to "Company." Read the excerpt and consider its effect on the people who created it, distributed it and read it.

HELP: Careers are destroyed with too much help. You, too, can learn to help people you want to get rid of. The following phrases will assist you:

a. "Help me understand that." Say this to your adversary at a large meeting after he has just made an amazingly silly statement. This will call everyone's attention to the fact not only that he is a complete idiot but that you are a tactful and modest person.

b. "How can I help Irving?" Say this to Irving's boss, then point out Irving's many good qualities ("He seems to be trying his best") while making it clear that he is totally incompetent ("But he doesn't appear to be making much progress, and I know it's important"). Irving's boss will immediately recognize you as a helpful and tactful person and will plan Irving as a "4" (Needs Help) on his next review. With any luck, Irving will be so incensed over his lousy raise that he'll quit Company altogether.

ISSUE: Issues are Company's most flexible product. There are lots of things you can do with issues:

a. Table the issue (meaning do nothing)
b. Address the issue (look into it and then do nothing)
c. Visit the issue (say you did, then don't)
d. Revisit the issue (oh no, not again)

e. Work the issue (spend a lot of time looking into details that have no bearing on the issue, then do nothing)

f. Let's work that issue off-line (let's not embarrass ourselves by talking about that mess in front of all these people)

g. I'm on top of that issue (I don't intend to do anything about it and don't want to talk about it)

OFF-LINE: This is the way we like to solve problems. Actually solving a problem during a meeting is disruptive to the process of the meeting (see **PROCESS**). So we take the problems "off-line" (look into them at some later date, preferably never).

PROCESS: We love process at Company. We even hold meetings to discuss the process of holding meetings. You can get instant recognition as manager material if you come to a meeting and say things like:

a. "We have a process question." This will free everyone at the meeting from doing any work at all and allow them instead to discuss how they propose to conduct the meeting. This usually begins and ends with rearranging the chairs and tables in the room.

b. "The process is what's causing the problem." This is a REALLY brilliant move, since now everyone can spend his/her time bitching about how impossible Company is to work for, instead of solving the problem. Better yet, the person who caused the problem is now free from all blame. Say this loudly when the person who is clearly to blame for the screwup is both high-ranking and in the room.

QUALITY CONTROL: Very important at Company. If we don't carefully control quality, it might get out of hand.

STUPIDITY: Never attribute to maliciousness that which can be explained by mere stupidity.

TASK FORCE: This is a group that generates a lot of memos (preferably EMS rather than hard copy), a lengthy recommendation report (lots of appendices, charts, and graphs) and then does nothing. The task force usually concludes its report by recommending the formation of another task force to really work the issue (see **ISSUE**).

Task forces are lots of fun to work on. They give you a good excuse for not doing your current job ("Gee, boss, I'm sorry, but you know that task force is taking up a lot of my time"), while making it possible for you to decline any really work-heavy assignments on the task force ("My current responsibilities prohibit me from volunteering for that task").[1]

Is the humor in this "dictionary" appropriate or inappropriate? Does it boost morale by demonstrating that the company can poke fun at itself? Or does it reflect a morale-draining cynicism? You be the judge.

THIRTEEN

Practice Makes Perfect: Exercises to Develop Your Humor Skills

Too many people confine their exercise to jumping to conclusions, running up bills, stretching the truth, bending over backward, lying down on the job, sidestepping responsibility, and pushing their luck.

—Anonymous

A tough athletic director at a health spa was putting some guests through their morning calisthenics. After push-ups and sit-ups, he said, "Everyone on your backs, legs up in the air, and move them as if you were riding a bicycle." A few seconds later one guest stopped moving his legs. "What's your problem?" barked the director. "No problem," replied the guest. "I'm coasting."

The guest's approach to exercise is familiar to many of us— we coast. We assume that we can get by on our natural abilities without making any effort to maintain or improve them. This assumption is unfounded and incorrect. No matter whether the ability is mental or physical, our skills will decline without regular exercise. How often do you exercise your sense of humor? It's a question that most of us never stop to ponder. Yet the answer is critical. Because sense of humor is governed by the principle that controls all aspects of human fitness: Use it or lose it.

Getting serious about humor means making a commitment. That means setting up measurable goals and regular workouts. You've got to devise a balanced program that's challenging yet achievable. And you've got to start today. You're not going to improve by talking about doing it.

Fortunately, the exercises in this chapter are easy to implement. They don't require any special equipment. They can be learned quickly. They can be performed indoors or outdoors, at home or at work, at any time of day. So don't make excuses for not starting a program. You don't have any.

Begin your workouts with simple warm-up exercises. These will stretch your mental muscles, provide positive reinforcement, and lower the risk of injury. After you're warmed up, proceed to the more difficult tasks. Be consistent. Develop a comfortable routine and stick with it.

How much exercise do you need? It varies with the individual. But a small investment of time on a daily basis will pay off in a large reserve of mental health. Your outlook will become more flexible. You'll feel more creative. People will perceive you as a better manager. And don't worry about overdoing it. Despite popular mythology I've never seen a documented case where someone died laughing.

Group I: Exercises to Change Perspective

The first group of exercises is designed to help you develop your ability to "see things in a funny way." These perspective changers can shift your mental gears when you're bogged down or stressed out.

In stressful situations it's not unusual to develop a distorted view of events. On-the-job crises or routine tensions can produce strange reactions from people working under pressure. Similarly a mental state of anxiety or depression can wreak havoc with normal perceptions and responses. Sometimes humor can restore the balance.

Research by Dr. Arthur Nezu, chief psychologist at Beth Israel Center and associate professor of psychiatry at Mount Sinai School of Medicine in New York, has shown that humor can moderate the harmful effects of stress. His research also suggests that people who display a sense of humor under stressful situations tend to be well liked and respected. He calls humor a "natural human resource."[1]

The following exercises will help you develop your natural resources:

1. SIGNS

Here's an easy warm-up exercise to stretch your humor muscles. It will put your mind in the slightly out-of-focus position so essential for comic vision. Based on the principle of incongruity, the exercise simply moves a common object from one setting to another. The "incongruous" result produces the humor.

Begin by making a list of your favorite signs. Here are a few to get you started:

SLIPPERY WHEN WET	KEEP OFF THE GRASS	CLOSED
NO SMOKING	NO LOITERING	LOW BRIDGE
GOING OUT OF BUSINESS	REST AREA	55 MILES PER HOUR
HELP WANTED	MAIN ENTRANCE	NO LIFEGUARD ON DUTY
FALLING ROCKS	BEWARE OF DOG	NO U-TURN
FOR SALE	DANGER	HALF OFF
WET PAINT	ONE WAY	BE BACK SOON

Now pick a sign and move it to a new location that will make it funny. After you select the new location, strengthen the image by filling in specific details.

Example: BEWARE OF DOG

Normal setting:	Sign on fence in front of someone's house
New location:	The boss's office

Where in office: The boss's desk
What else do you see: Boss sitting at desk growling

Now try it with some signs from your workplace. Move them to new locations in your office, warehouse, or factory.

Example: NO SMOKING

Normal setting: Sign on wall in company cafeteria
New location: The R&D department
Where in department: The conference room
What else do you see: Engineers   brainstorming   with
                          smoke coming out of their heads

Incongruity is a powerful perspective changer. Once you've warmed up with the signs exercise, look around at your co-workers. Instead of signs, try shifting colleagues, clients, and customers into unusual locations. The results can be very entertaining.

2. TAKE THINGS LITERALLY

Another simple way of developing a humorous perspective is to "take things literally." My favorite example of this technique comes from a Ziggy cartoon. Ziggy, a perpetual loser, is depicted holding a can labeled Bug Spray. When he presses the nozzle, bugs spray out of the can. The cartoonist who draws Ziggy has given us a literal translation of the term *bug spray*. The humor arises because we would normally interpret the term to mean a spray that repels bugs.

Language is an inherently ambiguous medium of communication. Our words and expressions can be interpreted in an endless variety of ways. That's why much of our daily conversation consists of efforts to clarify what we're trying to say. "I didn't mean it that way." "Do you know what I mean?" "Don't take this the wrong way?" These are just a few of the many expressions we use to make ourselves understood. Perhaps the most celebrated of these expressions is the one posted on office walls around the world: "I know you believe you understand what you think I said, but I'm not sure you realize that what you heard is not what I meant."

Despite our best intentions, there will always be many ways to "take" what someone has said. Taking things literally is one of the options. An excellent starting point for developing your "literal" sense of humor is provided by daily newspaper headlines. A quick scan usually reveals some fascinating events—if you take the headlines literally. For example, the *Rocky Mountain News* ran an article headlined, "LAWYER TO OFFER POOR FREE ADVICE." Does this mean the lawyer is doing charity work? Or does it mean you get what you pay for? You be the judge.

Here are a few more examples:

- "THREE STATES HIT BY BLIZZARD; ONE IS MISSING" (*Item-Tribune*)
- "FACULTY WIVES TO ADORN TREE FOR HOSPITAL" (*Sacramento Union*)
- "WOMAN FALLS THREE FLOORS AS SHE WATERS FLOWERS" (*Newsday*)
- "TWO GIRLS, DAD ALL JAILED IN WATCH CASE" (*New York Daily News*)
- "CHICAGO HEADS SPLIT ON RAILROAD MERGER" (*Philadelphia Inquirer*)[2]

Taking things literally changes your frame of reference and allows you to see things in a funny way. It unlocks your creativity. The silly image generated by a literal interpretation enables your mind to wander in new directions. It can start you on a path to new ideas. And if nothing else, it may give you a sidesplitting laugh—which can be very funny if taken literally.

3. NEW FUNCTIONS

One of the primary ways we identify objects in our perceptual universe is by looking at how they function. We define what something is by what it does. A chair is something you sit on. A table is something you sit at. A pen is something you use for writing. We are trained to view objects as performing certain functions. The problem is that any given object can perform a far greater range of functions than we are socially conditioned to perceive. For example you can use a chair as a ladder by standing on it. You can use a chair as a bookmark. Or you can use it as a hat. Thinking about a chair solely as a piece of furniture for sitting is an artificial limit.

Your first reaction to using a chair as a bookmark or hat is probably laughter. Your reaction is quite normal. Philosopher Alfred North Whitehead anticipated that response when he observed, "Almost all new ideas have a certain aspect of foolishness when they are first produced." What he was really observing is a phenomenon I call the humor-creativity overlap.

The humor-creativity overlap refers to our instinctive reaction to ideas that don't conform to our expectations—we laugh at them. The history of science is rife with examples. Basic scientific ideas that are unquestioned today were objects of hilarity when first proposed. Copernicus said the earth revolves around the sun. Louis Pasteur said disease is caused by microscopic creatures called germs. Newton spoke of an invisible force called gravity. These scientists could have been top comedians in their day just by standing on a stage and reciting their theories. The cycle of laughter and acceptance that accompanies many new ideas was best summed up by William James. He said, "First a new theory is attacked as absurd; then it is admitted to be true, but obvious and insignificant; finally it is seen to be so important that its adversaries claim they themselves discovered it."

Of course many new ideas *are* stupid, ridiculous, or absurd. They richly deserve the laughter they attract. However, snap judgments must be avoided. Because most new ideas seem funny at first, the great ones cannot immediately be distinguished from the clinkers. That's why changing an object's function is one of my favorite exercises. In addition to giving you a lot of funny ideas, it might give you a great one.

Many years ago I heard a story that illustrates this possibility. The story was told by a junior high school shop teacher who was trying to inspire greatness in his metalworking students. The teacher told them that scrap metal filings used to be considered garbage. Every day tons of filings would be hauled out of factories and carted to garbage dumps around the world. Industrialists had to pay a fee for this service. Then one day a Mr. Brillo offered to cart away the filings free of charge. He stored them in a warehouse, added soap, and sold them as Brillo soap pads.

The story is probably apocryphal, but it shows what can happen when you change your view of an object's function. Mr. Brillo didn't view scrap metal filings as garbage. He viewed them as a multimillion-dollar product. Although the world surely laughed at his idea, no one is laughing anymore. It turned out to be a great idea.

So here's the exercise: Pick a common object and make a list of its characteristics. What is its color, shape, and texture? How does it taste, sound, and smell? What is its height and weight? How is it structured? What are its normal functions? Record all of your observations on your list. Then use the list to think of new functions for the object. The more observations you make, the easier it is to perform the exercise.

Let's do a quick run-through. The common object that we will observe is the tomato. It is round and smooth. It has a skin. It contains seeds. It fits in your hand. It makes a squishy sound if you drop it. It can be red or green or a mixture of colors. It can taste rotten. Its normal functions include being put in a salad, turned into juice, and thrown at inept public speakers.

Now let's use the list to think up some new functions for tomatoes. We could use the tomato juice to paint graffiti on a natural foods store. We could flatten a tomato in the middle of a white pillowcase to make a Japanese flag. Or we could use the tomato skin to make gloves for petty thieves. When they wear the gloves, we would know that they had been caught red-handed.

Do these ideas seem absurd? You bet they do. That's the point—looking at objects in new ways evokes laughter. Will any of these ideas turn out to be great? You never know. Let's stop and think a moment. Tomato-skin gloves could probably serve as a great publicity gimmick for a group involved in the animal rights movement. Suddenly an idea that was laughable starts to have serious possibilities. By changing an object's function, you will begin to discover the comic potential of the universe. You will stretch your imagination. And you may even become the next Mr. Brillo.

4. SITCOM

This exercise is especially useful for putting workplace pressures and problems into perspective. It is designed to turn frustration into laughter. Imagine that your workplace is the setting for a situation comedy. Now create a new show as if you were going to sell it to a television network. Start with the characters. Your coworkers will be the main characters. Describe each of them in a few words. What are their personality traits? How do they relate to each other? What are their habits and foibles?

For example, Arlene is a loud, extroverted product marketing manager. She is a total yuppie—flashy clothes, cars, and boyfriends. Her temper is hair-trigger and she likes to delegate most of her work. Bob is vice president of engineering. He is a left-brain type who analyzes things to death. He wears corduroy suits to important meetings. David is an operations executive who hates to make decisions. He spends his day writing memos. He is extremely shy. Jim is a secretary. He is going to night school to become an accountant. He is the only sane one in the place. Jim gets along with everyone. Arlene and Bob can't stand each other. No one knows who David likes or dislikes.

Next develop some plots, the story lines for each episode of your show. Here's where your work-related problems come into play. Use them as plots for your show. Describe them in the style used in *TV Guide*. For example Arlene goes on the warpath when David refuses to sign a purchase order for a new trade show booth. Or, Jim screws up a memo after he receives conflicting directions from Arlene and Bob. Or, the CEO forgets his slides for an important presentation and blames his secretary.

You've got a million of them—they happen at work every day. Looking at your problems from a sitcom perspective won't automatically solve them. But it will create some psychological distance. Then maybe you'll be able to change the channel.

5. TITLES

The titles exercise provides another outlet for dissipating your work-related frustrations. Titles abound in the workplace. From business cards to business plans, everyone and everything has a title. But titles are not always accurate. In this exercise you will correct such gross errors by giving people the titles they really deserve. ·

Start by making a list of irritating people, projects, or events in your work environment. Then assign them movie titles. For example let's say you're in marketing. You're ready to roll out a new product in order to meet a critical window of opportunity. Suddenly Engineering objects. The engineers form a committee. Their committee is going to delay the product-release date and screw up your life. Whenever you think of that committee, your blood pressure rises. You'll probably feel better if you mentally refer to the committee with a movie title—*Revenge of the Nerds.*

Here are a few more common work situations and potential movie titles:

> Two superiors, who dislike each other, are always trying to manipulate you. One is a screamer. The other specializes in transparently false flattery. Now they're having an argument over which one will control your work—*Godzilla versus the Smog Monster.*

> The office gossip is meeting with your archrival—*Dangerous Liaisons.*

The boss's latest emergency project must take precedence over all previous emergency projects—*Apocalypse Now*.

If you don't like movies, use the titles of novels. Just pick some titles. Pick some problems. Then throw the book at them.

6. CROSSOVER

Comic perspective depends on a combination of factors. The crossover exercise emphasizes the "combination." It recognizes that humor is kaleidoscopic in nature, arising from the unique patterns formed by a collision of people and events. A crossover artificially induces these collisions. It takes characteristics from two different items and blends them together in a funny way. For example, what do you get when you cross a cup of flour with a bowl of alphabet soup? Monogrammed pancakes.

Here's how it works. Start by picking two items to cross, for example a homing pigeon and a woodpecker. Then make a list of characteristics that you associate with each item. (The longer the lists, the easier it is to do this exercise.)

HOMING PIGEON	WOODPECKER
Flies	Eats bugs
Carries messages	Knocks on trees
Lives in a nest	Flies
Trained to return home	Inspired a cartoon character
People keep them as pets	Lives in the forest
Lives in a coop	Pecks on telephone poles
Hangs around statues	

Look at the two lists and cross the characteristics until you spot a funny combination. Example: What do you get when you cross a homing pigeon with a woodpecker? A bird that not only returns home, but also knocks on the door.

The exercise is even easier when you cross the traits of two famous people. For example, what do you get when you cross Ivan Boesky and Frank Sinatra? Someone who shouldn't have done it "his way." Now that you understand the basic principle, try crossing people and objects from your work environment. The results should speak for themselves.

If you want to be more sophisticated, don't say, "What do you get when you cross...?" Instead use natural setups that *imply* the crossover. Natural setups are situations where two or more items are combined—recipes, marriages, inventions, corporate mergers. A good example involves IBM's acquisition of ROLM Corporation several years ago. IBM was famous for three-piece suits and a serious style. ROLM was noted for its employee swimming pool and laid-back style. This was a perfect natural setup for a crossover. The result: Everyone was concerned that IBM's takeover would change ROLM's relaxed life-style. Well, it's already happened. At ROLM they're now wearing three-piece bathing suits.

Group II: Exercises to Produce Humorous Artifacts

The second group of exercises is designed to produce physical artifacts capable of stimulating your brain's mirth centers. Some of the artifacts will be suitable for public display. Others will be more appropriate for private consumption. All of them will give you a laugh when you need one.

1. SANITY FILE

Ever have "one of those days"? You know what I'm talking about—everything, and I mean everything, goes wrong. Clients and customers scream at you. Your superiors scream at you. Your subordinates scream at you. And you just want to, well, scream. One way of preserving your sanity during such times is to reach into your desk, pull out a file of humorous material, and browse through it. The funny items will help pull you back from the brink. Hence the name sanity file.

The key to setting up a successful sanity file is making sure its contents are funny. How do you know what's funny? Simple—whatever makes you laugh. This file is a highly personal matter. It exists to preserve *your* sanity.

Start by designating a folder as your sanity file. Then fill it up. File items can include cartoons, news clips, jokes, photographs, letters, postcards, and memos—anything you think is funny. Whenever you come across a laugh provoker, save it for the file.

Use of the file need not be limited to times of stress, despair, and near-hysteria (although many workplaces provide such occasions several times a day). You can use the file to engage the humor functions of your mind at any time. This can be particularly helpful when you're involved in creative endeavors. There's nothing like looking at funny stuff to start you thinking funny.

2. CARTOON CAPTIONING

One way to get the "big picture" with humor is to start with a picture—a cartoon. Clip one out of a newspaper or magazine. Then remove the caption and write your own. If you relate it to your work environment, you'll probably find that your caption is funnier than the original.

A good way to get caption ideas flowing is to ask yourself a series of questions: Who are the characters in the cartoon? Does it feature people or objects or animals? What are they doing? What are they talking about? Where is the action taking place?

For example one of my favorite cartoons comes from *Herman* by Jim Unger. It depicts a clerk at a hardware store talking to a customer. The clerk is standing behind a counter and is holding a gigantic paint roller. The caption consists of what the clerk is telling the customer. During my seminars I ask people to create a new caption that relates to their work environment. Their ideas have included: "This can cover up all your mistakes at once." "It's perfect for a whitewash." "The time-management people will love it." The possibilities are endless.

3. MURPHY'S LAW

Many people believe in law and order as long as they can lay down the law and give the orders. Unfortunately you can't always give the orders. But that doesn't mean that you can't lay down the laws.

A good way to maintain perspective with humor is to create funny scientific laws that explain life's irritations. The classic example is Murphy's Law—"Anything that can go wrong will go wrong." Other examples include:

You can't depend on anyone to be wrong all the time.

Indecision is the key to flexibility.

A motion to adjourn is always in order.[3]

It's easy, as well as cathartic, to make up laws that reflect workplace problems. And it's comforting to know that when something goes wrong, there will be a law available to help you handle the situation. Never underestimate the illusion of control. After all, being able to laugh at a problem is the first step toward solving it.

The maximum effect can be achieved if you give your laws important-sounding names. The following examples from a medical clinic illustrate the process:

Hippocrates' Ratio: The last patient of the day is always the sickest.

Dr. Griger's Corollary: Especially if you're about to go on vacation.

Make a list of frustrating, stressful, or irritating situations that you experience on the job. Create some laws to deal with them. Then put the laws in your sanity file until needed. The mind you save may be your own.

4. PROVERBS

Proverbs provide excellent raw material for creating humorous messages about your workplace. After you twist the proverb into an amusing bit of wisdom, it can be easily displayed as a sign, poster, or button.

Start the exercise by compiling a list of proverbs. For example:

> Crime doesn't pay.
> Ignorance of the law is no excuse.
> Actions speak louder than words.
> Honesty is the best policy.
> It takes two to tango.
> Laugh and the world laughs with you.
> Two heads are better than one.

Then pick a proverb and create a funny message by adding, deleting, or changing words. For example:

> Crime doesn't pay—but it looks interesting on a resume.

> Laugh and the world laughs with you. Cry and you're probably looking at your telephone bill.

Try to make the new proverb relevant to your work situation. Let's say you're frequently surrounded by loud or angry people—a routine occurrence for customer service representatives and secretaries. You might create the following proverb:

> Two heads are better than one—unless they're shouting at each other.

Write it down and hang it up. You never know who might heed its advice.

5. GREETING CARDS

Funny greeting cards for office birthdays, holidays, and other events are easy to create if you invest a little time and imagination. Just pick an occasion, make a word association list, and write a funny line. Then take a piece of paper, fold it in half, and make the card. Yes, it sounds like something you did in kindergarten. But isn't that where you learned the important things in life? Here's how it works:

Occasion: Retirement of coworker

Word Association List for Retirement:

old age	Social Security	lack of energy
wrinkles	mentor	gold watch
emeritus	gift	party
consultant	pension	golf
hide your age	tire easily	hang out in bar

Write the setup line for the front of the card: "Congratulations on your retirement. You've finally reached that age..." Now look over the word association list and write the inside line that completes the joke: "...when you go to a fern bar to pick up a fern."

Sure you could go to a store and buy a card. But it will mean a lot more to your coworker if you make the card yourself. Besides, you'll save at least seventy-five cents.

6. ASTROLOGY CHART

If you could see into the future, you could prepare for all the irritating people that eventually confront you on the job. What? You don't possess the power to peer through time. Then do the next best thing—create a funny astrology chart.

For example:

AQUARIUS—January 20 to February 18: You are an emotional type who would cut off your nose to spite your face. Most people believe this would be an improvement. Your ability to make mistakes is only surpassed by your talent for covering them up. People laugh at you behind your back.

PISCES—February 19 to March 20: You have a vivid imagination and often think that you will soon be promoted. You are the only one who doesn't realize that your so-called career has plateaued. Your bullying behavior is a poor imitation of the executive prerogative you will never achieve.

ARIES—March 21 to April 19: You are a left-brain type and hate disorder. You'd probably make a good engineer if you weren't so dumb. That's probably why you ended up in [department].

You get the idea.

The chart provides a terrific outlet for venting your feelings of aggression toward "difficult" people with whom you must interact from time to time. You know who they are. The boss who screams about inconsequential matters. The junior exec who's always ready with a snappy put-down. The passive-aggressives who smile as they stab you in the back.

Encounters with these people will leave you seething with rage. However, your response to their boorish behavior will inevitably be restrained due to your inherent good manners and the fact that they can destroy your career. That's when the astrology chart comes in handy. Consult it whenever one of the "stars" in your office gives you a hard time. But keep it to yourself.

7. COMPANY CALENDAR

Many organizations issue "company calendars" that include information about business activities. You can adopt this practice with amusing results. In addition to standard holidays, your calendar can note other important work-related dates. These can range from holidays commemorating historic workplace events to special "theme" weeks or months.

For example:

February 19–25:	Engineers-Wear-Matching-Socks Week
May 9:	Purchasing-Says-Yes Day
July 21:	Company installed first photocopy machine
July 22:	Company installed first shredding machine

December 1–31: Leftovers-in-the-Cafeteria Month

Construct it as a desk calendar for maximum flexibility. Then, depending on what you write, you can put it either on your desk or in your desk. And remember, time flies when you're having fun.

Group III: Humor-Appreciation Exercises

The third group of exercises is designed to strengthen your humor-appreciation skills. You will develop the ability to identify, absorb, and react to an increasingly broad range of humor experiences. As you become more receptive to humor, you will find yourself immersed in a mirthful universe of constantly expanding dimensions. You'll discover just how funny people can be if you give them a little permission and encouragement.

1. RECOGNITION

Orville and Wilbur Wright tried repeatedly to get off the ground with their new flying machine. They had one disappointment after another. Finally one December day at Kitty Hawk, Orville did what no man had ever done before. It was one of the greatest events in history. They wired their sister Katherine, "We have actually flown 120 feet. We'll be home for Christmas." When she received the wire, Katherine ran straight to the local newspaper office and handed it to the editor. He looked at the wire and said, "Well, isn't that nice? They're going to be home for Christmas."

You're not always going to get the recognition you deserve— no matter how fantastic or important your accomplishments. People are busy. People are distracted. People are concerned with their own careers. It's a fact of corporate life: your colleagues are never going to recognize the full significance of your heroic efforts on that last deal or project. They may not even acknowledge that you did a good job.

Instead of becoming frustrated at such crass behavior, attack the problem from another angle. Start with behavior you can control—your own. Ask yourself a question: Do you give your coworkers the recognition *they* deserve? Probably not. You're probably blind to their achievements for the same reasons that your own accomplishments go unnoticed. You're busy. You're distracted. You have a million things to do.

This vicious cycle can be broken if you're willing to make the first move. Just force yourself to start giving coworkers the recognition they deserve. You may actually enjoy the process. After all, everyone knows it's better to give than receive—then you don't have to write thank-you notes.

Giving recognition is particularly important when humor is involved. Humor is an extremely fragile creature. It will not thrive without encouragement. If you don't respond when people offer humor, they will eventually turn their efforts elsewhere. The loss is far greater than missing an opportunity to hear some jokes. You also lose the desire for camaraderie that underlies your colleagues' attempts to share humor.

The first step toward improving your humor-appreciation skills is acknowledging humor when it occurs. Recognize appropriate humor offered by your colleagues. Smile. Laugh. Say, "That's a good one." Do something encouraging. Reward appropriate humor with appropriate recognition. Your own reward will be a payback in camaraderie and good will. You'll also get to hear a lot of jokes.

2. VISUALIZATION

Much has been written about visualization as a technique for achieving goals. A quick browse through the psychology section of any bookstore confirms the popularity of the topic. Leaders, winners, and peak performers attribute their success to visualization. Sports figures use visualization to improve their "inner" games. Famous executives credit visualization for their rise to the top. The technique is considered an indispensable arrow in the quiver of success.

The basic theory is that visualizing success helps you achieve success. Although the concept is as old as positive thinking, the modern version has its roots in the motivation and training programs used by top athletes. For example, Jack Nicklaus is said to visualize a successful outcome just before he swings a golf club. And Olympic runners reportedly imagine themselves running each step of their races and accepting gold medals. By mentally rehearsing the sequence of events leading to victory, the athlete is better prepared for victory. In a sense it is the ultimate self-fulfilling prophecy.

Transplanted to a business environment, visualization has been linked with being a successful entrepreneur. Steve Jobs had a vision of Apple Computer as a major company even when it was headquartered in a garage. Similar vision has been attributed to Charles Schwab (discount stock brokerage), Liz Claiborne (women's clothes), and Trammell Crow (real estate). By logical extension, common wisdom now dictates that superior business leaders possess a vision that can guide their decisions and actions.

The standard advice on harnessing the power of visualization is to imagine yourself achieving your goals. Pop psychologists suggest that you perform this exercise on a regular basis. Visualize yourself grabbing the brass ring. Visualize the scene as you triumph. Visualize yourself as number one. In short, visualize success. My advice is slightly different: I believe that you should visualize success—other people's.

While this may sound strange in an era populated by the "me generation," it really makes a lot of sense. The pop-psychology approach to visualizing success is shortsighted at best. It's selfish. It's egocentric. And it doesn't foster the leadership necessary for long-term success. A true leader is a person who can empower others, a process that begins by visualizing other people's success. In the long run it will make *you* more successful.

Now let's apply this technique to developing your humor-appreciation skills. When someone tells you a joke that falls flat, visualize how it could have been successful. If someone uses humor that doesn't click, imagine different circumstances where it would have worked. Then share your insights with the person who "bombed." If you practice this exercise frequently, you will soon notice three results. First, your tolerance for ineffective humor will grow as you come to appreciate its possibilities. Second, your instinctive response to failed humor will change from negative to neutral. Third, your stock will rise with the people who bombed. They will be grateful for your non-negative reaction.

The more you visualize other people's success with humor, the more you increase your own humor-appreciation skills. And the more you appreciate humor—well, that makes you a better person. The key to achieving these results is your ability to visualize humor. This ability can be enhanced by performing the other exercises in this chapter. It can also be improved simply by understanding some basic humor philosophy.

Humor philosopher John Cantu categorizes jokes as either "valid" or "funny." The distinction is important. A valid joke is one that you "get"—you intellectually understand why the joke is supposed to be funny. A funny joke is one that you personally find amusing.

Based on this distinction, Cantu postulates two basic laws:

1. A joke can't be funny without being valid. In other words, if you don't "get" a joke, then you can't possibly be amused by it.
2. People will always disagree about what is funny. If a joke is valid, it will seem funny to some people and not to others.

The proof of this second law is quickly evidenced by considering the relative talents of famous comedians. For example, do you think Woody Allen is funny? How about Joan Rivers, Henny Youngman, Steve Martin, Mort Sahl, Roseanne Barr, and Bob Hope? Ask this question to a large group of people, and disagreements arise immediately. Each of the comedians will be considered hysterically funny by some people and terrible by others. Yet each of these comedians makes a fortune by being "funny."

What does all this have to do with visualizing other people's success with humor? Everything. The Cantu distinction provides a framework for appreciating humor that you don't find personally amusing. This is quite significant. It enables you to offer constructive criticism of a bad joke instead of automatically dismissing it. For example when someone tells a joke that isn't "funny," you can still determine that it's valid. You can then visualize how it might be funny to other people or how it might be made funny to you. Evaluating humor in this manner vastly expands your humor universe. By spotting the potential in ineffective humor, you transform other people's failures into triumphs, a skill that guarantees your own success.

Putting It All Together

A prisoner with a long criminal record was on trial for his latest crime. The judge found him guilty on twenty-six counts and sentenced him to 130 years. Already middle-aged, the prisoner burst into tears. Noting this show of remorse, the judge reconsidered. He said, "I didn't mean to be so harsh. I know I've imposed an unusually severe sentence. So you don't have to serve the whole time." With a benign smile he leaned toward the prisoner, whose face showed newfound hope. "Just do as much as you can."

When you think about performing all the exercises discussed in this chapter, it may seem as if you've received a hopeless sentence. Not true. You haven't committed a crime and you're not going to prison. Your only crime will occur if you ignore the exercises. They are your key to success. Practice may not make you perfect, but it will definitely help your humor skills blossom. Don't get overwhelmed. If you can't do everything immediately, remember the judge's advice—"Just do as much as you can."

FOURTEEN

Secret Sources of Effective Humor

Originality is the art of concealing your source.
—Franklin P. Adams

Two Indian chiefs on opposite sides of Nevada were arguing about territorial rights to an atomic test site in the middle. They were sending smoke signals back and forth, when an atomic blast occurred. A giant mushroom cloud appeared on the horizon. One of the chiefs looked at it and thought, "I wish I'd said that."

The chief's thought occurs to most of us when we hear a witty remark, great joke, incisive quip, or amusing anecdote. We wish we'd said it. We also wish we knew where it came from. Did the person telling it make it up? Did he or she hear it someplace? Was it obtained from a secret newsletter mailed to a select group of clandestine subscribers?

The nagging suspicion that certain people can access a hidden supply of scintillating wit highlights the difficulty in locating such humor. Where does the search begin? To whom does one turn for help? Many managers and professionals regard the process as a complete mystery. Finding comic material suitable for business purposes is considered a task worthy of Sherlock Holmes. Its difficulty ranks with capturing the

Loch Ness Monster or getting a lawyer to return a telephone call.

As a humor consultant I have observed these frustrations firsthand. The second most frequent question I receive from businesspeople is "How do you find good material?" My clients want to know where they can procure usable quips, anecdotes, quotes, and funny definitions. They want to know where to look. And they want to know why certain people always have an endless supply.

I must admit that some people do seem to have a joke or story for every occasion. They greet you on the elevator with the latest political quip. They open meetings by telling a funny story that no one has heard before. They always have a witty line for birthdays, retirements, and other office celebrations. How do they do it? Does it require extrasensory powers? Does it involve a pact with the devil?

The explanation is neither sinister nor supernatural. People with a ready wit are just taking advantage of natural resources. You can do likewise. Let me describe several sources of humor that can transform an empty tank into a vast reservoir of usable comic material. Then the next time the phrase "I wish I'd said that" comes up in conversation, it will be someone responding to you.

Standard Sources

In the classic Humphrey Bogart movie *Casablanca,* a police official begins a homicide investigation with an order to "round up the usual suspects." This approach can also be applied to a humor investigation. Start with the obvious sources. Don't ignore the commonplace while racing toward the esoteric. In your search for comic material, the "usual suspects" should include books, newspapers, magazines, television and radio programs, records, and newsletters.

The simplest strategy is to begin with the media that you already receive. If you skim *The Wall Street Journal* every day, include the "Pepper...and Salt" feature in your reading. Located at the bottom of the op-ed page, "Pepper...and Salt" provides a daily dose of business-related humor—cartoons, funny definitions, rhymes, and one-liners. Similar features can be found in many business, trade, and professional journals. Examples include *Fortune*'s "Keeping Up" (a collection of amusing news events), *California Lawyer*'s "The Compleat Lawyer" (legal anecdotes), *Newsweek*'s "Perspectives" (topical cartoons and quotes), and *Forbes*'s "Thoughts on the Business of Life" (epigrammatic quotes). If you routinely read such publications, make the humor feature part of your routine.

Business and trade periodicals also use humor as "fillers"— short items that fill the space left when articles end before the bottom of a page. Collecting fillers is easy. It doesn't require extensive reading or concentration. You can spot them by flipping through the pages of a magazine. Your effort will be well justified when a great quip or anecdote suddenly leaps out at you.

After you've identified the humorous material in familiar sources, start expanding your search. Look at some magazines that you never read. Go to a library and browse through the periodicals section. There are thousands of publications waiting for you to mine the humor out of them. One particularly good source is *Reader's Digest*, a monthly magazine with four regular humor features, as well as numerous fillers.

While you're in the library, take a few minutes to become acquainted with the humor books. They can range from collections of celebrity wit and wisdom to treasuries of anecdotes and compendiums of humorous quotations. You will find them located under Dewey decimal number 808.8. You might also inquire if any additional humor resources are available. For example, many libraries now have record, audiocassette, and videotape collections.

You can also increase your humor collection by plugging into the electronic universe of radio and television comedy. A growing number of late-night TV talk show hosts initiate their programs with comic monologues about the day's events. Many radio personalities also lace their shows with topical humor. Tuning into these programs for just a few minutes a day can produce an excellent return on a small investment of time.

In order to maximize your return on investment, start a humor file. It can be as simple as tossing items into a shoebox. Every time you hear a good line, jot it down and put it in the box. When you see a funny item in a newspaper or magazine, clip it out and toss it in the box. If you want to get sophisticated, you can cross-reference your materials by topic and points illustrated. But it's really not necessary. Besides, it's much more fun to hunt through everything in the file when you're looking for a line. You'll come across all sorts of funny things that you forgot about.

Switching

Once you begin collecting humorous material, you may notice that much of it bears distinct similarities. In fact the same joke will often appear in several different sources with minor variations. This occurs for two reasons. First, it is difficult, if not impossible, to copyright a joke. Second, old jokes never die, they just live on in after-dinner speeches.

Mark Twain once observed that Adam was lucky because "when he said a good thing, he knew nobody had said it before." Twain's observation applies with special force to humor. Adam may have been the last person to tell a new joke. The popular phrase "Stop me if you've heard this one" suggests the scope of the problem. That's why a successful storyteller is a person who has a good memory and hopes other people don't.

The ancient status of much modern humor highlights the special nature of quips and anecdotes. They represent a form of immortality. Like the mythical Flying Dutchman, jokes pass from one vehicle to another without end. This process can be summed up as follows. A joke

Appears in *Playboy*,
Is reprinted in a local tabloid, then is
Told by a comedian on "The Tonight Show,"
Retold by a radio talk-show host,
Quoted by a syndicated columnist,
Retold by a politician,
Reprinted in a book of wit and humor,
Used as filler in a trade journal,
And mailed to *Playboy* as an original.

I've made a few changes to update this process, but its basic form comes from an ancient jokebook. And who knows where it appeared before that or where it will appear next.

Are there any new jokes? This is one of the great philosophical questions of humor. Answers and arguments abound. Debate on the issue is older than some of the jokes themselves. The question has perplexed scholars ever since the first chicken crossed the road to get to the other side.

Over the years three major positions have emerged. Some scholars believe there are only seven basic types of jokes. Others believe there are only three types of jokes. The compromise position holds that there is only one type of joke— old. All three positions share a common root. They are based on a thermodynamic model of humor: Jokes can neither be created nor destroyed—only their form can change. That's why, say its proponents, there are no new jokes, only an infinite variety of old ones.

My own view differs significantly. I don't believe that humor creation is constrained by the laws of thermodynamics. However, this debate need not be entered for our present purposes. Whether or not one believes that there are any new jokes, there are undoubtedly an infinite variety of old ones. Jokes mutate as they age. Details change through their constant telling and retelling. Some jokes are so old that they have spawned a multitude of altered versions of themselves.

Although this seems to suggest a negative outcome in our quest for fresh humor, it actually represents a tremendous opportunity. It reveals a way of obtaining large amounts of useful comic material. Instead of waiting for jokes to alter themselves randomly, you can consciously manipulate the process. The secret is called switching—taking an old joke and changing part or all of it.

Let's see exactly how switching works. A speech writer at a major utility company was preparing some remarks for an executive to deliver at a retirement ceremony. The executive wanted to include a joke about retirement. He wanted the retiree to leave with a smile and a fond memory of the company. The speech writer dutifully looked for an appropriate joke. He combed through his files of quips and quotes. He pulled joke books from his library shelves. He turned humor newsletters inside out. He ransacked his office trying to find the perfect bit of drollery. He even called other speech writers and begged.

The frantic search proved unsuccessful. Although the speech writer found many jokes about retirement, all of them were negative. They focused chiefly on four themes: The retiree would have a lot of time and nothing to do; the retiree would no longer have any clout at the company; the retiree's accomplishments at the company would not be adequately rewarded or recognized; and the retiree would soon suffer the physical and mental declines of advanced age. Jokes with these messages were deemed inappropriate for the occasion.

With the retirement ceremony rapidly approaching and no joke in hand, the speech writer turned to me for help. I asked if he liked any of the jokes uncovered by his research. It turned out that he was fond of one: "Retirement is when you and your wife can do what you haven't had time to do for the past ten years." However, he insisted that it was unusable. He didn't want to send a message that (a) the retiree hadn't had sex for ten years and (b) it was the company's fault.

The speech writer's concerns were certainly valid. But I pointed out that the joke sent an additional message: The retiree had been such a dedicated worker that he didn't have time for anything else. This message complimented the retiree.

If it could be emphasized and the other messages eliminated, the joke would be usable. That's where the switching came in.

I began by eliminating the sexual innuendo by dropping the wife from the joke. The setup became: "Retirement is when you can do what you haven't had time to do for the past ten years." The question then became what is a funny time-consuming activity? Understanding the tax code leaped to mind. Congress had recently passed a "simplified" tax code that nobody could understand. It was a popular topic of conversation among businesspeople in 1988. And it made a perfect punch line. Here's the final version: "Retirement is when you can do what you haven't had time to do for the past year— figure out the Tax Reform Act of 1987."

The beauty of switching is that it can be performed at various levels, from simple to elaborate. You just decide how much effort to invest. In the retirement-joke example, the switch was rather elaborate. It required a bit of thought and editing. However, a switch can be as simple as updating an old topical joke. For example a 1983 issue of *Comedy/Update* contains the following one-liner: "Pia Zadora wears a medical bracelet: 'IN CASE OF ACCIDENT, CALL A PRESS CONFERENCE.'"[1] Today the joke would work well simply by changing the name Pia Zadora to Donald Trump.

History repeats itself. The current event of today is often the current event of yesterday with a new identity. The stock market surges and declines. The economy recedes and inflates. Alliances strengthen and weaken. Switching lets you take advantage of these cyclical events. And sometimes you don't even have to change a word.

In *The Ad-Libber's Handbook*, a compilation of topical humor from the 1960s, jokesmith Bob Orben includes the following quip under the heading "Red China": "Remember the good old days? When the only problem we had in the Far East was Godzilla?"[2] The heading—"Red China"—is a tip-off. The joke was written during the height of the Cold War and reflects America's strained relations with the People's Republic of China. Subsequent developments eliminated this "problem."

Chinese leaders introduced Western-style economic reforms. China became an American trading partner. Relations improved. Then in 1989 the Chinese government massacred liberal students in Beijing, and relations were strained again. Suddenly, just by switching its unstated reference, the twenty-five-year-old joke about 1960s China applies to the current massacre.

This concept of switching the reference is very important. It allows you to switch one joke in a variety of ways without changing a single word. Let's reexamine the 1960s Orben joke: "Remember the good old days? When the only problem we had in the Far East was Godzilla?" We've already switched it to refer to the 1989 massacre in Beijing. We could also switch it to refer to current trade disputes with Japan; political unrest in Korea; or industrial competition with Hong Kong, Taiwan, and Singapore.

Like the philosopher's stone sought by the ancient alchemists, switching allows you to turn leaden jokes into gold. If a joke is old, switch it. If it's in poor taste, switch it. If it's too negative, switch it. All that's required is a little imagination and discipline. With switching, whole new vistas of potential arise in the stalest, least amusing stories. Suddenly a collection of old jokes is an asset to be highly prized and valued. There are no bad jokes in the world—only ones that haven't been switched yet.

Formulas

Formula humor offers another simple method for expanding your supply of usable comic material. Rather than tinkering with old jokes, you can follow simple formulas to create new quips and amusing observations. Some formulas even allow you to shape entire presentations. The key to success is locating the formulas. Let's discuss where you can find them and how they operate.

One of the best sources of simple quip formulas is *Reader's Digest*. Each month its pages are packed with fillers that are essentially formulas written up as short features. A good example comes from the February 1987 issue. The formula is "One good thing..." followed by a wry observation about a potentially negative situation.

One good thing...
...about middle-age spread is that it brings people closer together.[3]

...about children is that they never pull out photographs of their grandparents.[4]

You get the idea.

I especially like this formula because it forces you to look at the world in a positive way. And it can be easily applied to the world of work. Just think about the things that are most irritating in your business life and plug them into the formula. The possibilities are limitless—junk mail, endless meetings, working on weekends, competitors, rush jobs, computer glitches, budget disputes. Can we really find any positive qualities in such items? Sure we can. One good thing...

...about junk mail is that it makes your trash look important.

...about competitors is that they provide a career path for your problem employees.

A different type of formula, and one with widespread utility, is the reverse. How can I describe it? Using the reverse formula, you transform events or actions into their opposites or make them occur backward. Yes, I know this sounds strange. Perhaps the simplest way of explaining it is with an illustration.

A classic example of the reverse comes from a press release penned by Jeff Raleigh, a senior vice president at public relations giant Hill & Knowlton. In 1983 Raleigh received a major challenge. He was assigned to publicize the fact that the American Society of Association Executives was holding its annual convention in San Francisco. His problem: The story was nothing more than a routine convention announcement. Sure the convention would mean a lot of business for San Francisco, but that's not exactly big news in a city that hosts hundreds of conventions every year.

Raleigh solved his problem by using the reverse formula. Instead of telling the media what would occur at the convention, he told them what *wouldn't* occur. His press release began as follows:

> Even without representatives from the Society of Tongue Depressors or the American Council of Spotted Asses, the 63rd Annual Meeting and Exposition of the American Society of Association Executives (ASAE) will be San Francisco's most important 1983 meeting.

The rest of the release described the standard trivia about the convention. I'll spare you the details. However, the concluding sentence of the release referred back to the opening: "It is doubtful the lack of tongue depressors and spotted asses will be noticed at all."

The strategy was effective. The story was reported by the major local newspapers, the two largest local television stations, and a local network affiliate radio station. Raleigh's clever application of the reverse formula transformed a yawner into an attention-getting news item.

The reverse formula is extremely powerful. It can be used to structure entire presentations—particularly instructional messages. Instead of telling people how to succeed, you tell them how to fail. Rather than explaining how to do the job correctly, you explain how to make mistakes. You search for mediocrity. You make a case for destroying teamwork. You reveal methods for lowering quality. The formula, when used this way, derives its power from two fundamental principles. First, it's usually easier to teach someone to avoid a behavior than to perform a behavior. Second, it's always funnier to show what can go wrong than what can go right.

A good example comes from a speech by Sandy Kurtzig, chairman, CEO, and president of ASK Computer Systems Inc. Kurtzig is often asked to speak about how she started a part-time software business that grew into a $200-million company. Rather than deliver the standard bromides about hard work and perseverance, she uses the reverse formula. Here's how she sets up her discussion of entrepreneurship:

> Instead of telling you all the right ways to be an entrepreneur, I thought I'd tell you all the wrong ways. Since I followed all of them, I can tell you about them from experience.

She then offers advice such as "start with little or no planning" and "start with no money." Notice that she adds a nice touch of self-effacing humor by claiming to have made the mistakes herself.

One of the most popular applications of the reverse formula is the "how to" article. Typical titles include "How to Make the 10 Most Common Mistakes in Selecting, Implementing and Using an MRP-II system" (*Askhorizons*), "Ten Ways to Screw Up a Sales Meeting" (*Sales and Marketing Management*), "How to Turn a Professional Corporation into a Disaster" (*Medical Economics*), "Eleven Ways to Mess Up Your Business Succession" (*Air Conditioning, Heating & Refrigeration News*), and "In Search of Failure: How to Pave the Road to Ruin" (*Industry Week*). This format allows writers to elicit laughs about their subject matter while conveying practical information.

Networking

One last source of humor that is so obvious it's often overlooked is other people. If you assume that most people know at least one good joke, then you can jump-start your humor search by asking acquaintances to share their favorite quips or anecdotes. This is really just a form of networking. It operates on the same principles as a job search. Instead of asking everyone you know for job leads, you ask them for jokes. Your friends will probably be much happier to provide the jokes than the names of their contacts.

Like networking for jobs or new business, networking for jokes is performed most efficiently by talking to people who have the information you seek. In the case of jokes, certain occupations tend to be particularly fruitful sources. Lobbyists, salespeople, and stockbrokers should be high on your list for contact. Each of these occupations requires extensive interaction with numerous people on a daily basis. And practitioners in these fields thrive on exchanges of humor. In fact anyone who works with an "800" telephone line is probably exposed to a lot of good material.

Networking can also be pursued on a more formal level. In traditional networking, that might include joining a country club or professional association in order to generate new business. In humor networking it might include organizing a joke lunch. The joke lunch is a creation of Kip Witter, former vice president and treasurer of Amdahl Corporation. It is an almost monthly gathering of Silicon Valley businesspeople who meet at a restaurant for the express purpose of exchanging jokes. The ritual began when Witter decided he needed a new source of fresh comic material. "Five or six of us thought it was a good idea, booked a reservation, and did it," he recalls.

In order to ensure that the lunch accomplishes its purpose, a small number of formalities has been instituted. Each participant brings a notepad. The top of the pad lists the date and location of the lunch, members who attended, and any visitors. The rest of the pad is used for summarizing jokes. At the end of the lunch a vote is taken, and the person who told the best joke receives a trophy. "The trophy is an ugly-looking Oscar-type thing that says 'Joe Klunch,'" states Witter. "I have yet to win it and I refuse to take it on sympathy." The trophy winner is responsible for setting up the next lunch.

"The joke lunch is like a tidal pool," states Witter. "It washes things out and you get fresh material." He also notes that additional jokes come from waiters and waitresses, who inevitably gravitate toward the group's table. "The restaurant staff sees us firing jokes at each other and they come over to contribute," Witter explains. "One time we hit a gold mine. A waitress kept running back to the kitchen to get jokes from a cook who had a million of them." In order to maximize such occurrences, the group rotates its meeting among several restaurants. "We try not to go back to places for at least a year," states Witter. "That gives the staffs time to store up new material."

A Humor Action Plan

Now that you know how to develop a large supply of usable humor, my mission is almost complete. We've discussed the distinction between being funny and communicating a sense of humor. You have learned about various types of humor. You understand the importance of making humor relevant to your message. You know how humor can motivate people. We've reviewed how humor applies to conflict situations. And we've seen how humor can affect corporate culture. However, before we conclude, one last task remains. You must translate your knowledge into action.

You must create a plan that integrates humor into your regular routine of work-related activities. Without a plan your knowledge will remain unapplied. Or it will be employed haphazardly in largely wasted efforts. Management guru Peter Drucker expressed it best when he said, "Management by objectives works if you know the objectives. Ninety percent of the time you don't."

In order to ensure that you know the objectives, I recommend putting together a detailed humor action plan. Just follow four simple steps. First, review your overall work objectives and decide how humor can further those goals. Second, define your humor objectives and outline the specific tasks necessary to achieve them. Third, identify the sources of humor that will enable you to perform each task. Finally, establish a schedule that requires you to perform each task at a designated time. If you follow these steps, you'll be well on your way to achieving success with a light touch.

Now you are fully equipped to use humor as a management tool. I have no doubt that you will use it successfully and I wish you the best of luck. But don't rely on luck. Rely on action—your own. Don't postpone, stall, delay, or procrastinate. Don't worry about making mistakes. Dive right in.

A minister was trapped in a small country church during a torrential downpour. The rain kept falling and the water kept rising. The streets were flooding. Suddenly a rowboat came by and someone yelled, "Reverend, we're evacuating. Get in the boat." The minister said, "No, I'm staying with the church." An hour later the water had risen to the second floor. Another rowboat came by and someone yelled, "Reverend, we're evacuating. Get in the boat." The minister said, "No, I'm staying with the church." The water kept rising and a few hours later the minister was up on the steeple. A helicopter came by and dropped a rope ladder. Someone yelled, "Reverend, it's your last chance. Get in the helicopter." The minister said, "No, I'm staying with the church." Well, the rain kept falling and the water kept rising and he drowned. And he couldn't believe it. He was at the Pearly Gates and demanded to see God. God asked, "What do you want?" The minister said, "God, how could you let this happen to me? I was your most loyal, obedient servant. I stayed with the church." And God said, "Hey, I sent two boats and a helicopter. What did you expect, a miracle?"

Like the minister in this story, you must realize two things. First, don't expect any miracles. You've only spent a few hours reading a book about humor and management. The techniques will work, but you've got to practice and develop your skills over a meaningful period of time. Second, don't overlook opportunities. Every day you are presented with numerous occasions for using humor. Take advantage of them. As an old philosopher once said, "There are three types of people in the world. Those who make things happen. Those who watch things happen. And those who wonder what happened." Make something happen right now.

How to Create a Quip

Allison Spiller, corporate communications manager for ASK Computer Systems Inc., had a problem. She had to make a presentation about international public relations to a group of advertising professionals. And she didn't have the slightest idea why they might be interested in the subject.

Spiller had been volunteered to participate in a panel discussion organized by a local chapter of the Business and Professional Advertising Association. Billed as a "shirtsleeves session," the discussion was supposed to focus on nuts-and-bolts issues. The audience would really learn how to put together an international public relations program.

Spiller had impeccable credentials for the task. In addition to handling PR chores in the United States and Canada, she coordinated her company's PR program in the United Kingdom, France, Germany, and Australia. She could wax eloquent about the problems and pitfalls in running an international public relations program. She could offer a cogent list of dos and don'ts. She could provide expert advice on the subject. But the question remained, Why would advertising people want to know how to conduct a PR program?

Unable to secure a satisfactory answer to this question, Spiller pondered the potential outcome of her presentation. Success could prove elusive. An audience uninterested in her topic would be difficult to please. Worst-case scenarios ranged from high-decibel snoring to mass movements toward the exits. A negative outcome was rapidly becoming too frightening to contemplate. Disaster had to be avoided at all costs. Spiller had to find a way of creating some audience identification. She asked me to help.

The obvious solution was to begin the presentation by emphasizing similarities between advertising and public relations. The basic appeal would be that "we're really all in the same business." This would diminish the gap between speaker and audience, as well as provide a weak justification for the topic. In order to improve her chance for creating rapport with her audience, Spiller decided to explain the similarities of PR and advertising with a humorous quip.

A simple five-step process guided construction of the quip from start to finish.

STEP 1: STATE THE POINT TO BE MADE BY THE QUIP.

In this case we stated the point as a question: Why should advertising people be interested in public relations? What do they have in common?

STEP 2: CONVERT THE POINT INTO THE BASIC SETUP PORTION OF THE QUIP.

We accomplished this step as follows:

When I was invited to speak here tonight, I wondered why a group of advertising professionals would be interested in how to organize a public relations program. Then I realized that advertising and public relations have a lot in common.

STEP 3: BRAINSTORM A LIST OF ITEMS RELATED TO THE POINT OF THE QUIP.

We brainstormed similarities between advertising and public relations. Our list included items such as both:

> Involve getting a message across
> Require an understanding of human nature
> Manipulate information
> Employ "creative types"
> Require paying an agency
> Involve retainer agreements
> Require interaction with the media
> Cost a lot of money

STEP 4: CHOOSE TWO ITEMS FROM THE LIST AND USE THEM TO EXTEND THE
SETUP.

The two items we selected were that both "require an understanding of human nature" and "require interaction with
the media." They were used to extend the setup as follows:

> When I was invited to speak here tonight, I wondered why a
> group of advertising professionals would be interested in how
> to organize a public relations program. Then I realized that
> advertising and public relations have a lot in common. They
> both require an understanding of human nature. They both
> require interaction with the media. And they both _____.

STEP 5: LOOK FOR AN ITEM FROM THE LIST THAT CAN SERVE AS A PUNCH
LINE.

In this case the items "require paying an agency" and "cost
a lot of money" suggested that the punch line involve money.
We felt that nervousness over the subject of money—a per-
petually touchy subject between agency and client in both PR
and advertising—could be converted into laughter.

Several attempts were discarded before a satisfactory punch
line was developed. In order to shed light on the creative
process, some of the discards have been fished out of the
garbage can and displayed here for your examination.

> Attempt: And they both require dealing with money-grubbing
> account executives.
> Problem: True, but it insults many members of the audience.

> Attempt: And they both require a huge sum of money—better
> known as a retainer fee.
> Problem: First, it's not that funny. Second, retainer fees put the
> blame for money problems solely on the agencies and would
> offend many members of the audience.

These problems were avoided in the final version of the
quip:

When I was invited to speak here tonight, I wondered why a group of advertising professionals would be interested in how to organize a public relations program. Then I realized that advertising and public relations have a lot in common. They both require an understanding of human nature. They both require interaction with the media. And they both require more money than you have in your budget.

The quip worked, because it addressed the issue of money but didn't put the blame on the company or the agency. It allowed everyone in the audience to laugh at a common problem. And it made the audience receptive to Spiller's speech—which was a complete success.

Notice also that the quip did not require any special effort in comic delivery. It was merely a light observation designed to amuse and interest the audience. Anyone could use it successfully.

So now you know the secret: The best source of humor is your own imagination. It provides the raw material. The five steps provide the framework. Together they can provide all the quips you will ever need.

Source Notes

Chapter One

1. Heather Twidale, "Nowadays, Being 'Old Sourpuss' Is No Joke," *Working Woman*, March 1986, p. 18.
2. *San Jose Mercury News*, July 30, 1986, p. 14E.
3. Russell S. Reynolds, Jr., "Executive Recruiters Find Humor Is Critical," Letter to the editor, *Wall Street Journal*, August 15, 1988, p. 17. Reprinted with permission of *Wall Street Journal.* ©1989 Dow Jones & Company Inc. All rights reserved.
4. Don Oldenburg, "The Bottom Line is Laughter," *Washington Post*, March 4, 1986, p. B5. Reprinted with permission of *Washington Post.*
5. "A Cure for Stress?," *Newsweek*, October 12, 1987, p. 64.
6. Steve Swartz and Laurie P. Cohen, "Executive Anguish," *Wall Street Journal*, December 19, 1988, p. 1.
7. Rhoda Koenig in *New York,* quoted in *Reader's Digest*, January 1987, p. 161. Reprinted with permission from the January 1987 *Reader's Digest* and *New York.*
8. Hugh Sidey, "The Presidency," *Time*, December 28, 1987, p. 22. ©1987 Time Inc. Reprinted by permission.

Chapter Two

1. Laurie Itow, "Bottom Line on Humor: It's Cost Effective," *San Francisco Examiner*, February 13, 1983, p. D10. Reprinted with permission of *San*

Francisco Examiner. ©1983 *San Francisco Examiner.*
2. Lee Leonard, "Glenn Wows Delegation," *UPI*, July 20, 1984. Reprinted with permission.
3. *Vital Speeches*, March 15, 1989, p. 322. Reprinted with permission of City News Publishing Co.
4. *Vital Speeches*, July 1, 1986, p. 563. Reprinted with permission of City News Publishing Co.
5. *Vital Speeches*, May 15, 1989, p. 450. Reprinted with permission of City News Publishing Co.
6. *Vital Speeches*, February 15, 1989, p. 265. Reprinted with permission of City News Publishing Co.
7. *Vital Speeches*, September 15, 1987, p. 723. Reprinted with permission of City News Publishing Co.
8. *Vital Speeches*, April 1, 1987, p. 357. Reprinted with permission of City News Publishing Co.
9. *Vital Speeches*, March 1, 1988, p. 300. Reprinted with permission of City News Publishing Co.
10. *Vital Speeches*, January 15, 1989, pp. 203–204. Reprinted with permission of City News Publishing Co.
11. *Vital Speeches*, March 1, 1989, p. 309. Reprinted with permission of City News Publishing Co.

Chapter Three

1. *The Executive Speaker*® (Box 292437, Dayton, Ohio 45429), vol. 4, no. 4, April 1983, pp. 2–3. Reprinted with permission of The Executive Speaker Co.
2. *Vital Speeches*, August 1, 1984, p. 34. Reprinted with permission of City News Publishing Co.
3. *Vital Speeches*, November 1, 1977, p. 49. Reprinted with permission of City News Publishing Co.
4. *Vital Speeches*, October 15, 1984, p. 16. Reprinted with permission of City News Publishing Co.
5. Juliet Lowell, *Dear Candidate* (New York: Paperback Library, Inc., 1968). Reprinted with permission from Warner Books, Inc.
6. *Vital Speeches*, November 1, 1977, p. 42. Reprinted with permission of City News Publishing Co.
7. *The Executive Speaker*® (Box 292437, Dayton, Ohio 45429), vol. 2, no. 5, May 1981, p. 2. Reprinted with permission of The Executive Speaker Co.
8. *The Executive Speaker*® (Box 292437, Dayton, Ohio 45429), vol. 1, no. 1, June 1980, p. 6. Reprinted with permission of The Executive Speaker Co.

9. *Vital Speeches*, January 1, 1988, pp. 170–71. Reprinted with permission of City News Publishing Co.
10. "Utah Bankers Urged to Maintain Professional Integrity," *Deseret News*, June 30–July 1, 1987, p. D9.
11. *Vital Speeches*, November 15, 1977, p. 84. Reprinted with permission of City News Publishing Co.

Chapter Four

1. "Berman's Got H'wood's Number," *Daily Variety*, February 4, 1986. ©1989 Daily Variety Ltd. Reprinted by permission. ®Daily Variety is a registered trademark of Variety Inc. Used by permission.
2. *Vital Speeches*, August 1, 1987, p. 637. Reprinted with permission of City News Publishing Co.
3. Jacob M. Braude, *Braude's Treasury of Wit and Humor* (Englewood Cliffs, N.J.: Prentice-Hall, Inc., 1964), p. 86.
4. *Vital Speeches*, August 15, 1984, p. 670. Reprinted with permission of City News Publishing Co.
5. *Vital Speeches*, January 15, 1982, p. 201. Reprinted with permission of City News Publishing Co.

Chapter Five

1. Walter Kiechell III, "Executives Ought to Be Funnier," *Fortune*, December 12, 1983, p. 206. Reprinted with permission.
2. *Vital Speeches*, February 15, 1987, p. 266. Reprinted with permission of City News Publishing Co.
3. Jack White, "Survivor on the Track," *Time*, March 23, 1987, p. 23.
4. *Ibid.*
5. Evan Thomas, "Journey of a Small Town Boy," *Time*, March 26, 1984, p. 19.
6. "Brightness at Apple," *San Francisco Chronicle*, December 23, 1985, p. 23.
7. Unidentified newspaper article.
8. Reprinted with permission of Intel Corp.

Chapter Six

1. John Culhane, "Oscar: Little Statue of Dreams," March 1987, p. 54.

Chapter Seven

1. Laurie Itow, "Bottom Line on Humor: It's Cost Effective," *San Francisco Examiner*, February 13, 1983, p. D10. Reprinted with permission of *San*

Francisco Examiner. ©1983 *San Francisco Examiner.*
2. "Shop Talk, Did He Scream?" *Wall Street Journal,* November 19, 1987, p. 33. Reprinted by permission of *Wall Street Journal.* ©1987 Dow Jones & Company, Inc. All rights reserved worldwide.
3. Letter in "Dear Abby" carried in *San Francisco Chronicle,* March 14, 1984.

Chapter Eight

1. Robert Baron, "Reducing Organizational Conflict: An Incompatible Response Approach," *Journal of Applied Psychology* 69, no. 2 (1984): 272–79.
2. William D. Ellis, "Solve That Problem With Humor," *Reader's Digest,* May 1973, p. 189.
3. Walter Kiechell III, "Executives Ought to Be Funnier," *Fortune,* December 12, 1983, p. 206. Reprinted with permission.
4. Mark McCormack, *What They Don't Teach You at the Harvard Business School* (New York: Bantam Books, 1984) pp. 46–47.
5. William D. Ellis, "Solve That Problem with Humor," *Reader's Digest,* May 1973, p. 189.
6. Bill Strobel, "Laugh Maven Goes for the Belly," *San Jose Mercury News,* April 24, 1985, p. 3B.
7. Karen O'Quin and Joel Aronoff, "Humor as a Technique of Social Influence," *Social Psychology Quarterly* 44, no. 4 (1981): 349–57.
8. Diane Simmons, "My CEO Is So Slow...(How Slow Is He?)," *American Banker,* January 9, 1984, p. 16.

Chapter Nine

1. Walter Kiechell III, "Executives Ought to Be Funnier," *Fortune,* December 12, 1983, p. 206. Reprinted with permission.
2. Howard R. Pollio and Charlene Kubo Bainum, "Are Funny Groups Good at Problem Solving? A Methodological Evaluation and Some Preliminary Results," *Small Group Behavior,* Vol. 14, No. 4, November 1983, pp. 379–404.
3. W. Jack Duncan and J. Philip Feisal, "No Laughing Matter: Patterns of Humor in the Workplace," *Organizational Dynamics,* Vol. 17, Spring 1989, pp. 18–30.
4. Frederick Gray, "Humorists Who Wing It," Reuters, carried in the *Washington Post,* January 13, 1979, p. B6. Reprinted with permission.
5. *Ibid.*
6. Kirsten Downey, "Laughs Fill Empty Space," *San Jose Mercury News,*

March 6, 1986, p. 4F. Reprinted by permission of the *San Jose Mercury News.*

7. Ann Hughey, "Purple's Prose," *Wall Street Journal*, August 22, 1983, p. 1. Reprinted by permission of *Wall Street Journal.* ©1983 Dow Jones & Company, Inc. All rights reserved worldwide.

8. *Ibid.*

9. *Ibid.*

10. Herb Caen, *San Francisco Chronicle.* ©*San Francisco Chronicle.* Reprinted by permission.

Chapter Ten

1. Meg Cox, "The Frill Is Gone," *Wall Street Journal*, March 20, 1987, p. 32D–33D. Reprinted by permission of *Wall Street Journal.* ©1987 Dow Jones & Company, Inc. All rights reserved worldwide.

2. *Ibid*, p. 32D.

3. Don Oldenburg, "The Bottom Line Is Laughter," *Washington Post*, March 4, 1986, p. B5. Reprinted with permission of *Washington Post.*

4. *Letter from the Lion*, reprinted with permission of The Dreyfus Corporation.

5. "The Lion's Share of Quotes," *Letter from the Lion*, Spring 1983.

6. Reprinted with permission of ASK Computer Systems Inc.

7. "Losses and Laughs," *Wall Street Journal*, February 23, 1984, p. 31. Reprinted by permission of *Wall Street Journal.* ©1984 Dow Jones & Company, Inc. All rights reserved worldwide.

8. "Idaho Police Kept Sense of Humor in Wake of Hoax," Associated Press, carried in the *San Jose Mercury News*, September 12, 1987, p. 24A.

9. Source of original and author unknown.

10. Reprinted with permission of Adia Personnel Services.

11. Source of original and author unknown.

12. Source of original and author unknown.

13. Source of original and author unknown.

14. Source of original and author unknown.

15. Source of original and author unknown.

Chapter Eleven

1. Owen Ullman, "Aw Shucks, Mr. President," *San Jose Mercury News*, August 17, 1986, p. 11A. Reprinted by permission of the *San Jose Mercury News.*

2. "How the New Math of Productivity Adds Up," *Business Week*, June 6, 1988, p. 108.

3. Rock Miller, "Quality Is a Business Issue," *Managing Automation*, March 1988, p. 45.
4. Joani Nelson-Horchler, "Performance Appraisals," *Industry Week*, September 19, 1988, p. 61. Reprinted with permission.

Chapter Twelve

1. Reprinted with permission from Susan Jancourtz.

Chapter Thirteen

1. Arthur M. Nezu and Christine M. Nezu, "Sense of Humor as a Moderator of the Relation Between Stressful Events and Psychological Distress: A Prospective Analysis," *Journal of Personality and Social Psychology*, 1988, Vol. 54, No. 3, pp. 520–525.
2. Earle Tempel, *Humor in the Headlines* (New York: Pocket Books, 1969), pp. 130, 203, 89, 12, 65, 39. Reprinted with permission.
3. Compiled by John Peers and edited by Gordon Bennett, *1,001 Logical Laws, Accurate Axioms, Profound Principles, Trusty Truisms, Homey Homilies, Colorful Corollaries, Quotable Quotes, and Rambunctious Ruminations for All Walks of Life* (New York: Fawcett Columbine, 1979).

Chapter Fourteen

1. John Cantu, editor, *Comedy/Update*, January 1983, p. 1.
2. Robert Orben, *The Ad-Libber's Handbook* (North Hollywood, Calif.: Wilshire Book Company, 1969), p. 153.
3. Martin Buxbaum quoted in "One Good Thing," *Reader's Digest*, February 1987, p. 111. Reprinted with permission of the February 1987 *Reader's Digest* and Martin Buxbaum.
4. *Sunshine Magazine* quoted in "One Good Thing," *Reader's Digest*, February 1987, p. 111. Reprinted with permission of the February 1987 *Reader's Digest* and *Sunshine Magazine*.

Acknowledgments

Three people were instrumental in guiding this book from idea to reality. Matty Goldberg recognized its potential. Fred Hills provided superb editing. Norman Mitgang offered an endless supply of encouragement. Their exceptional efforts are deeply appreciated.

I would also like to thank all of my clients for sharing their insights and anecdotes about humor in the workplace. Special thanks to John Austin, Bob Brownson, Joe DiNucci, Nancy Evans, Martin Gonzales, Bob Powell, Allison Spiller, and Les Wright.

Valuable ideas, comments and suggestions, as well as unflagging support, were provided by D. Scott Apel, Daphne Bien, Rob Bragin, Brad Bunnin, Katherine Burns, John Cantu, Linda Carll, Lesley Czechowicz, Dana Fox, Steve Katleman, Hank Kushner, Helen Kushner, Monte Lorenzet, Mike Malone, Carol Marschner, Jeff Raleigh, Bob Reed, Ken Sereno, Bob Skovgard, Amy Tamarkin, Heather Tamarkin and Leigh Weimers.

Finally, special thanks to Christine Griger for eliminating typos, grammatical errors and major lapses in logic as the pages came out of the printer.

Index

bottom line
fertile
to be sloppy

shortcoming
nullify - свести к нулю